"The best book that I have read on speed. Weimann has thoroughly researched the subject and scientifically identified the aspects of speed."

Mark McClish
Former Defensive Tactics Instructor
U. S. Marshals Service Training Academy

"Warrior Speed is a wealth of insightful, reliable, and hard-to-find information written by a veteran martial artist who has learned his fighting method the hard way - in the ring and on the street."

Loren Christensen, 7th Degree Black Belt
Author of 11 martial arts books

"This book is for anyone who wants to expand their technical understanding of the generation of speed and power."

Howard Webb, 6th Degree Black Belt
Lead Training Officer
Montana Law Enforcement Academy

"Unlike so many authors Ted does not concentrate exclusively on just physical technique but he engages the very important aspect of real world confrontations. I can recommend it for the more advanced student of the martial arts as well; he debunks a number of myths and explains things with simple physics rather than mysticism."

Peyton Quinn
author of "Real Fighting : Adrenaline Stress Conditioning Through Scenario-Based Training"

Warrior Speed

by
Ted Weimann

Turtle Press   **Hartford**

To contact the author or to order additional copies of this book:
> Turtle Press
> 401 Silas Deane Hwy
> P.O. Box 290206
> Wethersfield, CT 06129-0206
> 1-880-77-TURTL

ISBN 1-880336-38-3
LCCN 00-023471
Printed in the United States of America

10 9 8 7 6 5 4 3 2 1

Library of Congress Cataloguing in Publication Data
Weimann, Ted, 1962-
  Warrior speed / by Ted Weimann
    p. cm.
  Includes bibliographical references and index
  ISBN 1-880336-38-3
  1. Martial arts--Training. 2. Speed. I. Title

GV1102.7.T7 W45 2000
796.8--dc21   00-023471

<u>Acknowledgments</u>

I would like to extend my sincere thanks to the following people for their part in helping me write this book.

First and foremost I would like to thank my wife Sharice. If it wasn't for her motivation, inspiration and support, I don't know if I would have taken on such a project.

Thanks to my friend Neil for his critical analysis of physics and techniques.

I would like to thank all my friends and training partners that have helped me in ways too numerous to enumerate upon. I would especially like to thank Neil, Jerry and Larry for their dedication to training. They taught me as much as I ever taught them.

About the Notes

Throughout the text, the author cites reference works. Because many of the works are cited in more than one chapter, the sources have been compiled in a single references section beginning on page 291 rather than at the end of each chapter.

Contents

INTRODUCTION

How many times have you said, or heard someone say, "Wow, he's quick!" Often, I am sure. All fighters have. Maybe you prefer, as many people do, to watch the welterweights fight because there is more action, their moves and reflexes are faster. Or you've seen someone particularly adept in the ring or on the screen and thought to yourself, "If only I had that kind of speed." Perhaps your thoughts soon wandered into the realm of genetics and you were wishing you had been able to choose 'faster' parents.

There is some validity to those thoughts. However, the issue of speed is far more complex than this. Yes, genetics does play a factor in how fast your muscles contract and therefore, how fast you move. But you can significantly influence and alter this rate of contraction as well as mentally condition yourself to respond faster to any situation.

It is also important to understand that physics plays a role in the equation. Physics can affect not only how fast you move, but it can help you decide which techniques to use and how to perform them. The many different aspects of speed over which you have influence have been broken down and grouped into three separate components for this book. They include physical speed, psychological speed and perceptive speed.

The chapter on physical speed discusses ways in which you can actually change your muscle structure, shape and metabolism to increase the speed of your muscular contractions. Using the latest research on exercise physiology and the laws of physics, you will learn not only how to train but why this training must be so specific in order to realize the maximum speed gains which are readily attainable.

And what about psychological speed? Have you ever had a day when you simply felt fast? Or a day where you seemed slow to react, without any apparent reason? Do you have a sparring partner with whom you generally respond quicker, or vice versa? Why is that? A great deal of research has been published on mind set, mental training and athletic performance.

Psychological speed is composed of analysis, decision, confidence and experience. The faster you recognize a movement for what it is, be it a glimpse, raised shoulder, etc., the faster you can prepare for appropriate action. Once the analysis phase is complete and the stimulus has been recognized, categorized and evaluated, you can begin to decide what response is desirable, if any. Both analysis and decision speed can be enhanced by experience, mindset, video tape analysis, and so on. *Chapter 5* closely examines analysis and decision speed, and ways to improve your skill in both areas. Altering your confidence or the confidence of your opponent can affect the speed of both of you. How to change confidence levels and how doing so affects speed is also covered.

Perceptive speed can be increased as well. Everyone's brain receives information from the eyes at the same rate. How fast your brain interprets that information depends on numerous factors. You can increase the speed at which you interpret stimuli.

Research in the last few years has proved some of the old theories wrong. This book incorporates the latest research in medical science, physics and psychology, and ties them all into fighting technique, strategy and performance. In short, you can dramatically increase your speed and this book shows you how to do it.

Chapter 1
SPEED

In English dictionaries, speed is defined as: "swift or rapid movement; quickness in moving from one place to another; the rate of movement." For the purposes of fighting however, speed incorporates more than just the rate of movement. If it takes a long time to decide which technique to use in response to an attack, then no matter how fast your physical action is performed, your speed, in terms of total response time, is slow. As you can see, speed has a psychological element to it. In fact, it has several additional elements to it. To incorporate all the various aspects of those components into the equation, speed has been broken down into the following parts:

PERCEPTION —> NEUROLOGICAL RELAY —> ANALYSIS —> DECISION —> NEUROLOGICAL RELAY —> ACTION

In the above diagram, speed has been broken down into six components, four of which can be enhanced through training. These areas are perception, analysis, decision and action. The exception is the neurological relay. The speed of the relay of information along the neurons and across the nerve synapses cannot be increased and is the same for all humans. Even if the speed of the transmission of electrical and chemical information could be increased with drugs, which the author researched and found no evidence to support, the time involved figures minimally in the total equation because our brains transmit messages with incredible speed. Once you realize the majority of the elements affecting response time are within the realm of things you can influence, you are on your way to increasing your speed significantly. (Note: Speed of information transfer from one neuron to another can be increased through repetitive training. As noted above, because of the great speed at which this already occurs, the increase is not significant. More important than the speed of the information transfer, repetitive training allows this transfer to occur automatically. This increases coordination and fluidity. It also permits you to concentrate on another area, such as perception. This process is thoroughly explained in *Chapter 5*, subsection, *Myelination.*

The physical aspect of speed is what most people refer to when involved in a discussion of speed. How fast can you throw a punch? How quickly can you execute a kick or move across the floor? Most people believe that the answers to these questions are inscribed in their genetic code. To a large degree that is true. However, there are many factors that directly or indirectly affect the speed of movement that can be influenced.

For instance, flexibility, just like tight clothing, can restrict movement and thereby affect speed. Obviously, fitness level affects speed and so does physics. Physics affects speed through two mechanisms: first, through physical fitness, and second, by way of economy of movement and the laws of movement. Speed of movement, to a large part, is a factor of the velocity of muscle contraction. The stronger a muscle is the greater the force of contraction it can generate, and therefore the faster and more powerful the individual is. The strength, or level of force generated by muscle, can be influenced by exercise, nutrition, health, mind set, drugs and training regimens.

As stated earlier, the four components of speed you can influence are perception, analysis, decision making and action. Perception speed is the time it takes you or your opponent to realize that an action is about to be taken or has been initiated. This component is discussed in *Chapter 7, Perception Speed.* Next follows a chapter on deception. Deception is included because an act of deception can be used to increase the time it takes your opponent to perceive that an attack is about to occur or has begun, or what the actual attack really is.

Analysis and decision making components of speed have been placed within *Chapter 5, Psychological Speed.* Since both analysis and decision making are functions within the brain, the mind sets of you and your opponent greatly influence the efficiency of those functions. Training also affects the efficiency of both the analysis of stimuli and decision making, however, you have to be in the proper mind set to take full advantage of your training. *Chapters 5 & 6* explain techniques designed to enhance your control over your own and your opponent's mind sets.

Action is the component of speed everyone desires. *Chapter 2* explains why specific training is so important to increasing your speed and how this training makes you faster. Subsequent chapters discuss training, tactics and techniques, and how they affect each of the four components of speed. Using certain techniques can increase the speed of your movements and your opponent's perception time. Training can increase the speed of your analysis and decision making through learning to pick up on minor cues and by association/response training.

Each of the areas of speed is very closely intertwined. For this reason, the chapters routinely mention how one action affects elements of speed discussed in other chapters. In many of these examples, the separate elements of speed affected by that action are listed. To avoid unnecessary repetition, the author has chosen not to do so in some of the examples. As you near the end of the book, you should immediately know what elements of speed are affected by each action. If not, read the book through a second time to develop a more thorough understanding of the complexities of speed.

The Basics

The Action-Reaction Principle

Generally, people who are more aggressive and attack first, end up winning. Is that simply because they are more aggressive? Or is it because a person cannot win by merely being defensive? Is it due to more confidence? Or, is it because of the action-reaction principle? Much of the time it's a combination of the above with numerous other factors. Nonetheless, the person who attacks first has a significant advantage because of the action-reaction principle. The action-reaction principle is based upon a simple equation and it provides the person who initiates the action with an advantage in time.

When you initiate an action, your opponent has to take the time to perceive that action and then respond. This would involve perception, the neurological relay, analysis, decision, neurological relay, and finally action (P-NR-A-D-NR-A), in response to your attack. An unavoidable time delay exists between your action and your opponent's reaction.

As an example, suppose you held your hand up and another person held up his hand 18 inches away from your hand. His objective is to strike your hand and your aim is to move your hand out of reach. Assuming your natural reflexes are roughly equal, it would be virtually impossible for you to do so based upon the action-reaction principle. Once movement was initiated, your opponent's hand would be striking your hand by the time the total P-NR-A-D-NR-A sequence was completed. This is still true even if your analysis, decision, and action sequence were already preprogrammed in your mind. He would strike your hand before you would have the opportunity to initiate a reaction, or at least shortly afterward, before you had time to move it out of the way. Therefore, everything else being equal, the fighter who initiates the attack will be the winner. He will also appear faster in the process.

Tension

There are five areas of tension to be concerned with in terms of their influence upon speed. They are static tension, clothing, flexibility, stress and temperature. Static tension is the tension that exists in all muscles to some degree. Have you ever heard someone describe what the body of a dead person looked like? Frequently, part of the description describes how totally relaxed the body looked, how the body appeared to sink into the ground. Static tension exists because our muscles carry some tension within them at all times. Some of this tension is stress related, some maintains posture and balance and some of it exists as a form of protection.

Static Tension

This tension that serves as protection is a physiological safeguard that prevents muscle fibers from contracting too drastically or dynamically at one time. This prevents injury to the antagonist muscles that would be stretched at the same rate as the contracting muscles. For instance, if you could contract every fiber in a given muscle at will, say for instance, your quadriceps, and therefore kick your leg outward extremely quickly and with great force, there would be a relatively high probability of injuring your hamstrings.

Fortunately, your body has built in preventive measures, such as static tension, which prevent you from doing just that. However, there are certain physiological loopholes built into our neuromuscular systems to circumvent this when necessary such as emergency-type situations like when you stumble and begin to fall forward, yet are able to catch yourself with one leg. This is an example of what is referred to as a plyometric action. A plyometric action is a sudden, forceful, contraction of a muscle following a sudden stretch of that muscle. The force exerted upon that one leg (and then generated by that leg in response), primarily your quadriceps, is so significant that it goes beyond what you can consciously generate yourself. Under those circumstances, your body is able to override the normal safeguards provided by static tension to prevent injury because your mind senses immediate danger and signals the necessary muscles to act at near maximal level in order to prevent a more serious injury.

For the most part, there is little that can be done to influence the level of static tension in your body. However, you can subject your body to a specific type of exercise, plyometric exercise, which simulates conditions where your body automatically overrides the static tension and causes intense, dynamic muscular contractions. This will not change the base level of static tension. What it will do is work to increase the amount of voluntary control you have over both the force of your muscular contractions and over the level of relaxation of the antagonistic muscles. A thorough discussion of plyometric exercises and how they produce these results can be found in *Chapter 2*.

Clothing

The second type of tension we will be discussing is that type caused by clothing, particularly that which binds or restricts your movements in any way. One study suggested that if you were to go hiking in a typical pair of blue jeans, by the end of the day you would have exerted enough energy in overcoming the friction and restrictive action of those jeans to have hiked an additional mile. Whether that estimate is accurate is not important. The implications are clear enough.

Tight clothing can make a significant difference concerning friction applied to your movement. This will inevitably slow down your rate of movement and thus your overall speed. If you would like to test the significance of this, try the following experiment.

First, throw a series of 50 high kicks with one leg while wearing restrictive clothing. Note the speed and height that you are able to attain. Then change into a pair of loose fitting shorts and proceed to throw 50 kicks with your other leg. It should be apparent which activity is more fatiguing. Also note the difficulty in attaining the same height and speed while wearing the more binding clothes.

Flexibility

The third subject in our discussion of tension is flexibility. Just as restrictive clothing provides tension that causes you to exert more energy to move, inflexible muscles and tendons apply tension and friction when it comes to resisting and restricting physical movement. Do not underestimate the importance of flexibility training in any area of physical conditioning, including programs designed to increase speed and power.

Suppose you wish to throw a high front snap kick, involving a contraction of your quadriceps muscle and a stretching of your hamstrings. If your hamstrings are tight, the quads must apply some of their contractile force to overcome the resistance applied by your hamstrings. Consequently, your rate of movement would be slowed due to the smaller portion of the force generated by your quadriceps that's available to be applied to the speed of the muscle contraction. This is because a portion of that energy must be used to overcome the unnecessarily high level of resistance being exerted by your hamstrings. Furthermore, if your hamstrings, or any other body parts, are unduly tight, there is only so much force the antagonist muscles (in this case, your quadriceps) can apply without causing injury.

The simple fact is, tight muscles only stretch so far and so fast. In addition, the plyometric action that occurs at the midpoint of a snap kick, when the hamstrings begin to dynamically contract as quickly and forcefully as possible, is very stressful on a muscle that has been stretched near its limits of flexibility. Increasing your flexibility increases the fluidity of your movements, increases the speed of certain movements, increases your range of movement, and decreases your risk of injury.

Stress

The fourth type of tension that affects speed is stress. Psychological stress, including generalized tension, anxiety and fear, all cause muscular tension throughout the body. Much of this tension is concentrated around the head, neck and shoulders of the average individual. This causes headaches, sore necks, shoulder and back problems, etc. There are numerous physiological and medical problems caused by people carrying too much stress.

However, at the moment we are discussing muscular tension. Has a friend ever massaged your trapezoids muscle, located in upper back and shoulder region, and mentioned how tight you felt? That muscle tension is stress induced. If that level of tension was in your hamstring or biceps muscles, how slow do you think your kicks and punches would be? Fortunately, the level of stress related tension held in those muscles is much lower. It is there though and this type of tension plays a significant role in slowing down your movements. It also speeds the onset of fatigue and increases the likelihood of injury.

Another example illustrating how muscular tension slows down your movements involves relaxation twitches. Most people have a tendency to twitch as they are falling asleep. If you are one of them, have you noticed how quickly your hand moves? The hand seems to move quicker than it does when performing a back-fist. The reason the contraction is so fast is that the level of muscular tension is very low. When are you more relaxed than when you are falling asleep? By learning how to reduce the level of muscular tension, the speed of your movements will increase.

Temperature

Finally, cold also causes muscular tension. Actually, it is a combination of an increase in the viscosity of blood and fluids within the muscle tissue and a decrease in the oxygen and nutrient supply to the muscle. The latter factor is a physiological adaptation to the cold. When the body becomes cold, it responds by vasoconstriction, resulting in a slowing of blood flow to the extremities. This results in less oxygen and nutrients to the tissues, decreasing their ability to work at maximum efficiency. This is similar to the adverse effect upon mountaineers. In the oxygen deprived high altitude, their mental functions slow and they lose the ability to think clearly and rationally.

In the cold, your body is deprived of warmth, which results in vasoconstriction. The vasoconstriction deprives the limbs of oxygen. The brain maintains its oxygen supply. However, in its effort to conserve warmth, the limbs are shorted their supply of oxygen. As far as the viscosity is concerned, just as engine oil thickens as it cools, so does blood and the interstitial fluids found within your muscles. (64) Do not underestimate this effect. Remember how slowly your hand closes when it is cold. It can only be closed at a fraction of the speed compared to when it is warm. As an interesting side note, dehydration can also adversely affect muscle viscosity.

As further evidence of the adverse effects of cold upon muscle stiffness and performance, think about cold weather and your injuries. For those of you who have suffered any injuries, you may have noticed that cold causes a stiffness in those areas. In your neck, shoulders, hips, knees, or wherever the injury site may be, cold causes either an additional tightening, or an awareness of the tension in those muscles that have already been compromised by injury. So, not only is it beneficial to warm yourself up with light exercise before stretching or working out to prevent injuries, but warming up and stretching will make you faster for their own independent reasons.

As the body temperature rises, the efficiency of the biochemical reactions supplying energy for muscular contraction also increases. As mentioned, blood flow is increased which supplies oxygen and fuel and removes waste products. The increase in temperature also speeds the process of muscular relaxation and reduces stiffness within the contractile muscle fibers and stretch fibers (Intrafusal fibers.) Each of these benefits resulting from an increase in muscular temperature can help increase the speed of movement.

---

5 Types of Tension

1. Static tension
2. Clothing
3. Flexibility
4. Stress
5. Temperature

Physics

The Principle of Motion

The laws of physics affect speed and force production through several mechanisms. One of these laws you should be aware of has to do with motion. Through the law of inertia, we know that an object in motion tends to stay in motion, and an object at rest tends to stay at rest. This leads to the principle of staying in motion, of always keeping your hands, and sometimes your body, in motion. It is faster to alter the direction of movement of your hands than it is to initiate movement of your hands when they are still. Also, it is harder for your opponent to perceive a significant change of movement (e.g., an attack) if you and/or your hands are in constant motion than it is to perceive the initiation of an offensive movement of the hands when they have been motionless.

This last point relates directly to perceptive and deceptive speed because it increases the perception time of your opponent. Another benefit of remaining mobile is that you are a harder target to hit. Because a mobile target is much harder to hit, your opponent has more difficulty striking you. This may result in frustration and a decrease in his confidence. Therefore, psychology also comes into play in this example.

Power/Force/Speed

Physical speed is what most people think of when they think of speed. Of the four components of speed, it is the one everyone desires. Quickness of movement, physical prowess, power, these are all associated traits of speed. Why do physical prowess and power relate to speed? To answer this question, power, force and speed must all be discussed.

Power is a misnomer, at least where lifters and fighters are concerned. Technically speaking, power is a measurement for the rate at which work is done, e.g.,: foot pounds per minute. Force is what everyone wants. Force is defined as any influence or agency that causes a body to move, accelerate or stop. Force is equal to mass times acceleration. (4) This book is written in layperson's terms. Therefore, other than this section on physics and how it affects fighting, the term power is used in place of the technically correct term of force.

For purposes of clarification, it is necessary to define two other terms, momentum and kinetic energy. Momentum is defined as mass times velocity. Kinetic energy is defined as one half the product of the mass and the square of its velocity. (4)

Force

A tennis ball and a baseball are traveling toward a wall at the same speed. For the sake of this example, the baseball has twice the mass as the tennis ball. The baseball will have twice the force upon impact than will the tennis ball. Simple enough. The baseball will transfer slightly more than twice the force of the tennis ball, however. This is because of the elastic qualities of the tennis ball. Some of the force carried by the tennis ball will be absorbed by the tennis ball rather than imparted to the wall. This absorption of force takes place as the tennis ball indents and then pushes back. Referring to the definition of force, "any action causing a body to move..." The tennis ball is moved as it is indented. It obviously takes force to indent the ball. Therefore some of the force carried by the ball is used to indent the tennis ball and can not be imparted to the wall. For the remainder of the examples, assume that the tennis ball does not have any elastic qualities.

For the next example, two identical tennis balls are traveling toward a wall. One is traveling two times faster than the other. The faster ball will impact the wall with twice the force of the slower one. Also easy. If the tennis ball hits the wall two times faster than the baseball, the impact force generated by the balls is equal.

Now something a little more involved. The tennis ball and baseball are hurled toward the wall by an identical amount of force. The tennis ball will hit the wall first because it travels faster. (It travels faster because having less mass allowed more of the force supplied, to propel it, to be used toward acceleration.) When the baseball hits the wall, if it had sufficient velocity to reach the wall, it will generate the same amount of force that the tennis ball did. In this example, where the tennis ball is one half the mass of the baseball, it can be determined that the tennis ball will hit the wall twice as fast as the baseball. If the mass of the balls were not known, only the equation "mass times acceleration of the tennis ball equals the mass times acceleration of the baseball" would be known. Note: In this last example, assume that the machine propelling the balls toward the wall is very close to the wall. Otherwise, to be technically accurate, friction would come into the equation. The size and texture of the ball would affect the amount of resistance with the air.

Application of Force in Martial Arts

Ever try breaking a board? Easy if it breaks. If it does not however, it hurts, possibly damaging your hand. This is because the unbroken board acts like a mirror, redirecting the force back into your hand. If you failed to break it, you failed to move it. If you fail to move the board, the board causes your hand to STOP. Refer to the definition of force: any influence or agency that causes a body to move, accelerate or stop. Punching a board does not hurt nearly as much as punching a cement wall. This is because the board did move, even though it did not break. The person holding the board probably was moved to some degree. Also, the board was most likely dented, evidence of movement within the board itself.

Punching a cement wall does not cause the wall to move, nor does the punch indent the wall. Therefore, none of the force is absorbed by the wall, i.e., the wall does not move, accelerate or stop. If the wall does not absorb any force, then the fist must absorb it. The fist absorbs the force through the quick stop and by movement. Movement within the hand includes the deformation of the fist, broken bones or tissue damage.

Now add a twist to this scenario. Why does a punch to the ribs cause so much more damage when the opponent's back is against the ground or a wall? When an opponent is punched in the ribs, it usually moves him backward. This backward movement requires force (an influence that causes a body to move or accelerate). Therefore, some of the force behind the punch is used to move the opponent backward. This diminishes the amount of force available to cause internal damage, e.g., broken bones and/or bruising. When his back is against a wall, he can not move backward, therefore, more of the force delivered by the punch goes toward bodily damage.

For the same reason, attacks are much more "forceful" when they strike the opponent as he is coming toward you or if they strike upward, for example, a rising groin kick or an uppercut. If you hit your opponent when he is advancing, the amount of damage will be significantly higher for two reasons. First, the amount of force supplied by his forward moving mass will be added to the amount of force delivered by your hand or foot. Second, his forward movement prevents much, if not all, of the backward movement that his body would initiate in its attempt to dissipate some of the force delivered by your attack. Upwardly directed techniques are more damaging because the pull of gravity helps decrease the amount that his body can move up, thereby, increasing the amount of force that his body must absorb.

What happens when you hit a new, pliable, heavy bag versus an old, hard one? It can hurt hitting the hard one, can't it? Both bags absorb some of the force by initiating movement. The softer bag however, absorbs more force because of the additional movement within the bag, i.e., compression of the stuffing. If you are not concentrating when hitting the hard bag, it can hurt your hand and sometimes buckle your wrist. This point illustrates the importance of using good technique, especially when hitting something hard like a board or a skull. If you don't, some of the force carried by your fist will not be able to transfer over to the opponent and therefore, must be absorbed by your hand or wrist, possibly causing an injury.

Then, if force is acceleration times mass, then why isn't a five inch punch more forceful than a punch that is near the end of its range and at its full velocity? The five-inch punch is certainly accelerating more than the extended punch. If the extended punch is at its full velocity, then acceleration is zero. Would force then not be zero because the equation would be mass times zero? Obviously not. But why? Because force is any influence that causes a body to move, accelerate or STOP. Stopping the punch is an influence. The opponent absorbs this force as he stops the punch. Since the extended punch was traveling faster than the five-inch punch, it takes more force to stop it. Think of it as deceleration. The extended punch has to decelerate more than the five-inch punch. Deceleration times mass also equals force.

Force & Technique

As you know, the amount of force behind a punch depends on many factors. Some of these include drive off the ground, hip involvement, proper bone alignment, etc. Since this book is about speed, not power, these factors will not be discussed any further.

For a more thorough understanding of force, it is necessary to address two factors concerning technique. The first factor involves how the force is delivered. Some would call this focus. For example, fighter 1 side kicks his opponent, connecting with the entire bottom of his foot. Fighter 2 side kicks his opponent, contacting with his heel only. Everything else being equal, they will deliver the same amount of force against their opponents.

Fighter 2 causes more damage though. This is because the force must be absorbed by less tissue, concentrating the force. This, in turn, causes more tissue damage to the area absorbing the force. The equation is simple. More force absorbed equals more damage. Yes, the damaged area will be smaller, but the injury will be more severe. On a technical point, fighter 1 may deliver a less forceful impact on his opponent because some of the soft tissue on the bottom of his foot may absorb some of the impact, like the tennis ball indenting. The heel of fighter 2, a bone designed to withstand much force, makes a very efficient transfer of force.

The second factor concerning technique involves driving versus snapping techniques. Driving techniques usually involve more commitment, more follow through and more force. (Note: More commitment is another way of saying more body weight. The reason a power punch that incorporates the body's mass behind it delivers much more force than a snapping punch is because a power punch has much more weight behind it. The snapping punch would have to be faster than the power punch to the same degree that it is lighter than the power punch. The difference in their speed is not enough to make up for the difference in their mass.) Because snapping techniques are usually less committed, have less follow through and less force, they are usually faster and allow the fighter to return to the on guard position more quickly. In fact, this snapping back to the on guard position is one reason why they deliver less force to the opponent. Some of the force generated in the technique is used to snap the body and limb back, thus, subtracting from the amount of force that is available to impart to the opponent.

Why then are snapping techniques so effective, other than the fact that being faster makes it easier to strike the opponent? The answer involves time. A driving right cross or a front kick is in contact with the opponent for perhaps, .10 of a second. A snapping right cross or a front kick is in contact with the opponent for perhaps, .02 of a second. The difference in the amount of time that the hand or foot is in contact with the opponent is significant. The consequence is that the tissue must absorb the force in less time. This tissue does not have the time to disperse some of the force to other parts of the body. During a driving kick, the skeletal system has time to absorb some of the force and then disperse this force around the body in the form of movement, e.g., being knocked backwards. During a snapping kick, the skeletal system does not have time to absorb, transfer and disperse the force as movement. Therefore, even though the technique may be considerably less forceful, it may actually inflict more damage to the target tissue.

Technique execution plays an important role in determining how much force is delivered to your opponent. If you do not put your body behind the punch, then this lower amount of mass behind the strike reduces the amount of force delivered at impact. Joint alignment and driving through the opponent also are very important. To test your understanding of the physics of fighting so far, why are uppercuts so effective? Yes, you may be striking a vulnerable area, but the answer I was looking for was this. For one thing, they are delivered with the limb remaining close to the body. This maintains strength within the arm. (This rule of biomechanics is explained in *Chapter 13*.)

The added strength that the arm maintains allows it to transfer more force to the opponent with less re-absorption and continue driving through the target. Also, because the target is over your legs, you are in a better position to continue driving off the ground, through the target. Lastly, because you are striking the target in an upward manner, attempting to punch him into the sky, the opponent's body is held in place by gravity. Therefore, less of the force is dissipated by moving the body upward or backward.

Momentum & Force

In definition, the momentum and force appear very similar. Perhaps they are. However, the following example should illustrate the difference between the two. Take two identical rockets, identical in size, weight, velocity, shape and materials. Both impact a wall, however, one runs out of fuel just prior to impact. The momentum is the same at impact, however the force is not. The rocket with some fuel remaining continues to drive into the wall at impact, thereby, increasing the force. Punches and kicks act in the same manner. With good technique, a punch drives off the ground, through the legs and continues driving into the target after impact. If you continue this drive through the target, you will deliver more force, and therefore, cause more damage to your opponent.

Kinetic Energy & Force

The PR 24, also known as the side handled baton or tonfa, has been adopted by police departments across the U.S. Knowing that kinetic energy increases significantly more when velocity is doubled than it is when mass is doubled, the departments reasoned that the PR 24 should be the more effective weapon when compared to the straight baton. A properly wielded PR 24 hits its target much faster than a club does.

The PR 24 has a higher impact velocity than a club for two factors. First, all the speed a club has a PR 24 has for the same reasons. The arm and body work to swing the PR 24 into the target similar to a club. Second, as the PR 24 is swinging toward the target, the shaft of the weapon has a separate swinging motion. The shaft arcs around the handle and into the target. The impact velocity is the summation of the velocity of the primary swing and the velocity of the shaft arcing around the handle.

Why then have so many officers had such poor results with them? Perhaps, under stress, their technique suffered. But there are too many stories where an officer, after failing to drop the assailant with the PR 24, began swinging the weapon like a club and the assailant dropped like a rock. The answer is not a simple one. For starters, kinetic energy is really a term used for astrophysics. It is a way of measuring how fast something happens, including a change from momentum to heat energy. For example, when an asteroid slams into the Earth, how much heat is going to be released? Kinetic energy is not the appropriate unit for measuring an action occurring as slow as the impact of a PR 24.

The reason the club was more effective against the assailant is that the force delivered by the PR 24 was less than when it was used like a club. This explains why the club was more effective. The reason the club imparted more force on the assailant is that the officer put his body weight behind the strike. Momentum is the appropriate measure to predict how much force will be delivered to the target, not kinetic energy. Remember, momentum is defined as mass times velocity. Therefore, mass and velocity play an equal part in determining the amount of momentum, whereas, velocity plays a more important role in determining kinetic energy. The PR 24 may have been moving twice as fast, but with less than half the mass behind it, it would deliver less force than the club.

This explains why a lightweight fighter finds it difficult to knock out a heavyweight fighter. For the sake of simplicity, assume fighter 1 weighs 100 pounds and fighter 2 weighs 200 pounds. Just to deliver an equal amount of force, fighter 1 would have to throw his punches twice as fast as fighter 2. The author believes that every person has a force knockout threshold. In other words, someone has to hit you with enough force to knock you out, or to break your jaw. That's why a 50 pound seven year old cannot hurt you when a slow, 300 pound couch potato can. Suppose your force knockout threshold was 600 units. The 300 pounder would then have to hit you with a velocity of 2 units to knock you out. Three hundred times 2 equals 600. The kid would have to hit you with a velocity of 12 units to reach your threshold. Fifty times 12 equals 600. No human could ever achieve such velocity. Another reason the small fighter finds it hard to knock out a large fighter involves the concept of energy transfer.

To illustrate the idea of energy transfer, think of a rubber ball tossed through the air and striking another rubber ball of equal mass. The first ball stops and the second ball absorbs the energy and continues along the trajectory of the first ball at almost the same speed. If, on the other hand, the ball hit a much heavier ball, the heavy ball would barely move at all. The first ball would bounce off in the opposite direction, having lost little speed. This ball was not able to transmit much of its energy to the heavy ball. It absorbed most of the force of the impact. A small fighter hitting a large opponent faces the same problem. When his hand contacts the skull of the large opponent, his hand absorbs much of the force of impact. The large, heavier skull or jawbone is like the large ball, and the fist is like the small ball. This is not a perfect example because the movement within the hand changes the equation some, however it illustrates the point. (23)

Here's another example to illustrate the laws of energy transfer and why kinetic energy is not what fighters desire in their strikes. A group of scientist tested the physics of breaking a pine board versus a cement slab using the hammer fist. It requires three times the amount of kinetic energy to break the board as it does the cement, yet everyone knows that the cement is the harder one to break. It requires five times the force to break the cement as it does to break the board. The reason the wood has the higher threshold of energy to break it is that the board must be bent to a degree that is 16 times greater than the degree that the cement must bend before it breaks. Energy is the product of force and deflection. The wood is deflected 16 times farther than the cement before breaking.

The reason the cement requires more force to break it is that it has more mass than the wood. The amount of energy the hand needs to break the object depends on how easily energy can be transmitted from the hand to the target. This in turn depends on the relative masses of the hand and the target. When the target has less mass than the hand, such as the wood, it accepts most of the energy. When the target has more mass than the hand, as is the case with cement, it only accepts a small fraction of the energy. Therefore, more force must be present when the fist hits the cement. (23)

Physics & Physical Fitness

Both strength and weight affect speed and force through physics. If you lose weight without losing strength, you will increase your speed. If you gain weight without gaining strength, you will decrease your speed. In the following example, both individuals are of the same height, weight and bone structure.

Individual 1 is a 200 lb. man with 20% body fat.
Individual 2 is a 200 lb. man with 10% body fat.

The second individual is a leaner, more muscular person, and would be more powerful and faster for two reasons. First, he would be more powerful because his greater muscle mass would give him increased contractile strength. Second, he would be faster because he would have more strength available to move his body weight. Therefore, he could move it more quickly. Thus, the principles of physics dictate that, as the ratio of muscle to fat is increased, there is a corresponding increase in speed and power.

In the next example, a 200 lb. man with 20% body fat diets and loses 25 lbs., without increasing or decreasing his muscle mass. This man now has 8.6 percent body fat. Because he has the same muscle mass, there has been no increase in strength. However, having 25 pounds less of useless body mass means less energy is being expended on moving nonproductive body weight (weight that cannot contribute to the production of speed). Therefore, the more efficient use of energy results in a faster individual.

If you gain weight and strength, you will most likely increase the speed of your lunges and decrease the speed of your kicks and punches. For example, if you gain ten pounds of muscle, you have most likely increased the strength of your lower body to a significant degree, perhaps by 20 percent. Yet this ten pounds is perhaps just 6 percent of your body weight. Therefore, the increase in the strength to weight ratio is in your favor. Your lunges will be faster.

A lunge is much slower than a punch because the driving leg has to move your body weight, whereas, the arm only has to move the weight of the arm.

The 20 percent increase in strength of the leg versus the 6 percent increase in weight translates to a faster lunge.

The increase in strength of the arm is not as relevant. There is not a large amount of mass within the arm that the muscles must move along. Therefore, the increase in strength will not necessarily increase the speed of your punches. If your arms and upper-body increase in strength and not weight, then your punches would become faster. If your arms and upper-body increase in strength and weight, it is possible that your punches may slow down. This is because there is not much mass to a thin arm. Great strength is not necessary to move the arm and change its direction quickly. Increase the weight of the arm and you may slow it down. Put a three pound weight, or a heavy weapon such as a padded baton, in a strong fighter's arm. Of course, his hand movements will be even slower. Now put the same weight in the thin fighter's hand. The strong fighter will punch, or swing the baton, faster than the thin fighter. Even though the thin fighter may have faster hands, he is disadvantaged when attempting to manipulate a heavy weapon. The additional inertia created by the weapon requires additional strength to manipulate it quickly. The same rule applies to kicks, however the differences are not as noticeable.

Don't think you need huge guns to swing a baton quickly or to knock out your opponent. You don't. Most of the power generated in a punch comes from the body and legs. For those of you who like numbers, biomechanical analysis found that the arm muscles contribute only 24% of a punch's force. The trunk contributes 37% and the legs 39% of the force. (73)

From a physics point of view, as speed increases, so does force. Physics tells us that, everything else remaining the same, if you increase the speed of a kick by two times, then the amount of force delivered to the target is increased two fold. This is not the case in reality, however. In the practical application of fighting techniques, as speed increases force decreases and vice versa. This is true because of the laws of inertia and biomechanics. This rule of biomechanics is explained in *Chapter 2*. Inertia explains why it is slower to move the entire body 18 inches forward than it is to move a hand by way of the back-fist 18 inches forward. To deliver a forceful punch with your body weight behind it takes just that, your body weight. The inevitable consequence of this is a decrease in the speed of your punch.

Now that you understand how physics, biomechanics and technique come into play concerning fighting speed, which body and corresponding attributes do you want? A strong, heavily muscled body, capable of lunging with great speed, delivering substantial amounts of force in the strikes, applying a crushing grip when wrestling, wielding weapons quickly, and being better able to withstand blows from the opponent? Or a thinner, strong body, capable of lightening fast punches and kicks, and more stamina? The increase in stamina in a lighter body comes from a conservation of energy because there is less mass to move. Endurance would be decreased once the bout turned to wrestling however, because the fighter with the lower level of strength would have to work harder to manipulate the mass of the stronger, heavier opponent.

One more comment regarding the speed versus power equation. There will be opportunities for you to take advantage of both facets if you know what to look for. Use your speed techniques when the opponent is stepping in toward you. When you hit him as he is coming toward you, you do not need power. The power will be greatly increased because the force behind his body coming forward is added to your technique. Many fighters have been dropped by nothing more than a jab that caught them as they were stepping in.

Based on the above lesson in physics, you should now understand why speed, body size, bone structure, technique selection, target selection, and joint alignment, all play a role in determining how much force will be imparted on your opponent with every technique. Body positioning, the movements of both you and your opponent, leg drive, follow through, hip and body rotation, and focus, also must be factored into the equation.

*Adaptability means that cross training may
decrease performance in a desired area. As a
result, the serious athlete must carefully design a
training program with the principle of specificity
of training in mind.*

Chapter 2
PHYSICAL SPEED

The human body is incredibly adaptable. Muscle physiology changes to become more efficient to optimize performance for the type of work being performed. This is good news for athletes. It means that an athlete can enhance his muscle and aerobic physiology to be sport specific through proper training. On the other hand, this adaptability means that cross training may decrease performance in a desired area. As a result, the serious athlete must carefully design a training program with the principle of specificity of training in mind. In fact, sports specific training has been proven to be more effective than generalized training at increasing performance in a particular sport.

For example, if you are a runner, you should not train on a bicycle, even though running and biking both use the same energy system, the aerobic system. This is because a lack of sport specific training prevents you from reaching your optimal level. If you trained by running and biking, you would not reach as high a level of proficiency at running as you would if you only trained at running. This holds especially true if you combine aerobic and anaerobic training. Doing so produces mixed results, with neither energy system reaching optimum levels. (7) Unfortunately, this fact also means that the benefits of your training are very sport specific. (Note: The anaerobic system will be discussed in more detail later in this chapter. For now, know that high intensity weight training receives its energy from the anaerobic system, therefore, resistance training is anaerobic training.)

One study compared the aerobic improvement gained from the rowing machine versus the stationary bicycle. Both groups improved their aerobic fitness levels substantially. Then the two groups switched equipment and were tested again. Their aerobic fitness levels dropped dramatically. Even though their aerobic fitness levels had significantly increased as a result of the training, this increased level of fitness was sport specific. There is little carry over from one sport to another. (65) As a result of this research and the research described below, every serious athlete should set highly detailed fitness goals in order to facilitate the development of an effective and appropriate physical training program.

Exercise affects muscle physiology in myriad ways. The changes that affect power production are explained below. Research suggests that the sarcomere, the part of the muscle fiber affecting force / length properties of the muscle, can also be changed through training. (Note: The force/length properties determine how much force a muscle can generate while it is stretched to any given length. For example, if the leg is bent at a 90 degree angle, the quadriceps would be capable of generating X amount of force. Changing the degree of the bend in the leg to 45 degrees, the quadriceps would be capable of generating Y amount of force.) Dr. Walter Herzog of the Human Performance Lab at the University of Calgary tested the effects of running versus cycling on the sarcomere force/length relationships and discovered a significant difference between the two groups. As a result, running to cross-train for cycling and vise versa is not advised. (38) Dr. Herzog stated that the results suggest that a triathlete (who trains with running and cycling) can never be as good a runner, or cycling specialist, even if he runs, or cycles, as much as the specialist and is equally talented as the running or cycling specialist.

Velocity of muscular contraction is affected by, to name a few factors, fiber type, fiber length, fiber diameter and the numbers of sarcomere in series. Each of these factors can be influenced in various ways by different forms of exercise. In addition, mechanical properties and enzymes necessary for energy production differ in the different types of muscle fibers. Each of these factors, including the process by which the fibers generate and burn fuel can be influenced by exercise. (15, 24, 44) In fact, these changes are immensely exercise specific. If you are not following a specific training program, not only could you miss out on some speed gains, but you could cause changes that decrease the speed of your muscle fibers. Make a recorded goal of your athletic ambitions so that the most effective training program to accomplish this goal can be designed. Techniques proven effective for making such a written goal are discussed in *Chapter 6, Psychological Speed.*

Speed of Muscular Contractions

There are three types of muscle tissue: they are skeletal, smooth and cardiac. Skeletal (or striated), muscle is attached to the skeleton. It performs the function of body movement and is under voluntary control. Smooth muscle is found within and around the digestive system. It is not under voluntary control. Cardiac muscle is unique to the heart and is also not under voluntary control.

Within skeletal muscle there are two primary types, slow twitch (Type I) and fast twitch (Type II.) Fast twitch is further broken down into Type IIa, Type IIb, IIx, and possibly IIax hybrids. Type IIa is the slowest contracting fast type, followed by IIax, IIx, and finally IIb. Type IIb is the fastest contracting muscle fiber type. These types are classified based on their functional and metabolic properties.

Type I Muscle Fibers

Type I fibers are slow oxidative fibers that require oxygen to burn fuel. Type I fibers have slower contractile properties, are smaller in diameter, have a lower strength of contraction and have a higher mitochondrial density. Mitochondria are very small, usually rod-like structures found in the cytoplasm (protoplasm of a cell, outside the nucleus) of most cells that serve as the center of intracellular enzyme activity. In other words, they are like little power stations that burn the fuel, providing the energy cells need to function. Type I fibers have a higher percentage of oxidative enzymes, a 15 to 20% greater capillary to fiber ratio versus Type II, and have a lower level of ATP activity. These factors translate to more oxygen delivery, waste removal and energy production, all of which help maintain conditions for prolonged activity. (Note: The breakdown of ATP is what provides the muscles with energy.) (7, 24)

Not only are Type I muscle fibers slow to contract but they are slow to fatigue as well. Part of the reason for their endurance is that they contain more, and larger, mitochondria as mentioned above. The additional mitochondria provide the fibers with more energy than Type II fibers receive. The smaller diameter of the Type I fibers causes an increase in the surface area to mass ratio. This facilitates gas and chemical exchange. That fact combined with their greater number of capillaries per fiber when compared to Type II fibers results in a significant gas and chemical exchange advantage.

These factors improve oxygen and energy delivery as well as waste product (primarily CO_2 and lactic acid) removal from the fibers. As a result of the above, Type I fibers tire less quickly than Type II fibers. (28, 65, 66) Type I fibers are known as slow oxidative fibers. This refers to the type of energy they burn. Type I fibers need oxygen to burn fuel. They are therefore, the primary energy producers during aerobic exercise.

Type II Muscle Fibers

Type II muscle fibers have fast contractile properties, higher ATP activity, fewer mitochondria with a lower mitochondrial respiratory capacity, and are 20% larger than Type I fibers. Type IIa fibers have relatively fast contractile properties, however, they display metabolic characteristics similar to Type I fibers. (66) Type IIa are fast oxidative-glycolytic fibers that can use either oxygen or glycogen for fuel production. Type IIb are fast glycolytic fibers that burn glycogen for fuel. (7, 24)

Type IIa, fast oxidative-glycolytic fibers, can produce fuel with or without oxygen. Energy produced without the consumption of oxygen is produced by the anaerobic energy system. Type IIb, fast gylcolytic fibers, are characterized by high adenosine triphosphatase (ATPase) activities and come into play during maximal effort when the cardiovascular and mitochondrial systems cannot keep up with the energy demands. (24) As stated above, the breakdown of ATP provides the muscle with energy. Both the aerobic and anaerobic energy systems can produce ATP, however, the aerobic system, Type I fibers, must have oxygen to produce ATP. It also takes Type I fibers longer to produce ATP. Type II fibers can produce ATP faster and without oxygen, but the production of ATP through the anaerobic system is not nearly as efficient as it is with the aerobic system. In other words, Type II fibers burn more fuel and receive less ATP. As a result, they have higher ATP activity so that they can produce ATP quickly and without oxygen.

The latest available research indicates that humans cannot change slow twitch fibers to fast twitch. Some animals can apparently make such a change and a few studies have provided evidence that humans can as well. The testing methods used in those studies however, carried a high degree of error and therefore, most researchers do not believe that any such change occurs within human muscle tissue.

<u>Muscle Fiber Type Summary</u>

Type I fibers

Type: slow oxidative fibers
Common Name: slow twitch
Energy Source: require oxygen to burn fuel
Properties:
• slower contractile properties
• are smaller in diameter
• have a lower strength of contraction
• have a higher mitochondrial density

Type II fibers

Type: fast oxidative fibers
Common Name: fast twitch
Energy Source: breakdown of ATP
Properties:
• fast contractile properties
• higher ATP activity
• fewer mitochondria with a lower mitochondrial respiratory capacity
• are 20% larger than Type I fibers

Type II Sub-groups

Type IIa (slowest of Type II fiber)
Type: fast oxidative-glycolytic fibers
Energy Source: either oxygen or glycogen

Type IIb (fastest contracting muscle fiber)
Type: fast glycolytic fibers
Energy Source: glycogen

Muscle Speed & Force Relationship

There is a relationship between speed and force. As more force is needed, speed decreases. This property of skeletal muscle is known as the force-velocity relationship. (8, 70) With the front-snap kick, very little force is generated, however, the foot travels to the groin and back very quickly. If you attempt to raise your opponent off the ground with your kick to the groin, the kick will not travel as quickly because additional force is required to perform the technique.

Consider how you would execute a front snap kick to the groin versus a front thrust kick where you attempt to knock down a door. The snap kick is light, involves little commitment, and is fast. The thrust kick is fully committed, involves much more body action, and is much slower. These examples illustrate the difference between the speed of contraction and the speed of tension development. The more tension, or force, that you want your muscle to generate, the longer it takes. That's one reason why you sacrifice speed when striking with maximal power.

The reason a power technique involves more commitment is different, however. Physics, specifically inertia, explains why a speed jab is less committed than a power jab. More of your mass is behind the power technique, creating more energy that must eventually be stopped. Thus, it takes more effort to mobilize the additional amount of mass when starting the technique and it takes more energy to slow down and reverse direction of your body mass after striking. Therefore, a power jab involves more commitment.

Muscle force is affected by several factors including neural firing rates and frequencies, strength, and relaxation capabilities of the antagonist muscle. Untrained subjects may not be able to voluntarily maximally recruit muscle fibers. Weight training can improve the level of voluntary activation. (44) Additionally, plyometrics can take the weightlifting athlete one step farther. (See *Plyometric Training, Chapter 9*.)

How you can increase the amount of relaxation of the antagonistic muscle is also explained under *Plyometrics*, found later in this chapter. However, on a related topic, highly trained athletes may be able to inhibit slow twitch fibers and activate the fast fibers to generate more explosive force. This adaptation can only come from repeated, maximal training. Dynamic training (plyometrics) is one such method of training. Plyometric training also can result in significant increases in Type II fiber area. (24) Therefore, even if you cannot inhibit the firing of slow twitch fibers, the higher ratio of Type II fiber area will, in essence, have the same effect because the hindrance from the Type I fibers becomes a smaller percentage of the total equation. Thus, its effect becomes less significant. (Note: Activation of slow twitch fibers can actually hinder the performance of fast twitch fibers.) (44)

Research & Physical Conditioning

Resistance training causes the following advantageous adaptations:

· It increases inhibition of the antagonist muscles, creating greater relaxation of those muscles. (An antagonist muscle is the muscle opposing a muscle performing work. For example, the biceps are the antagonists to the triceps muscles.)

· Resistance training decreases neural protective mechanisms (inhibition reflex). The inhibition reflex is a natural protective mechanism prohibiting maximal firing of all neurons. This protective mechanism decreases speed and power by not allowing maximal contraction of the muscle. Resistance training decreases the level of this inhibition, allowing for a faster, more powerful contraction. (26)

· Resistance training increases coordination of stimulation of synergistic muscles and it increases activation of synergistic muscles.

· It also increases motor neuron excitability (primes the motor neuron for stimulation). (26)

Each of these changes, by and of itself, increases speed and power. Together, the potential increase in contraction speed and power output is substantial. Resistance training for speed and power targets Type II fibers and the anaerobic system. As this chapter explains, the anaerobic system responds to high intensity training with biochemical, neural and anatomic adaptations. Unlike the aerobic system that produces changes throughout the body including changes to the circulatory system, respiratory system and VO2 efficiency, the response to anaerobic training is a local phenomenon with little systemic adaptation. (7, 37) Therefore, each muscle that plays a part in a technique that you want to improve upon needs to be targeted and trained.

Some studies show no significant difference in the maximal activation of muscle fibers in vivo (living subjects) versus in vitro (lab studies). Other studies show that as much as 25% of the test subjects cannot achieve maximal activation because of neural inhibition. The degree of inhibition for most people is relatively small during concentric contractions. However, it is significant during eccentric contractions. (Concentric contractions involve a shortening of the muscle fibers while eccentric contractions involve a lengthening of the fibers.) It is theorized that this is a protective factor, helping to prevent muscle tears, especially as the muscle lengthens. (15, 24) This protective mechanism normally decreases speed and power by not allowing maximal contraction of the muscle. Resistance training decreases the level of this inhibition, allowing for a faster, more powerful contraction. (26)

Doctors Robert Fitts and Jeffery Widrick reported in *Exercise and Sports Sciences Reviews* that variations in muscle fiber type account for only 25% of the difference in peak power output between different individuals. Therefore, other factors play a substantial role in determining variations in muscle performance. Two probable factors include muscle fiber diameter and neural drive, both of which are easily increased with proper training.

Neural drive refers to the efficiency of stimulation of the muscle by the central nervous system. Many researchers believe that neural drive is the primary factor for the significant gains in strength observed during the first six weeks when subjects begin a weight training program for the first time.

A third factor may involve co-activation of the antagonist muscle. As co-activation of the antagonist muscle is decreased, the level of relaxation of this muscle is increased. This increased relaxation results in less resistance being applied to the working muscle. Co-activation of the antagonist muscle decreased by approximately 20% during the first week of weight training according to one study and it continues to decrease with training. (24) Training to reduce the co-activation of the antagonist muscle is discussed later in this chapter. Neural inhibition is discussed in detail under *Plyometrics*, also in this chapter.

Over-Training

Some trainers argue that the number one factor causing diminished results concerning resistance exercise is over-training. There are three elements of over-training that may or may not be inter-related.

The first involves rest and recovery. Theory holds that the body adapts to the microscopic tears created during training by repairing those tears to a level infinitesimally stronger than before. This adaptation occurs during rest. A minimum of a full night rest is necessary. Also, be it good or bad, the skeletal muscular system is not on the top of the repair list. If you are fighting a cold, illness, or more serious injury, these microscopic tears in the muscle may go unrepaired. Therefore, take good care of yourself in every way to increase the speed of attaining desired results. This includes diet, rest and mental health (stress).

As an example of how inter-related these factors are, take note that one bad night's sleep can reduce the immune system's efficiency by as much as 50%. Studies have also shown that sleep deprivation slows reaction time as much as and sometimes more than alcohol. Miss a good night's sleep or catch a cold and your strength and speed may suffer. At the least, any gains you may have been making will stop until you are over the cold. Fortunately, the immune system can return to its full fighting form during the next night if it is a good sleep. (22)

The second element of over-training involves intensity. One study using experienced lifters had one group, group A, perform ten squats daily. Each squat consisted of the individual's one rep maximum. Test subjects in group B performed one set of ten squats daily. The weight used was 50% of their one rep max. After two weeks, subjects in group A had lost a significant amount of strength. Individuals in Group B did not suffer any loss in strength. The researchers also noted that it took between two and eight weeks before the level of strength returned to its pre-test condition for the subjects in group A. (27)

The third element of over-training involves weight training in conjunction with aerobic training. The physical shock of weight-bearing aerobic training, especially running, combined with a high intensity resistance training program tends to lead to over-training. It is for this reason that you see bodybuilders performing their aerobic work on the bicycle. (15)

Plyometrics

Plyometrics involve a sudden overloading of the muscle while the muscle is being stretched. In other words, it is a negative (eccentric) repetition performed dynamically (explosively). The benefit of plyometrics is derived from the inherent ability of the exercise to force the muscle to generate a more powerful contraction than any voluntary maximal stimulation could achieve. As stated before, there are inhibitors in the nervous system that prevent you from consciously contracting all muscle fibers maximally and simultaneously. This inhibition is a built in safety factor. If you could consciously stimulate your neuromuscular system to fire all muscle fibers within a muscle simultaneously and maximally, the risk of injury to that muscle and to its antagonist muscle would be high.

This natural inhibition can be overridden though. For example, you are walking down a sidewalk and stumble over a lifted section of cement. Your right leg automatically shoots out in front in a lunging position and prevents your face from kissing the concrete. The force generated by your right leg and gluteus muscles the instant your foot hits the ground is greater than what you could generate consciously. In fact, for most people, it is greater than the amount you can generate if you place yourself in this lunging position and try to spring backward off your right leg. By repeatedly subjecting a muscle to sudden overloads, you increase its eccentric strength and your ability to recruit this strength consciously, thus increasing your explosive abilities. (15)

Plyometric training was developed to increase the number of fibers that an athlete can simultaneously recruit, thus increasing speed, strength and power. (Reminder: The layperson's usage of the term power is used here and in most other sections of this book.) To understand how plyometrics work, it is necessary to first discuss the correlation between absolute and maximum strength. Absolute strength refers to the total contractile capacity of a muscle. It quantifies the amount of force generated if ALL muscle fibers fired in response to MAXIMAL stimulation by the nervous system. As discussed above, this is not possible due to protective mechanisms in the nervous system. Maximal strength is the greatest amount of force you can generate voluntarily. For example, your max on the bench press.

Some plyometrics come close to generating absolute strength levels of power. It is for this reason that plyometric training is high risk for injuries. Plyometrics should only be performed after a thorough warm up, after a good level of fitness has been achieved and then only twice per week per body part. Refer to the training section for more on plyometric cautions and routines.

The reason plyometrics can approach absolute strength levels lies in the stretch receptor reflex. Using the above stumble example, when the foot hits the ground and you start to stimulate the fibers, intrafusal fibers in the muscle spindles are stretched because the muscle is working eccentrically. These fibers do not contract like Type I & II fibers. They register the amount of stretch within the muscle. This information is then relayed to the central nervous system (CNS.) The CNS, attempting to save your face, overrides the normal inhibitions, sending stimulus to the muscle for a fast and forceful contraction.

There are several benefits of plyometric training, all of which increase speed, strength and power. Plyometric training does this by three mechanisms. First, it increases voluntary fiber recruitment, bringing your maximal contraction strength closer to your absolute contraction capacity. Second, it increases strength by increasing the effectiveness of the training session. More fibers are stimulated during the workout, resulting in an increased stimulation for growth. Third, it trains the muscle and neuromuscular system to perform at a faster rate.

This adaptation occurs through several mechanisms. The neuromuscular system adapts by decreasing the time required to switch from eccentric to concentric contractions; e.g., springing back off that right leg after the initial lunge. This depends on: 1) absolute strength, which can be increased by plyometric and resistance training, and 2) how efficiently the neuromuscular system can make the transition from eccentric to concentric contraction. In other words, as the neuromuscular system becomes familiar with plyometrics, it 'learns' to fire more fibers at a greater speed, or better yet, simultaneously. The rate of switching to concentric from eccentric contractions and the overall speed of conscious muscular contractions increase as a result. (15) Plyometric training also increases speed, strength and power by increasing the speed and level of relaxation within the antagonist muscles.

Exceptional athletes seem to perform even the most difficult tasks with ease, grace and fluidity. One of the reasons for this is the athlete's ability to relax the antagonist muscles. This has a direct impact on making the movements easier, thus faster, more powerful and economical, more graceful and fluid. This ability may be more pronounced in some athletes than in others, however it can be improved upon by everyone.

Concentric contractions are always more powerful when preceded by eccentric contractions. This is due, in part, to the decrease in inhibiting factors caused by the stretch reflex. This is also due to the elastic properties of muscle. When muscle fibers are stretched, they store elastic energy within the muscle. Think of a muscle like a rubber band. Both easily stretch beyond their normal resting length. However, when released, both return to their normal state. This pull beyond its resting length is stored energy. When contraction switches from eccentric to concentric, i.e., the stretching stops and the muscle starts to contract, this elastic energy is released and is added to the concentric contraction. Plyometrics strengthen elastic properties of muscle and therefore increase the elastic storage capabilities of muscle. (6, 15)

Intense exercise can produce effects on power production similar to the effects of plyometrics. Tests have shown that if an athlete performs maximum isometric contractions or near maximum concentric contractions before jumping, the athlete will be able to jump higher than if he did not perform that type of warm up. Specifically, after an athlete warms up, if he then performs a set of squats consisting of five repetitions with nearly his maximal weight and then rests for four minutes or a little more, he will be able to generate more power when jumping or lunging. A beginning weight lifter does not receive nearly as much benefit from this technique as does an advanced lifter. This benefit is short lived and would therefore be difficult to apply to sparring applications. (76)

A group of scientists studied the effects of plyometric training versus high intensity weight training. The training lasted 9 weeks and test subjects were tested in the 100 meter sprint before and after the training. The sprint was sectioned into three categories: initial acceleration, maximum speed and overall time reflecting speed endurance. The weight training group significantly increased their abilities in the areas of initial acceleration and muscular strength. The plyometric group did not increase their strength significantly. The plyometric group increased their abilities in the areas of initial acceleration and maximum speed. They were not able to maintain that higher speed, and therefore, even though their overall time was faster, it was not fast enough to meet the standards of statistical significance. Even though both groups significantly increased the speed of their initial acceleration, the plyometric group's gain in initial acceleration far exceeded that of the weight training group. (30)

Other tests have compared the results of different training regimens consisting of weight training, plyometrics, and weight training combined with plyometrics. The participants of the different studies were tested for increases in strength, speed and power. All three training regimens resulted in increased strength, speed and power. However, the group that trained with both weight training and plyometrics realized gains which were significantly greater than the gains achieved by the groups performing either weight training only or plyometrics only. (19)

Age & Speed

Everyone gets slower, weaker, fatter, and less flexible as they get older, right? Eventually, yes, but you will be amazed, and encouraged, as to just how long you can continue to improve and put off the inevitable. The four main areas athletes worry about as they age can all be improved upon for a very long time. These areas of concern are identified below.

1) FLEXIBILITY

Decreased flexibility can be overcome with stretching. You do not have to lose any flexibility, however, it takes more time and effort to maintain what you have and progress is harder and slower with age. Even seventy year olds can improve their flexibility.

2) NEUROMUSCULAR SYSTEM

At about the age of 55 a decrease in the proficiency and voluntary control of the neuromuscular system begins. This process is very slow, picking up pace at about the age of 65. Of course this process begins at a different time and at a different rate for everyone. Daily training helps slow this process. Even Olympic lifters continue to increase the efficiency and voluntary control of their neuromuscular system. There does not appear to be an upper limit that cannot be surpassed. Their highly developed neuromuscular system continues to make small improvements. Like flexibility, strength and body composition, the neuromuscular system can be maintained at a proficient level into the sixties. It simply takes more time and effort. (43)

3) BODY COMPOSITION

Most people experience an increase in the percentage of body fat as they get older. This is because they lose muscle mass. Approximately 95 to 98 percent of all calories are burned within muscle tissue. Therefore, less muscle mass means that less calories are being burned. This is the cause of the slowing of the basal metabolic rate (BMR.) Maintain your muscle mass and activity level and your BMR will remain the same. Also, a decrease in muscle mass equates to an increase in the percentage of fat that composes your body. Increase your muscle mass and the percentage of fat decreases. First, because it represents a smaller percentage of your total weight, and second, because the actual amount of fat will decrease because your BMR will increase. That's assuming your activity level and calorie consumption do not change for the worse.

4) MUSCLE MASS

At approximately the age of 50, people start to lose muscle size and strength, especially in fast twitch Type II fibers. Another study stated that this trend can begin in the thirties. (5) Low intensity resistance exercise was not shown to be very helpful in stopping this trend. However, high intensity resistance exercise was shown not only to stop the decline but to reverse the process. The test subjects became larger and stronger. (7, 43, 44) Based on this research, weight training is much more important for older athletes than it is for younger athletes when trying to maintain, or to improve, speed and power. Without training, older people lose type II fiber size through nerve denervation. (Note: The test subjects also maintained their balance, another ability that starts to fall with age, as a result of the resistance training.) (44) To be discussed in *Chapter 12*, balance is an important element in the production and maintenance of speed.

Below, you will find a list of the many effects age has on the human body. Unfortunately, none of these lead to an increase in performance. All the adverse effects of aging listed below can be delayed, if not reversed, for many years. Some of the effects of aging include:

1) Decrease in muscle fiber size, and therefore strength, especially Type II fibers, starting first with Type IIb, then IIx, IIax and IIa. Note: Most scientists do not believe that the number of fibers decreases with age, only that their size and type changes.
2) Decrease in the basal metabolic rate (BMR.)
3) Increase in the percentage of body fat.
4) Decrease in flexibility.
5) Decrease in the ability of balance.
6) Decrease in function of the neuromuscular system, including the

decreased ability & possibly complete inability to activate Type II fibers.

7) Decrease in the elasticity of muscle.
8) Increase in the susceptibility of muscular damage, especially from eccentric exercises. This is primarily due to the decrease in the elastic properties of the muscle.
9) Decrease in the efficiency of the repair of muscular damage. Refer to notation below.
10) Decrease in VO2 Max.
11) Increase in muscle collagen.
12) Decrease in recovery rate after muscle fatigue.
13) Weakening of the skeletal system due to osteoporosis.
(5, 7, 10, 43)

Additionally, to repair muscular damage, the repair and replacement of myofibers after injury depend on satellite cells. The number of satellite cells declines with age, however, the number of satellite cells increases with exercise, at least with endurance exercise. (10) The author could find no studies regarding the effects of resistance training on the production of satellite cells. Based on all of the above noted benefits of exercise in reference to the aging process and on conversations with some of the researchers of these studies, it seems a reasonable assumption that, like endurance training, resistance training would increase the number of satellite cells and therefore increase the speed of muscle repair.

As you can see, many of the above factors are inter-related and all can affect speed. All the above factors can be improved with regular training. In fact, most of these factors can be continually improved upon until the approximate age 55 and sometimes 65. After this 'very individual' age, training cannot keep up with the aging process. It can, however, dramatically slow it down. (10) For individuals with no physical activity after the age of 65, the implementation of a training program can bring dramatic improvements to all the above noted areas of fitness.

Rogers and Evans of the Noll Physiological Research Center at Pennsylvania State University (66), go as far as to say that the loss of strength and the decline of the muscle's metabolic capacity can no longer be considered as an inevitable consequence of the aging process. Studies have shown that the loss of strength and size of muscle, especially Type II fibers, in the elderly can be attributed largely to a progressive neurologic process beginning at the age of 50. At the approximate age of 50, Type II fibers undergo a denervation. Type I fibers then begin reinnervating, partly making up for the loss to the

Type II fibers. (5, 7, 43) Weight training has been shown to reverse this effect, reinnervating Type II fibers, resulting in hypertrophy and an increase in strength. One of the test subjects who realized such changes was 96 years of age. (7)

Muscle collagen has many functions, some of which include alignment of muscle fibers which enhances force mechanics through an increase in structural support and strength, conferring elasticity and storing elastic energy during stretching. (10) The alignment of muscle fibers and storage of elastic energy contribute directly to increasing speed. As far as conferring elasticity to the muscles, this increase in the elasticity of the muscle helps prevent injury. This results in fewer interruptions to training, and therefore, can indirectly lead to an increase in speed.

There is conflicting research data concerning age and the commonly observed decrease in contractile strength of the muscle and the increase in the fatigue factor (diminished aerobic capacity) of the muscle. Many researchers believe that the decrease in strength is primarily due to a decrease in fiber size resulting from inactivity. They also believe that the decrease in muscle aerobic capacity is due in part to the loss of fitness characteristics (for example, decreased muscle mitochondria) as a result of inactivity and a decreased contractile strength of the muscle. This last element plays a factor in speed production and is demonstrated by simple math.

To illustrate the point, if benching 100 pounds used to be 50% of your max, a decrease in strength could, for the sake of this example, cause this 100 pounds to be 75% of your max. When pressing the 100 pounds as many times as possible, you would not be able to press it as many times after the decrease in strength because more fibers must be recruited for each repetition, thereby shortening the time involved to exhaust the metabolic capabilities of the muscle. What is very clear from the research is that exercise can stop and even reverse the above noted effects of aging by increasing fiber size (contractile strength) and muscular endurance. (10, 43) In this example, not only is speed reduced during the later repetitions because of the earlier onset of fatigue, but the first repetition is also slower because the 100 pounds is now 75% of the your maximum. No longer is it 50% of your maximum. It would be as if you add 33 pounds to the bar. Of course it could not be pressed up as quickly.

At the approximate age of 45 to 50, humans begin to suffer from a slow decrease in strength and speed. At age 50 the rate of decline increases. Between 50 and 60, most people lose 18% of their strength. Between 60 and

70 they lose another 18%. This rate increases after age 70. (66) Up to the approximate age of 70, most of this loss comes from a reduction in size of Type II fibers. Therefore, speed and power suffer significant losses. After age 70, the loss in size becomes more generalized over Types I & II fibers. (66) Older studies indicated that there is a change from Type I fibers to Type I fibers with aging. This theory is no longer accepted. The results were most likely due to a loss in Type II fiber size rather than an actual change. Note: Data does exist to contradict this. Researchers have found a decrease in the fiber numbers in older individuals. They attribute this loss to a neurological deficit at the level of the motor neuron. However, they have not yet established any mechanisms to account for this loss. (43, 66)

Rogers and Evans (66) reference a study conducted by Young et al. that determined that the reduction in strength begins by the age of 30. Most, if not all, of this loss can be attributed to the loss of muscle size. There is some evidence however, indicating that some of the loss in strength comes from an alteration of the muscle's capacity to generate force, possibly due to a reduced activation of motor units (muscle fibers) and/or a loss of contractile or mechanical properties of the muscle. (7, 66) However, other studies, including those of Frontera et al., also referenced by Rogers and Evans (66), concluded that the major factor in the age related decline in strength can be attributed to the loss of muscle mass rather than a deterioration in the contractile capacity of the muscle.

Again, good news. These depressing effects of aging can be reversed. The above effects pertain to sedentary individuals. If you train consistently as you age, you can continue to increase your abilities and adaptations in many areas of fitness. In those areas that inevitably decline with age, training slows the rate of decline. You may also compensate for the loss by continuing to improve in another area. Here are some statistics for sedentary people placed on a training program at varying ages:

1) Subjects 60 to 72 years of age who trained with weights for 12 weeks. They increased their fiber size by an average of 28%. They also increased the number of capillaries per fiber by 15%. (Frontera et al., referenced within 66)

2) Test subjects were 30 year old men who endurance trained for five months. They increased the fiber size in Type I fibers by 23%. There was no observed change in Type II fiber size. Type IIb fibers did change to Type IIa fibers, however. (66)

3) Cogan, (referenced within 66), studied 70 year old men placed on an endurance training program. These test subjects realized an

increase in fiber areas of both Type I and Type II fibers. The conflicting data of these results and those within number 2 above can be theorized to be because the 70 year old men had already undergone a significant decrease in Type II fiber size. They simply regained some of what they had lost. The 30 year old men should not have lost Type II fiber size, and as you know from information provided above and from research quoted elsewhere in this book, endurance training does not increase fiber diameter in Type II fibers.

4) Resistance training in older subjects, age not stated, increased neural adaptations and therefore, increased the strength of the test subjects. This was concluded because the significant strength gains resulting from the short study duration could not be attributed to gains in hypertrophy. (66)

Age, Natural Antioxidants & Hormones

Pycnogenols, specifically proanthocyanidine, catechol and gallocatechol, are the most powerful antioxidants known. They are also produced naturally within the body. DHEA, which is short for dehydroepiandrosterone, is also considered to be important for health and longevity. It is a hormone produced naturally in human bodies by the adrenal glands and appears to act as a precursor to other hormones such as estrogen and testosterone. Testosterone levels have a direct relationship with muscle size, strength and aggression. Pycnogenols and DHEA are produced at their peak during our 20s and 30s. The levels gradually fall off after that. DHEA continues to fall until production is down to roughly 10% of peak by the age of 60. Exercise has been shown to increase levels of production of these beneficial chemicals. (72) How antioxidants can affect your speed by affecting your strength is discussed later in this chapter.

A side note not related to speed: although there are conflicting studies concerning the decline of VO2 Max with age, the consensus is that VO2 Max will inevitably decline with age. However, master athletes, over 50 years of age, have been shown to have significantly higher muscle respiration capacity over younger athletes, thereby making up for lost ground in the VO2 arena. This is believed due to the years of training and the continual adaptations resulting from their endurance training. (43, 66)

Kirkendall and Garett of Duke University Medical Center summarized their recent paper on the effects of aging and training of skeletal muscle with a motivational and optimistic view toward training throughout your life. They stated that the negative effects of aging on the structure and function of skeletal muscle can by minimized, if not eliminated, by a lifetime of proper physical activity. (43)

Youth & Power

Prepubescent children are at a disadvantage when it comes to speed and power production because their anaerobic system is under-developed. Studies have estimated that the anaerobic system of 11 to 13 year old boys may be only 65% developed. These studies have provided some evidence that high intensity training may significantly increase the function of their underdeveloped anaerobic system, however the training intensity needs to be quite high. Sprinting was the type of training used in the two studies from which this information was taken. (7)

Improper dieting methods can cause you to lose much of the muscle mass for which you worked so hard. Food supplements can increase the effectiveness of your workouts, improve workout recovery, increase your strength, and potentially waste your money.

Chapter 3
Supplements, Drugs and Diet

Health and nutrition affect speed through several mechanisms. If you are sick, overweight and out of shape when competing, you are obviously not going to be as fast as you could be if you were healthy, lean and in shape. Nutrition can not only affect your health and body composition, it can affect your energy level and endurance as well. Improper dieting methods can cause you to lose much of the muscle mass for which you worked so hard. Food supplements can increase the effectiveness of your workouts, improve workout recovery, increase your strength, and potentially waste your money. Drugs can affect your speed by affecting your health, strength, physiology and psychology.

If you wish to maximize the effectiveness of your speed training and to reach your full speed potential, read this section on health and nutrition. No training program is complete without incorporating the sciences of health, nutrition, diet, food supplements and drugs. Likewise, no speed training book would be complete without a section referencing those areas.

Food Supplements

There are at least five supplements for every possible bodily function. They all work, too. At least that's what all those advertisements say. "Dr. Scheister says this all natural supplement increases libido, or muscle mass, or whatever, by 23%." Don't buy it, literally. In the author's opinion, there is only one supplement proven in numerous double blind studies to increase strength and power. Don't waste your money on the rest. This wonder supplement was used by 3 out of 4 Olympic athletes at the 1996 Games. (62) So what is it?

Creatine Monohydrate

Creatine monohydrate, methylguanido-acetic acid, is produced naturally in the liver to supply energy to the muscles. Once absorbed by the muscles, it is converted to creatine phosphate by the enzyme creatine kinase. It is then stored in the muscle cell until needed, whereupon it is used to produce ATP. (58) Creatine Phosphate is primarily used in Type IIb fibers. (7) Creatine supplementation consistently increases weight, strength and power. Creatine kinase levels are two times higher in Type II fibers than in Type I muscle fiber cells. (9) This may indicate that the majority of the benefits of creatine supplementation are realized by Type II fibers, leading to more speed and power increases than if the Type I fibers were the beneficiaries.

Users generally gain five to ten pounds in two weeks. Most of the gains are attributed to water uptake by the muscle cells. Strength gains of 20 to 33% in one to two months are common, although most are closer to 15 to 20%. Creatine also increases energy stores in the muscle, thereby increasing muscle endurance because of increased strength and increased available energy. Creatine decreases blood lactate levels, delaying fatigue and speeding recovery. It may also reduce oxygen free radicals, reducing tissue damage and speeding recovery. (20) (Refer to *Antioxidants* below for more information on free radicals.) Creatine does not appear to increase aerobic capacity. This is attributed to the increase in overall weight with no apparent increase in VO2 Max. Therefore the total energy demands of endurance training are increased without any corresponding increase in aerobic capacity. (20, 44)

Is creatine safe? The author was not able to locate any research indicating adverse effects from taking creatine. There have been a few short-term studies concerning creatine supplementation and health effects. Only beneficial results were observed, however, the author did not find any articles addressing the possible effects of water uptake on high blood pressure. No long term study regarding the effects of creatine supplementation exists at this time.

Some scientists believe that creatine, when taken in high doses, causes dehydration because it reroutes an excessive amount of water to the muscles, impairing the body's ability to cool down through sweating.

Because of a lack of knowledge in the scientific community concerning creatine and food supplements, the author is not recommending that any supplement be taken, and certainly not without the approval and advice of your physician. Final note: Many bodybuilders and others with a near perfect diet do not seem to realize the gains from creatine that others do. This is most likely because creatine is found in meat, and therefore, their high protein diets supply them with sufficient amounts of creatine.

HMB

It was stated above that there is only one supplement proven to increase strength and power. Well, there may be two. Another one appears to offer benefits to those that suffer from protein breakdown (catabolism), either from age, strenuous exercise, or from an insufficient diet. This supplement is beta-hydroxy beta-methylbutyrate (HMB.) There are studies that have found that HMB increases muscle mass and strength and decreases fat percentages. These researchers attribute the results listed above to HMB's believed effect of minimizing the protein breakdown that occurs after strenuous activity, thereby decreasing recovery time and allowing the body to redirect efforts to building new tissue and subsequently burning more calories. (57, 62) Note: 98% of all calories are burned by muscle. Therefore, increasing muscle mass increases caloric expenditure, 24 hours a day. Thus, HMB may help change body composition by increasing muscle mass and by reducing fat.

HMB would most likely be of the most value when dieting, helping to reduce, and perhaps stop, the catabolic (protein consuming) effects usually associated with dieting. Of course, this assumes that the athlete continues resistance training during the diet. Dieting without exercise causes a loss of fat, AND muscle. HMB supplementation without exercise did not cause the test subjects to gain any muscle mass. (58) Like creatine, HMB occurs naturally in the body. Also like creatine, no known studies attribute adverse effects from supplementing HMB to the diet. However, there have not been any long term studies on the effects of HMB or creatine.

Antioxidants & Free Radicals

Free radicals are highly reactive molecules possessing unpaired electrons. They are produced during metabolism of food and during energy production (exercise). They are believed to contribute to the molecular damage and death of cells. (40, 62)

We have all seen articles and news reports proclaiming the beneficial effects of taking antioxidants, specifically vitamins C, E & A. Antioxidants are believed to reduce the number of free radicals, and therefore, reduce the risks of cancer, as well as postponing the effects of aging. It is theorized that strenuous exercise causes an increased production of free radicals and that these free radicals contribute to the muscle damage incurred as a result of the exercise. Vitamins C & E, particularly vitamin C, were shown to decrease recovery time after strenuous exercise. Subjects taking vitamin C regained significantly more of their original strength in days 0, 1, 2 and 3 after exercising than did other test subjects. (24)

This translates to more speed through three mechanisms. First, gaining 87% of their strength back on the day after exercising, for the vitamin C takers, compared to regaining only 75% of strength back for the vitamin E takers, means more strength to move mass, therefore, the ability to generate greater velocity. Second, if you exercise those same muscles within three days, you have more strength available, therefore, you are able to place a greater training stimulus upon the muscle fibers. This will lead to greater strength gains. Third, less muscle damage should translate to increased growth because a larger percentage of the nourishment available to the muscles can be directed at growth, instead of repair. This third point is just a hypothesis. However, this is a hypothesis accepted by the scientific community to explain how HMB supplementation can increase muscle growth through the same mechanism.

A recent study indicated that as little as 1000 mg of vitamin C a day significantly reduced serum cortisol levels. Cortisol is a hormone that is released as a result of tissue stress. It interferes with the anabolic (muscle building) effect of testosterone. It is possible that the reduced levels of cortisol during recovery can result in a greater retention of protein. Through this mechanism, vitamin C can act as an anti-catabolic agent. (Catabolic refers to muscle break down.) (50)

Preliminary studies indicate that vitamin E may improve athletic performance at high altitudes by improving oxygen utilization. (65) The exact mechanism(s) that makes this possible is still unknown. Why does it not improve performance at sea level if it improves oxygen utilization? Perhaps the benefits of vitamin E are only realized in low oxygen levels, or, because athletes performing at sea level have more oxygen readily available to them, the beneficial effects of vitamin E are less apparent. Nonetheless, since vitamin E is known to provide a host of other benefits to all individuals, it appears to be well worth supplementing your diet with it, should you wish to do so.

Other Supplements

GABA

GABA, or gamma-aminobutyric acid, accepted as a neurotransmitter, has been touted to increase growth hormone production and the BMR (basal metabolic rate). It also has some interesting side effects, like a flush tingling feeling, or sometimes a shortness of breath, but as yet nothing serious. Don't waste your money on it, though.

Ginseng

Don't waste your money. There is no sound evidence that supplementing ginseng to your diet will benefit your speed in any direct or indirect manner. Besides, long term heavy usage of it causes adverse side effects. (63)

Yohimbe Bark

Some people feel yohimbe bark is valuable as a fat burner. However, research for this book did not reveal any double blind studies conclusively showing an increase in the metabolism of fat as a result of supplementing the diet with yohimbe.

Chromium Picolinate

This was another highly promoted supplement. After 12 or 18 months of praise for chromium picolinate, studies concluded that it did not produce the athletic benefits that it was promoted to. In fact, some studies determined that prolonged usage of it can be harmful. Taking this supplement will not increase your speed.

Diet & Nutrition

Carbohydrate Loading

Carbohydrate loading is an accepted practice designed to enhance performance in long, intense endurance events by increasing the body's storage of glycogen. This practice extends the amount of time the athlete can maintain a desired level of performance by providing more available fuel. The larger the gas tank, the farther the car can go. The larger gas tank, full of fuel, weighs more though. This essentially happens with humans as well. For every gram of glycogen stored in muscle, the body must store 2.7 grams of water as well. Carbohydrate loading can hinder short term, high intensity performance through this mechanism. (65) In short, it can slow you down.

There is one reason why you may wish to consume plenty of carbs. If you are training twice a day, consuming carbohydrates during and after the first workout results in an increased energy level for your second workout. This can help delay fatigue. Even if both workouts are resistance training, carbs can help. A recent study revealed that group B, made up of lifters that consumed the carbohydrates during and after the first workout, realized substantial gains in strength and power when compared to group A. Group A did not consume any additional carbs. Their diet remained unchanged. Group B had more muscle glycogen, therefore more energy to exercise. This resulted in an increased training stimulus placed upon their muscles. (33)

Protein

Eat lots of protein, chicken, tuna and eggs, right? You have probably also been told that Americans consume far more protein than they need and that bodybuilders eat so much protein that it can cause digestive problems. Like most arguments, the answer lies somewhere in the middle. Most nutritionists argue that Americans eat far too much protein. They state that we eat more than needed to build muscle and more than the digestive tract can absorb. This may all be true. However, hypertrophy cannot occur if protein intake is inadequate. Vegetarians need to be especially aware of their protein intake. (68) Protein advocates would argue that one gram of protein for each pound of body weight is too low and nutritionists will argue that this is far too high. If you choose to limit your protein intake under the advice of a nutritionist, or for any other reason, supplementing your diet with HMB may help.

Athletes sustaining a moderate to high degree of muscle damage due to repeated strenuous exercise, or older subjects engaged in exercise programs, have been shown to benefit from supplementary protein beyond the levels recommended by nutritionists. (66)

There is a limit to how much protein the human body can digest in any one meal. Some bodybuilders argue that it is as low as 20 to 25 grams. (63) Many nutritionists will argue that the amount is higher. Either way, consuming your protein during several meals is more effective for absorption of protein than it would be if you were to eat all your protein during lunch and dinner. Several small meals are healthier than a few large ones anyway.

Hormones

As you know, hormones, which include testosterone, insulin, growth factors and growth hormones, influence muscle growth. The endocrine system regulates hormonal concentrations. Endocrine function is highly integrated with nutritional status and intake, stress, sleep, disease and overall health. Suffer from stress at work and your training results may suffer because of decreased endocrine function. (44) Physical training can alter hormonal concentration in the blood stream. Different types of training cause different alterations. (44, 72) Although research has just begun to look at how resistance exercise affects hormone levels, it is believed that it increases growth hormone production as well as testosterone production.

Thyroid Hormone

Since seven million Americans are affected by hypo- or hyperthyroidism, a brief discussion of how this affects muscle properties seems appropriate. Hypothyroidism causes a shift to Type I fiber characteristics and possibly a change from Type II to Type I. Hypothyroidism causes a slowing of the force-velocity relationship, it retards muscle growth and causes an increased rate of relaxation. It also decreases calcium intake, thus slowing the rate of fiber stimulation. It lowers levels of myosin enzymes necessary for energy breakdown and it causes an increase in muscle endurance. It also tends to cause a slowing of the metabolism. Hyperthyroidism causes the reverse of the above, resulting in an increased capacity for speed and power. (8, 16)

Growth Hormones

There is much conflicting data on the benefits of taking growth hormone enhancers and testosterone boosters. The majority of the research tends to indicate that both are only beneficial when the subject has a low level of growth hormone or testosterone. Growth hormone may be beneficial to subjects with naturally occurring low levels and in the elderly because levels decline naturally with age. (75) For the normal athlete, growth hormone supplementation does not appear to increase contractile protein, hypertrophy, strength, performance or muscle function.

Growth hormone supplementation can, however, have some very serious side effects. These may include water retention (due to increased nitrogen retention), carpal tunnel compression, and insulin resistance that can cause an increase in weight, specifically fat. (75) For those of you who insist on taking growth hormones, take them periodically. After four to six weeks, what small benefits you may derive from them, i.e., nitrogen sparing effects if you are not consuming enough protein, disappear. The body adapts to the supplementation and reduces the amount of its own growth hormone production. Therefore, if you feel you must take it, take it for about a month and then take three weeks off before supplementing again. (75) The best news is that heavy resistance training has been shown to increase blood levels of growth hormone naturally. (26, 72)

One night of bad sleep can reduce the effectiveness of the immune system by 50 percent. It also stops the secretion of growth hormones. Growth hormones are released in the third stage of sleep. Without this deep state of sleep, there is no release of growth hormones. As you have undoubtedly experienced, many factors can affect sleep, such as stress, drinking, disease, etc. Very strenuous exercise also can affect sleep. After those killer workouts where your entire body aches, you may not fall into third stage sleep. This results in a slowing of growth, recovery and of course, speed. (53)

Testosterone

Pretty much the same holds true for testosterone boosters. The two biggest testosterone boosters on the market are Androstenedione and Tribulus Terrestris. There is much hype about both, each being marketed with research citing great benefits to be gained from taking them. The Androstenedione fans are citing a 1962 study involving women where supplementation significantly raised their testosterone levels. Researching for this book, no unbiased research was found showing that it significantly raises levels in healthy males. It appears that Tribulus Terrestris does not raise testosterone levels in healthy males either. Its benefits appear to be for those who have low levels of testosterone, perhaps steroid users whose bodies have shut down production of testosterone.

Like growth hormones, testosterone boosters may only be beneficial to those individuals with naturally occurring low levels, most frequently including women and the elderly. Note: You may be interested to know that the NFL has decided to ban Androstenedione supplementation. (62)

There may very well be adverse effects from artificially boosting your testosterone levels. These could include increased aggression, hair loss, acne, and increased cardiac stress.

Diet & Exercise

The science of weight loss is beyond the scope of this book. However, if you do go on a diet, follow these two simple rules so that you will not lose strength as well.

When dieting, the body's natural reaction is not only to slow the BMR down, which will cause you to gain weight more easily when you stop dieting, but it also attempts to retain what it needs for survival. Unfortunately, it needs fat for warmth and other bodily functions. As a result, in its effort to retain some fat, dieting causes you to lose muscle mass. This is another reason why the BMR slows down. To prevent, or at least decrease the loss of muscle mass, perform resistance training regularly. To increase your chances of maintaining your muscle mass, lose weight slowly and train using heavy weight and low repetitions. Also, perform functional exercises that involve several body parts at once, e.g. bench press, squats, pull-ups, etc. These exercises are best for helping to maintain overall muscle mass during the diet.

Here's a second tip for dieting that you will not find in most dieting books. When dieting, the best meal to cut back on is dinner. If you consume 2000 calories per day, you will lose weight faster if they are consumed between 7: 00 a.m. and 3:00 p.m. than if they are consumed at 3:00 p.m. and at 8:00 p.m. Likewise, calories consumed at night have a higher probability of being stored as fat than they would if they were consumed during the day when they may be immediately used for fuel. Yes, the basic rule of weight control is calories burned versus calories consumed, however the equation is more complicated than that. As predicting weather is much more complicated than just factoring temperature and moisture content, the mechanics behind the above facts, including metabolism, weight, set points, etc., all of which are beyond the scope of this book, make the dieting equation just as complicated.

Also, research indicates that for people seeking to increase their metabolic rate through exercise, it is best to exercise shortly after eating. Eating alone temporarily speeds up your metabolism. Exercising shortly afterward further speeds up your metabolism and keeps it at this higher rate for several hours. This may also decrease the number of calories directed to fat storage.

Dehydration

Studies have demonstrated that dehydration is directly linked to fatigue. In an extended bout, dehydration will speed the onset of fatigue and that will slow you down. Dehydration also increases muscle viscosity. (63) Remember from *Chapter 1* that an increase in muscle viscosity can decrease the speed of contraction? Think of it like motor oil. The thicker the oil, the slower it flows.

Drugs

NSAIDs

Non-steroidal antiinflammatory drugs [NSAIDs] are the most commonly used prescription and non-prescription medications available. They are taken for everything from headaches to heart disease prevention. This group of drugs includes aspirin, ibuprofen, naproxen sodium and ketaprofen. These drugs work by inhibiting the enzyme cyclooxygenase. This enzyme is responsible for the production of prostaglandin, a hormone-like substance that contributes to pain and inflammation. It is theorized that prostaglandin, and the resulting soreness, are a natural consequence of the repair process that occurs after strenuous exercise.

Previously in this book you learned that the current theory suggests that growth comes from the repair of microscopic injury caused by exercise. Researchers believe that NSAIDs may inhibit muscle growth by inhibiting the production of prostaglandin. (22, 53) Therefore, to avoid the possible adverse effects of NSAIDs on your training, take acetaminophen, i.e., Tylenol. If you are taking aspirin for the health of your cardiovascular system, do not make any alterations in your dosage without first consulting your physician. Many athletes take NSAIDs to reduce pain and inflammation resulting from over training, arthritis, tendonitis and bursitis. If you are one of them, unfortunately, you don't have many options. Acetaminophen has very little effect on reducing inflammation.

Anabolic Steroids

Every one knows that anabolic steroids will make you faster and stronger. Remember the Canadian track star Ben Johnson? Fortunately, most people know that there are serious adverse side effects from anabolic steroid usage. All too often side effects, both temporary and permanent, are numerous and range from acne to death. Additionally, the benefits of anabolic steroid usage, such as increased strength, speed and power, only last as long as you are taking them. Once usage stops, the gains realized begin to fade. As noted above however, some of the adverse side effects may be permanent. Some athletes believe that if steroids are not 'stacked' and are taken conservatively, the risk of side effects is greatly diminished while many of the rewards can still be achieved. This is wishful thinking by desperate individuals. These temporary gains are not worth the serious consequences. In addition, there have been numerous studies documenting the adverse, and positive, effects of anabolic steroid usage. No long term studies were found indicating that conservative usage is safe.

Stimulants & Depressants

Obviously, depressants tend to slow, or adversely effect an athlete's performance. The only exception to this is if the athlete is suffering from anxiety. Then a depressant may help him to relax enough to increase his speed and/or performance. Depressants include alcohol, valium, marijuana, cough syrup, muscle relaxants and pain pills other than aspirin, ibuprofen or Tylenol. Even though nicotine is a stimulant, most physicians believe that cigarettes will tend to slow down, or hinder performance for numerous reasons. See smoking later in this chapter for more details.

Colds, motion sickness and traveler's diarrhea, of course, affect performance. The drugs used to treat them do as well because they have an anticholingeric effect, meaning they block transmission of nerve signals. These drugs include Contact, Marezine and Lomotil, among others. (64)

Stimulants, on the other hand, can enhance performance and speed. Most of the studies involve endurance events and they found the advantage to be gained from the drugs is marginal. In top level competition, this slight edge can make a difference. Of course, one should not learn to rely on something that drug testing would reveal and may subsequently lead to disqualification from competition. For most athletes, increased speed can best be realized through proper training, discipline, nutrition and rest.

Caffeine

Caffeine definitely increases endurance. (11, 65) Therefore, it can increase speed by offsetting fatigue. It also may enhance the strength of contracting muscles. If it does, then it directly increases speed. This, however, is a big IF. In research for this book, no studies were found that were specifically designed to measure the effects of caffeine on force production. Also, caffeine increases respiratory rate, kidney function and stimulates the central nervous system (CNS.) This stimulation of the CNS is what increases alertness. It is also what makes some people jittery. This increase in 'jitteryness' could potentially slow some people down as it increases their nervous tension. The equivalent of two cups of coffee is the recommended amount prior to an endurance event. Note: The effects of caffeine stated above are not seen in habitual caffeine users due to the body's increased tolerance. (65)

Psychomotor Stimulants

Amphetamines, cocaine and speed are all psychomotor stimulants. These drugs can have the following effects. They may increase endurance, decrease recovery time, improve reaction time and increase muscular strength. (65) The increase in endurance has been well documented. The improved reaction time is not through an increase in the speed of information transmission. Therefore, like caffeine, it must be from an increased alertness.

As far as the increase in strength, the author is at a loss to explain this. He has researched the topic and interviewed numerous researchers, physicians, neurosurgeons and pharmacologists. It appears that the mechanism for the sometimes dramatic increases in strength is not known. The author's theory, at least for cocaine and PCP, is that these drugs may block the normal safety inhibitors. Recall from above that the CNS has inhibitors preventing all muscle fibers from firing maximally and simultaneously. The author believes that the drugs may decrease or even prevent this inhibition, thereby permitting great performances in strength. Also, while on such drugs, the individual may not feel any pain from injuries incurred during such an exertion. That may explain stories of super human performance. (Note: PCP is a hallucinogen, not a stimulant.)

The risks inherent with taking psychomotor stimulants are numerous and severe. These include heart problems, sudden death, injury, digestive difficulties, sexual dysfunction, psychological problems and addiction. (65) Any possible benefits are completely overshadowed by the unavoidable risks.

Smoking

Since the ill effects of smoking upon one's health are generally well known, it's not necessary to detail them here. But, insofar as this book is dedicated to maximizing one's speed, what follows is a discussion of the effects of smoking on an athlete's speed.

First however, it is necessary to discuss carbon monoxide (CO) and gas transfer into and out of the blood stream. Hemoglobin bonds with carbon monoxide more than 200 times more easily than with oxygen (O2.) Because of this, carbon monoxide does not unbond from hemoglobin as readily as oxygen. (Note: Hemoglobin is a protein containing iron found in red blood cells. Its purpose is to deliver oxygen to the tissues and to transport carbon dioxide away from the tissues.) Not only does carbon monoxide bond to the hemoglobin, but it bonds to enzymes in the blood as well. The effect of this is to lower the efficiency of the cardiovascular system. The carbon monoxide ties up the hemoglobin sites on the red blood cells, thereby decreasing the number of available sites that oxygen could bond to. This is how carbon monoxide kills.

A carbon monoxide poisoning victim literally suffocates because the hemoglobin has bonded to the carbon monoxide, preventing the transfer of oxygen into the blood from the lungs. Carbon monoxide also bonds more readily to hemoglobin than carbon dioxide does, impairing the elimination of carbon dioxide. Because of its bonding properties to hemoglobin, it can take from nine to twelve hours for the circulatory system to eliminate carbon monoxide once inhaled. (64)

Smoking causes a loss of up to 20 percent of night vision capability. This loss results in decreased perception abilities, decreased depth perception and a decreased sense of balance. (59)

For those of you who choose to smoke, if you can avoid smoking on the day of competition without raising your anxiety levels, it is highly recommended for the following factors:

· Smoking raises normal carbon monoxide levels in the blood stream by three to twelve times.

· This causes the rate of circulation to increase so that the uncontaminated red blood cells can meet tissue gas-exchange requirements. In other words, since the blood no longer carries oxygen as efficiently, the rate of circulation must increase to make up for the decreased efficiency of the red blood cells. This obviously causes an increase in heart rate and blood pressure. This is why smoking stimulates the heart. (64) This alone should not have any effect on speed, at least not initially.

· Aerobic capacity is obviously diminished after smoking because the heart is already somewhat stressed as a result of the carbon monoxide intake. This reduced aerobic capacity affects speed by causing the fighter to tire more quickly, slowing the speed of muscle contractions and mental processing due to fatigue.

· The heart rate is also increased because of increased peripheral resistance. Nicotine causes the small arteries to contract, causing an increase in the resistance of blood flow. This increased peripheral resistance causes a lowering of temperature in the extremities. There have not been any studies on the effects of this on athletic performance, but it certainly is not going to help and it may decrease speed and dexterity. Remember how much slower your fist clenches when cold and how much harder it is to tie or untie a knot with cold hands. Although smoking does not lower the temperature to this degree, the degree to which these effects are realized after smoking are unknown. These temporal effects last for approximately 30 minutes after smoking.

*Just recently is it becoming understood how
significant the anaerobic system is in every
sport. All physical activity is initiated with the
anaerobic system.*

Chapter 4
RESISTANCE TRAINING

Weight training has been touted for its importance to athletic performance for many years. Just recently is it becoming understood how significant the anaerobic system is in every sport. All physical activity is initiated with the anaerobic system. In power sports, energy is derived almost exclusively from the anaerobic system. The anaerobic system is the primary energy system for football, weight lifting, baseball, street fights, many military combat activities, and even dart throwing. (7)

Resistance training has been shown to enhance neuromuscular systems by increasing voluntary fiber activation. In other words, more muscle fibers can be voluntarily stimulated, resulting in an increase in the speed and power of that muscle. It is also hypothesized that morphological (structural) changes in the neuromuscular junction occur. These changes include the growth of additional dendrites connecting to the muscle fibers. (44) This explains the rapid strength gains beginners realize within the first two to eight weeks of lifting. Increases in muscle mass cannot account for their initial increases in strength. This increased neural capacity (voluntary fiber recruitment) has also been shown to increase with Olympic lifters. Therefore, keep training because the neuromuscular system continues to improve.

Endurance training is not conducive to developing speed. Weight training on the other hand does increase the speed of muscular contractions in all regards except one. Weight training increases muscle fiber diameter. It increases the myofibrillar density of muscle fibers and it increases the average force capacity of each cross bridge. Each muscle fiber is made up of myofibrils. Cross bridges are structural supports for the muscle. The number of cross bridges and their locations affect how much force a muscle can generate.

Levels of contractile protein are increased by weight training as well. The above four factors are morphological changes. In other words, the structure of the muscle changes so that it can generate more force production. Weight training also causes an increased expression of fast acting proteins, thereby increasing the speed of the chemical reactions. All of these factors contribute to an increased speed of muscular contraction and power. (24, 39, 65) Therefore, weight training increases muscle speed and muscle strength. Both of these factors can increase speed of movement.

Weight training not only increases maximum strength, i.e., the one repetition maximum, it also increases submaximal strength. In other words, if an untrained individual can complete seven to ten repetitions of 70% of his one rep maximum, a weight lifter could perform seven to ten reps of 80% of his one rep maximum. This is true even though the lifter will have a higher one rep maximum. (49) These training effects increase not only the speed of the initial movement, but even after a little fatigue sets in, the lifter's movements will be faster than the non-lifter's.

The above referenced exception pertains to all forms of exercise. Every form of exercise studied caused a change in fiber type in the fast twitch muscles. Exercise causes Type IIb fibers to change to Type IIa, Type IIx or Type IIax. (24, 44, 45) The exact effect of this change is unknown. It should cause a decrease in the velocity of contraction. However, the totality of all the above referenced changes, including this change in fiber type, appears to cause an increase in contraction velocity. So don't worry about Type IIb fibers changing to other Type II fibers. The overall result of proper training is an increase in the speed of the muscle's contractions. And for the apparent contradiction of weight training causing Type IIb fibers to change to Type IIx, IIax or IIa, the exact effect on velocity is not really known. However, as long as speed does not decrease, the athlete is better off because he now has more muscular endurance.

Although most studies on the effects of resistance training observed an increase in fiber contraction velocity, a definitive answer is very difficult due to sampling procedures. With in-vivo studies, it is very difficult to measure contraction velocity due to subject variability and to the risk of having humans perform muscular contractions at maximal velocity. With in-vitro studies, the testing procedures are much more accurate, however, the problem arises in the number of fibers tested. Only a small percentage of the fibers within a muscle can be extracted, thereby creating the possibility of having tested fibers that do not accurately represent the proportion of Type I fibers to Type II fibers contained within the muscle. Remembering the above research problems, most studies conclude that resistance training increases the speed of muscular contraction. It is theorized that the change from Type IIb fibers to Type IIa, Type IIx and Type IIax, is a give and take adaptation. Yes, this change may slightly decrease from some of the gains in speed resulting from weight training. However, the muscle increases its aerobic capacity by changing from fast glycolytic fibers to fast oxidative glycolytic fibers. When training is ceased, the fibers tend to change back to Type IIb. However, begin training again and the change occurs at a faster rate. (44)

(Note: Because of the testing difficulties, most studies have examined the effects of endurance training rather than strength training. It's easy to get a rat to run a treadmill, but how do you get it to lift weights? These test rats can then be dissected, resulting in an accurate examination of the muscle tissues. The other option is to perform a painful biopsy on a human that results in a small, possibly inaccurate sampling of the tissue.)

Besides the above noted changes, mathematics plays a role in the increase in speed of muscular contractions. Since the muscle is stronger as a result of lifting, any load placed upon it is a smaller percentage of its maximal load. This means the work it is performing is easier than before. This benefit is more easily noticed with an increased work load. In other words, this mathematical equation plays a minor role with a back-fist. The workload is insignificant, therefore, the increase in strength does not necessarily translate to an increase in speed. It would take an increase in the speed of contraction and a decrease in the tension of the antagonist muscles to increase the speed of a back-fist.

However, if swinging a heavily padded stick, the increase in strength plays a significant role in initiating movement and changing direction of the stick. This also holds true for kicking with boots on, or for lunging toward the opponent. Both involve significant work loads and therefore, the increase in strength increases the speed of movement. This benefit is in addition to the other benefits of resistance training. The following example of the bench press should clearly demonstrate the point. If 200 pounds is your maximum bench, then pressing 150 pounds, 75% of your maximum may take .25 seconds. If you increase your strength so that 250 lbs. is your maximum, now the 150 pound barbell is only 60% of your max. Pressing the bar now would take, perhaps, .17 seconds.

Kraemer et al. (44) tested fit athletes training for three months under several categories:
1) Strength training only
2) Strength & endurance
3) Endurance only
4) Upper body strength & endurance

The strength only and strength & endurance groups resulted in an equal and almost complete change from Type IIb to Type IIa. The endurance only and upper body & endurance groups showed a lower rate of conversion of fiber types from IIb to IIa. At the end of the three months, the athletes in these last two groups lost only 50% of their Type IIb fibers, resulting in approximately four times the amount of Type IIb as the strength only and the strength & endurance groups had at the end of the study. This indicates that the strength and strength & endurance groups incorporated more of the anaerobic system in their training.

Changes in the cross sectional area of the fiber types occurred as well. An increase in fiber diameter results in an increase in the speed of contraction capabilities. The strength group had an increase in the cross sectional area, otherwise known as hypertrophy, in fiber types IIa and IIb. In fact, this group increased hypertrophy in both types of fibers more than any other group. Hypertrophy results from an increase in myofibrillar protein. (7) The strength & endurance group showed significant gains in the cross sectional area of Type IIa fibers and a 6% decrease in the Type IIb area. This is quite remarkable considering the combined effect of endurance training and the significant loss of Type IIb fibers. The upper body strength & endurance group had an insignificant decrease in the cross sectional area of both fiber types. The endurance group had a 7.4% decrease in the cross sectional area of Type IIa fibers and a 6% decrease in Type IIb fibers. All groups compromised power and strength gains when compared to the strength only group. (44) If tested, the strength only group should have achieved the greatest gains in speed as well. This provides still more evidence of the importance for sport specific training.

Muscle Bulk and Speed

Remember that the extra strength possessed by powerlifters and bodybuilders gives them an advantage when fighting gravity and inertia. Keep in mind the property of inertial mass is that the heavier an object is, the harder it is to change its speed or direction. With bodybuilders, the extra leg strength helps them move quickly from a stand still to a fast lunge. However, the extra mass on an arm is not going to be of benefit. A person with big legs may broad jump farther, but he probably cannot snatch that fly out of the air as quickly as a thin, well-defined fighter can.

Additional strength always helps speed, but additional mass will not necessarily. There is a balance between the two and it varies for each individual. If you increase strength without increasing mass, you will increase your speed and power. This is true because you have increased the amount of strength available to perform work without having increased the amount of work necessary to move the limb or body. Therefore, just like increasing your strength in bench press without increasing the weight of the bar translates to a faster, more explosive repetition, increasing the strength of a limb without increasing the weight of the limb translates to a faster, more explosive punch or kick.

Frequently though, as athletes get stronger, they get heavier. This changes the equation some. As a rule, fighters with thin arms and legs have fast punches and kicks. Listen to any boxer who moved up a weight division. He'll tell you how much faster his hands were when he was lighter. Watch a welterweight match versus a heavyweight bout. The lighter fighters punch much faster than the heavyweights. They will not necessarily lunge any faster though. Increasing the weight of your legs, due to an increase in strength, increases the speed of your lunge even though an increase in the strength and weight of the arms may not translate to an increase in hand speed. This is because the increase in leg strength is proportionally higher than the increase in total body weight. Think of it this way. If you perform squats regularly and develop large, strong legs, your broad jump will increase. If you increase your broad jump, that means your legs contract faster, more explosively. Lunging is in essence, a one-legged broad jump.

Isometric vs. Concentric Training

Isometric contractions are those which do not involve either a shortening or a lengthening of the muscle as it performs work. Placing your palms together in front of your chest and squeezing them together while the hands remain stationary is an example of an isometric exercise.

Concentric contractions involve a shortening of the muscle fibers as the muscle works. Pressing the bar up on bench press is an example of a concentric contraction. Eccentric contractions involve a lengthening of the fibers as the muscle works. Slowly lowering the bar on bench press is an example of an eccentric contraction.

Animal and human experiments have shown that speed of contraction and power output adapt to the pattern of muscle activation. Jacques Duchateau and Karl Hainaut of the University of Brussels tested the physiological adaptations of the hand muscles to isometric and concentric training. All subjects were initially couch potatoes. They trained their weak hand daily for three months, some isometrically and others concentrically. The concentric group only exercised with 30 to 40% of their maximum contraction. As you lifters already know, this is very light. For the test results, the muscles were stimulated electrically, thus eliminating the psychological and neuromuscular elements that could have tainted the results.

Both concentric and isometric training increased the power and speed of contraction of the muscles. However, concentric training primarily increased the speed of contraction against light loads, whereas isometric training did more to increase the speed of contraction against heavy loads. Isometric training did little, if anything, to increase the speed of contraction against light or no load contractions. (18) Again, this points to the importance of having a specific training regimen. The isometric training increased the peak power of contractions more than the concentric training did. This makes sense because the relationship between force and velocity indicates that the speed of contraction for light loads is essentially related to the speed of force development, whereas for heavy loads it is closely related to the maximal power of the muscle. (18, 24)

The maximum speed of contraction increased 20% after isometric training and by 25% after concentric training. The maximal speed of muscle relaxation also increased by 12 and 16% for isometric and concentric training respectively. These results indicate that concentric training increases the speed of contraction more than isometric training. Remember, this pertains to work against light loads. (18, 24) Remember that most athletes lift at a level in which the exercise is between the level of stimulation for the isometric training and the concentric training used for this experiment. Duchateau and Hainaut stated that a fast muscle stimulated at a low frequency becomes slower and a slow muscle stimulated at a high frequency becomes faster. This does not mean that bench presses and squats will slow you down. Remember that isometric training increased both power AND speed even though there was no fiber movement. When you are exerting 100% to perform that seventh repetition on the bench press, your neuromuscular system is firing at a very high rate (high frequency of stimulation).

In another study, concentric training resulted in only 33 to 55% of the gains received through isometric training when testing for peak isometric force. However, isometric training did not result in any hypertrophy where the concentric training did. This study indicates that isometric training will develop much greater gains in isometric strength. It did not state how the training affected speed or force production with concentric training. The speed of contraction should have increased for the concentric group because of the increase in strength due to hypertrophy and to neurological adaptations.

Concentric training with light loads performed quickly increases speed more with light loads but not as much with heavy loads. If you want to increase the speed of contractions during heavy loads, you need to train with heavy loads. You can make both training goals a reality by combining light loads with heavy loads. If training to move light loads quickly, keep most of your training light with some heavy workouts to continue increasing your maximal strength. If training to move heavy loads quickly, keep most of your training heavy with some light load workouts. (24)

In yet another study, both isometric and dynamic training (lifting light weights explosively) were shown to increase the muscle's peak speed of tension development. The researchers attributed this increase in the speed of tension development to an increase in hypertrophy. (34)

Genetics plays a role, not only in how much speed you start with, but also how much increase you can receive from lifting. Hakkinen et al. (34) reported that Type II fibers increased in cross sectional area more than Type I fibers. Due to the difference in the amount of hypertrophy between Type I and II fibers, athletes with a greater percentage of Type II fibers realize more gains in the cross sectional area of the muscle as a whole and therefore more gains in the peak rate of tension development.

A different study compared dynamic training to isometric training regarding their effect on the speed of muscle contraction. Only dynamic training increased the speed of muscular contractions. In fact, after a three-month study, the subjects that trained dynamically experienced a 21% increase in the speed of contraction. It is theorized that this was due to an increase in the speed of contraction within individual fibers. (24) What does all this mean? It means that if you want to increase the speed of a front-snap kick, dynamic training will do so, whereas isometric training will not. However, if your foot is placed against a door and it takes X amount of force to break the door in, both dynamic and isometric training will increase the speed at which you can develop the necessary amount of force.

Eccentric vs. Concentric Resistance Training

Eccentric training, or negatives, increases hypertrophy and peak isometric power more than concentric training. Training with both eccentric and concentric exercises causes hypertrophy in Types I and II fibers. However, eccentric-only training results in a higher portion of hypertrophy in Type I fibers. This is attributed to a greater training stimulus due to the higher forces placed on the muscle during eccentric exercises, primarily the added effort required to overcome the additional weight commonly used during eccentric training. In other words, you can bench more on a negative repetition than you can press upward. (24) Therefore, except for the possible adverse effects of increased hypertrophy within the Type I fibers, eccentric training increases your speed more than concentric training.

You can also draw the conclusion, based on this study, that exercising concentrically using sets of six is more beneficial towards increasing speed than using sets of ten is. This assumes that the weight used prevents you from performing a seventh or an eleventh repetition respectively. Mayhew, Rothstein and Finucane (52), also proved that eccentric strength training results in more increases in isometric, concentric and eccentric strength, than does concentric training. They noted that this is only true when the concentric and eccentric training routines are conducted at a maximal level. When the routines are conducted at the same relative load, concentric training results in more size and strength gains. This is true because the concentric work-out is harder, resulting in more training stimulus. Therefore, if you train eccentrically, use a weight that you are not able to move concentrically. (24, 52)

Another study verified what coaches and trainers already knew. That eccentric strength increases in response to near maximal resistance training, whereas fast, low-resistance strength training results in no increase in eccentric strength. (70) (Note: Eccentric training, like isometric training, increases your speed when working against heavy loads. Therefore, your lunges would be faster and you could manipulate a heavy stick, sword or staff, faster.) Whether eccentric training increases the speed of a jab is unknown. (Dynamic training and shadowing boxing increase the speed of your jab.)

As stated before, an increase in strength without a corresponding increase in mass will always make an increase in speed possible. Training with heavy loads obviously slows down the speed of your repetition. This may appear that you are not training specifically to increase the speed of your movement because the speed of your movements during resistance training is slow. It is important to explode with every repetition. Even though the movement may be slow because of the high amount of resistance, the muscle fibers are firing at near maximal rate. The neuromuscular system is working at a rapid rate and is therefore training specifically to increase speed. This is known as the size theory for motor unit recruitment. According to the theory, exercising as fast as possible against loads between 70% and 100% of 1 rep maximum results in the maximum recruitment of motor units and in a significant increase in maximum strength. (13)

Recently, studies have shown that the intention to accelerate each repetition as rapidly as possible is key to improvement of power. Even if there is no easily discernible difference in the speed of the contraction, the attempt to accelerate during each contraction results in significant gains when compared to training regimen that completes the rep, but does so without attempting to complete it as fast as possible. (41, 72)

Bodybuilding vs. Powerlifting

Which athlete will be faster, a bodybuilder or a powerlifter? If all factors are the same, e.g., genetics, size and weight, body composition, skill level and technique, etc., the answer lies in muscle physiology as it has adapted to the different methods of resistance training. To properly answer this, it is important to illustrate how the two training methods differ.

Powerlifters strive to increase their one-repetition maximum. They take long rests in between sets to be fully rested before the next maximal effort consisting of a very heavy weight with very few reps. Bodybuilders, on the other hand, are less concerned with their absolute maximum and more concerned with the fiber-fatigue factor. Bodybuilders, striving to develop a desired level of muscular stress, force more repetitions out, thus requiring a lower weight. They also take a shorter rest period between sets. The bodybuilder is thinking that by not allowing his muscles to recover fully, they will develop a greater level of fatigue, ie, muscular stress, during the next set. This occurs because the amount of fatigue created during the second set is added to the amount of fatigue still remaining in the muscle as a result of the shorter rest period. (36) Physiologically speaking, this has several athletic ramifications.

The differences in muscle physiology between powerlifters and bodybuilders include:

· Bodybuilders have a higher ratio of oxidative enzymes in Type IIa
  fibers over Type IIb fibers. (44)
· Bodybuilders have a higher capillary density. This is believed to
  be due to the higher levels of lactate build-up during training. (44)
· Bodybuilders have a greater lifting capacity when working at a
  raised lactate level. (44)

Heavy resistance training results in increased fiber size in both Type I & II fibers. However, the majority of the hypertrophy occurs in the Type II fibers. Powerlifting increases the ratio of these gains, resulting in an even larger portion of the hypertrophy occurring in Type II fibers when compared to bodybuilding. (26) Therefore, powerlifting should increase speed more than bodybuilding because it develops greater maximal strength. This is especially true with lunging. However, the powerlifter is not physiologically adapted for any lasting activity. The bodybuilder is better adapted for a sustained effort. Keep in mind that powerlifters often carry substantially more body fat and they have much less endurance. Once a fighter is tired, he is no longer fast. The muscle endurance that the theoretical bodybuilding fighter would have over a powerlifting fighter is vitally important in a fight lasting more than a few seconds.

Mental Commitment during Resistance Training

If resistance training is new to you, it will not take long to become familiar with muscle burn during certain exercises. It is especially prevalent when working the quadriceps, calves, upper abdominals and arms. With experience, part of which includes physiological adaptations and mental commitment, you can work beyond the burning point. By doing so, you more thoroughly exhaust your muscle, creating more stimulus for hypertrophy. This translates to increased strength and increased speed and power. If you push past the pain barrier set after set and workout after workout, you are bound to realize substantial improvements. If you have the drive and discipline to stick with this, the only way you cannot realize results is if you are over-training and/or your diet is significantly inadequate. Along with the increase in size and strength, your determination, concentration and pain tolerance also increase.

When you are training for strength and endurance, if you want to continue improving, you must constantly push yourself harder with every successive workout. If you are training for speed or skill, you must strive to be faster or better than the day before.

High Intensity Weight Training & Flexibility

Trainers, coaches and many researchers believe that loss of flexibility is due to disuse of the muscle, injury, or to a lesser extent, a lack of flexibility training. Many also believe that strength training will improve flexibility as long as: 1) exercises are performed through the full range of motion, 2) both agonist and antagonist muscle groups are trained, and 3) stretching exercises are included in the program.

Several studies have been conducted and the results are mixed. Some investigators report increases, others no changes, and one reported losses in flexibility with strength training. The methodologies of the studies differed. Some did not include stretching with the training while others used only low resistance exercises. Perhaps this explains the mixed results. Girouard and Hurley with the University of Maryland published a study in 1995. They tested the effects of ten weeks of heavy resistance strength training on adults between the ages of 50 and 74. Although those subjects involved in the strength and flexibility training did increase their flexibility, it was to such a small degree that the changes were not statistically significant when compared to the control group.

Just the flexibility only group substantially increased their level of flexibility. This group only stretched, they did not lift weights. (30) Based on the results of this study, at least for older individuals, the inclusion of heavy resistance strength training in a flexibility program will significantly impede the gains in flexibility that would otherwise be attained. For young subjects, the addition of heavy resistance training to their flexibility program would also slow their gains in flexibility, at least insofar as the weight training makes their muscles sore. The lifter would not be able to attain his or her maximum level of flexibility until the muscle repair was completed and the soreness gone.

Weight Training for Beginners

For those of you who have not been involved in a serious weight lifting regimen, start slowly. Not only will you be less sore, but research shows that for beginners, one high intensity set per week for each muscle produces the same results as three high intensity sets per week for each muscle. (71) Since lifting more will not provide you with any additional gains in size or strength, spend the time saved learning how to perform the exercises correctly and synergistically.

To lift synergistically, start with the muscles of the torso and move out to the limbs. This provides for a more effective training stimulus. Continue with the one set per week routine until you hit a plateau and do not make any gains for five or six weeks. Then change the exercises. This change of stimulus should result in additional gains. When you hit another plateau, either change the exercises or increase the routine to two high intensity sets per week for each muscle. Continue in this fashion, changing the exercises, the rest between the exercises, the number of sets, and the number of workouts per week, whenever you hit a plateau.

At some point, you will hit a plateau and it will appear that you can not break through it. At that point, consistency and discipline are what it takes to continue making gains. If you had started lifting with three sets per week, you would have hit the difficult plateau sooner. This would most likely rob you of some of the potential gains had you started under the recommendations noted above. (71)

Weights vs. Sprinting

As previously noted, weight training causes an increase in fiber size in all fiber types. High speed running, or nearly sprinting, does not cause an increase in fiber size, therefore, it does not increase the speed of contraction through this mechanism. Sprinting does, however, increase the oxidative enzyme in the Type II fibers, thus increasing their aerobic capacity. (24)

Fitts and Widrick referenced a study that showed that sprinting causes an increase in power output and an increase in concentric shortening speed. Since the study indicated that sprinting caused no increase in fiber size, possible explanations for the above noted increases in speed and power output include changes in fiber length, sarcomere numbers and properties, etc. (Note: A muscle fiber is made up of many myofibrils. Myofibrils are long, rod like structures. Myofibrils are further broken down into sarcomeres. Sarcomeres are bundles of thin and thick filaments. These filaments are made up of contractile protein. The thin filaments are made up of actin and the thick filaments are made up of myosin. Sixty-five percent of total muscle protein is myosin.) (12, 65)

Running decreases fiber size and power output by decreasing the number of cross bridges. (24) (Note: Cross bridges provide structural support. The number of cross bridges and how they are arranged affect force production.) Therefore, if you want to run to increase your endurance, sprints would be best. If you jog, you will not reach your maximal speed potential.

Endurance Training vs. Weight Training

Doctors Fitts and Widrick studied the effects of endurance training on muscle characteristics. From one group of sedentary individuals, two groups were created. Group One remained sedentary. Group Two followed an endurance training regimen. At the end of the study, the endurance group had a 10% decrease in peak power output in Type I fibers and 38% decrease in peak power output in Type IIa fibers. These results were attributed to the adaptations for endurance in that fiber diameters were reduced (one of the adaptations of endurance training) and a lower peak isometric force production resulted. (24)

Endurance training causes an increase in the number of mitochondria, an increase in mitochondrial connections and an increase in capillarization. (21,

28, 39) Each of these adaptations, as you might expect, can be attributed to the muscle's enhanced endurance capabilities. Weight lifting on the other hand causes a decrease in the mitochondrial density, mitochondrial connections and capillarization. (39, 44)

Prolonged voluntary aerobic activity in rats resulted in a 17% increase in Type I fiber area and a 20% decrease in Type II fiber area. A weight training program with humans resulted in an increase in the diameter area of both Type I & Type II fibers, although Type II fibers increased more than Type I fibers. (66)

In addition to changing the physical characteristics of muscle fibers, endurance training also has the following undesirable effects where speed is concerned:

1) It causes a fast-to-slow transition in the calcium handling system and the myofibril properties.
2) It causes a change in contractile protein, including a decrease in fast myosin and an increase in slow myosin. Myosin chains are known to influence fiber shortening speed. (24)

The result of this causes changes in the metabolic properties, creating conditions that favor endurance and hamper power production. (45) Weight training causes the reverse effect on the above factors, as well as causing Type I fibers to change to a light chain free form, thereby causing an increase in velocity.

Endurance Training for Maximum Speed

To understand how to avoid training Type II fibers aerobically, it is necessary to be familiar with VO2 Max. VO2 Max is expressed as milliliters of oxygen metabolized per kilogram of body weight per minute. (65) In plain English, it is the maximum amount of oxygen (O2) that your body can metabolize at a given time. The figure is different for everyone. It is affected by fitness level, type and length of training you are engaged in, genetics and gender. (Females are continuing to narrow the gender gap, even though they currently make up a small percentage of competitive athletes. This suggests that there may not be a gender difference for VO2 Max in the future.)

To illustrate VO2 Max, take the following example. If you started running up a hill, slowly increasing your speed, the amount of O2 consumed and metabolized would increase as well. If you continue to increase your running speed, eventually you would reach a speed at which no additional O2 was metabolized. The additional energy demand must then be met by anaerobic means. The point at which no additional oxygen is metabolized is your VO2 maximum (VO2 Max).

This understanding is important because of the relationship between VO2 Max and fiber type recruitment. Type II fibers are not recruited during weight training until approximately 70% of your one repetition maximum is performed. (Note: It is possible to recruit these fibers with low weights and high repetitions. However, these fibers are not recruited until you near the end of your set, after your muscles have fatigued.) They are recruited with every repetition when using heavy weights and low repetitions. Type II fibers are recruited during aerobic training only after the athlete has gone beyond 50% of his VO2 Max. When endurance training involves Type II fibers, those fibers take on endurance characteristics including loss of overall size, an increase in mitochondrial size, and a decrease in speed, strength, and ultimately, force production. (65) Therefore, if speed is the primary goal, but cardiovascular fitness and/or weight loss are also goals, then endurance training should be conducted at or below 50% VO2 Max. This strategy should minimize the conversion effect on the Type II fibers.

If a relatively high level of cardiac fitness is desired, once that fitness level is reached, it is possible to maintain it with less work. As few as two endurance training sessions per week will maintain that level of aerobic fitness as long as the intensity of the training remains the same. (65) Improvement in the level of aerobic fitness would not be realized unless the intensity were to increase, and even then progress would be slow because of the few aerobic training days per week. Of course, this increased intensity would recruit more Type II fibers.

If you adopted this two days per week maintenance program, it is theoretically possible that this smaller proportion of endurance training to resistance training would allow some of the Type II fibers that may have taken on aerobic characteristics to revert to power-based characteristics. The cardiovascular system and Type I fibers should maintain their aerobic characteristics and fitness levels, allowing you a reasonable compromise. No known studies have been conducted to either prove or disprove this theory. It is also worth mentioning again that such a program would not allow you to realize your full power or aerobic potential.

This theory of maintenance work only requiring two or three training days per week applies to weight training as well. 1-2 sessions per week are sufficient to maintain strength gains for most people. If you have a high level of strength, it may take 2-4 sessions per week to maintain your level. (72) If you are happy with your current level, you could reduce the time spent lifting and dedicate this time to sparring or technique training.

Do not quit your strength training altogether though. Your strength would decrease. How much and how fast? Most people have heard that muscles start to deteriorate within two or three days of inactivity. That's not necessarily true. If you have just completed a high intensity, eccentric workout, it can take seven to nine days for the muscles to repair, rebuild and fully recover. Once recovery is complete, then the clock starts to tick. For those of you who like numbers, a study measured the amount of loss after five weeks of bed rest for the triceps muscle. The test subjects had an average of a 46% decrease in maximum torque. This decrease was explained by a loss of 33% in neural activation of the muscle and a decrease of 19% in the muscle force generating capacity. The decrease in the muscle force generating capacity resulted from a loss of muscle mass. (17)

So what is 50% VO2 Max? An easy, unscientific method of training at, or below, 50% VO2 Max is not to train aerobically beyond a pace at which you can maintain a conversation. Once you start having to pause to catch your breath to continue your sentence, you are training at a level more than 50% of your VO2 Max. At this point you start recruiting Type II fibers. If your muscles start to take on that familiar burn, you know you have engaged your Type II fibers in the training. If you are endurance training, when your muscles start to burn, you are well above the 50% VO2 Max level.

Obviously, training at this low level of VO2 Max will require more training time to burn calories and to develop cardiovascular fitness. However, the trade off is that you maintain more of the power gained through resistance training. (Note: Aerobic fitness is very intensity specific. In other words, one hour of bicycling at 50% VO2 Max develops your aerobic capacity at that level.) If you want aerobic fitness at a high intensity level, you have to train at that high level. This as you know, recruits Type II fibers and decreases your speed and power. On the other hand, a fighter who does not train aerobically at a high level of intensity may maintain more speed and power than you, but while competing against him at a high intensity level, he will tire faster and lose his speed and power faster than you.

Bodybuilders are, of course, not concerned with this. Therefore, they do not train aerobically at high intensity and definitely do not partake in interval training. (Note: Because of its high intensity, interval training is extremely quick at adapting the body for aerobic performance.) Bodybuilders train aerobically to lose fat. This must be done in a manner to minimize, if not prevent, the loss of muscle mass. Fighters could consider training in the same manner but for a different reason. The fighter wishes to lose fat to increase speed and power. This training involves endurance work at approximately 15 heartbeats per minute below 50% VO2 Max. This is determined by taking your pulse when you have determined that you are training aerobically at 50% of your VO2 Max. Calculate you pulse rate for 60 seconds and subtract 15. Next, determine what level of aerobic training maintains that heart rate. (65) Unfortunately, this level is fairly slow and boring. On the bright side, you can use the time on the exercise bicycle to read this book again.

Where loss of weight is concerned, one of the most important adaptations to endurance training is the increase in fat metabolism and corresponding decrease in carbohydrate use during submaximal exercise. To maximize this effect, endurance work should be performed at a level between 50% to 65% VO2 Max. (51) (Note: to reach 65% VO2 Max, add approximately 15 beats per minute to 50% VO2 Max.) If losing weight is a necessary requirement to enhance speed and there is not sufficient time to lose it performing resistance exercises combined with low level endurance work, increase the level of intensity in the endurance training. This will speed the loss of fat. After attaining the desired weight, reduce the aerobic training to 50% or lower of your VO2 Max (with no weight bearing aerobic activities, such as the treadmill), to increase muscle mass and change the muscle characteristics back to fast acting properties.

Some researchers and trainers would argue that the endurance training should be performed at a more intense rate, thereby burning more calories and increasing the rate of weight loss. This may be true, however, additional muscle mass would also be lost. Also, muscle characteristics would make a dramatic change from power to endurance adaptations.

Velocity Training Specificity

The velocity training specificity concept states that training at a specific velocity results in an increase in strength mainly at that velocity. For endurance training, this theory has been proven in numerous studies. As for the speed of muscle contraction and power output with resistance training, this theory has yet to be proven.

The only study to date to address this question divided test subjects into two groups. Both groups performed squats. One group trained at a slow rate, the other at a fast rate. The fast group took two seconds to perform each repetition, one second down and one up. The slow group took twice as long. Both groups were tested in their pre and post study abilities for broad jumping and in the strength of the individual muscles of the legs. The squat test results did not support the concept of velocity training specificity for resistance exercises. There were mixed results between the two groups. The fast group increased in the broad jump significantly more than the slow group. The power output of their hip and ankle joints also increased more than the slow group. Conversely, the slow group's training results were superior to those of the fast group's for increasing the power output of the knee joint. Overall, even though the author of this study concluded that the velocity training specificity for weight training could not be supported by this study, he did find that the increase in power output for the legs was higher overall for the fast group. (55)

Physiological Summary

The single most effective method for increasing strength is resistance training. Resistance training involving heavy loads (80-90% of maximum) and few repetitions per set (4 to 8) has been shown to be superior for increasing power and movement speed to a greater extent than training with relatively light loads. (67) Another researcher concluded that the most important variable for increasing strength was the load placed against the muscle. (3) Plyometric training has been reported to provide greater improvements in the maximum rate of force development when compared to resistance training. (34)

A group of researchers combined resistance training with plyometrics, creating dynamic weight training. This involves plyometrics with light weights added. The scientist compared the effectiveness of weight training, plyometrics, and dynamic weight training in enhancing performance in five tests. The tests included a 30 meter sprint, a stationary squat jump, a counter movement squat jump (a squat jump that starts with a quick bending of the legs before jumping up), a six second maximum cycle test and a leg strength test. The experiment ran for 10 weeks, and unlike most studies, the test subjects had been training with weights for at least one year.

The weight training group improved the most in the leg strength. They also increased significantly in all other groups except the sprint. The weight training group did not improve in the sprint. The dynamic training group improved the most in all areas except in strength. They improved performance to a statistically significant level in all areas except the sprint. However, this group approached a statistically significant increase in the sprint. The plyometric group only obtained statistically significant improvement in the counter movement jump. Considering this study, it seems logical to include dynamic weight training in your program. The researchers found that 30% of one's maximal load is optimal for this type of explosive weight training. (74)

There is one area of concern with this study. The researchers used sophisticated equipment. This equipment allowed the test subjects to explode through the full range of motion. Using the bench press as an example, if you pressed 30% of your maximum as fast as you could, you would have to slow down before reaching the end of your range. A significant portion of your repetition would involve deceleration. This could negate the effectiveness of the dynamic strength training. You will have to use your ingenuity to overcome this obstacle. One possibility is to bench on a smith machine. At the end of each rep, toss the bar into the air and catch it on the way down for your next plyometric rep. It may not be necessary to have a training partner prevent the bar from going too high.

Resistance exercises are an excellent method of increasing force and speed production, however, they are not sport specific. If possible, perform resistance exercises that are sport specific. Examples of this include jabs, crosses, back-fists, etc., with a bungee cord in each hand that is attached to a wall at the other end. Kicks can be rigged up similarly. Lunges can also be performed using bungee cords to provide resistance or done wearing a weight vest. This type of movement specific training is called resisted speed training.

For those of you holding out on resistance training because you think it slows you down, consider the results of a study conducted on the US National Boxing Team. Weight training and interval running significantly increased punching velocity and punch endurance. (14)

*If you can control your opponent's mind, you
can conquer your opponent. Before you can
control your opponent's mind, you must first
learn to control your own.*

Chapter 5
PSYCHOLOGICAL SPEED

The psychology of fighting is multifaceted. It is imperative to learn to alter the mindset of your opponent while thwarting any efforts he might make to alter yours. It is also important to know what types of situations influence your psychological state and how training can help you maintain an optimal state of mental preparedness. This chapter teaches you how to alter your opponent's psychology to your advantage, how to enter and maintain a high performance frame of mind, how to avoid "losing it" under survival situations, and how to train your mind mentally to increase your physical abilities.

Sparring and Emotions

One of the biggest obstacles to improvement is stress. Many people have a great deal of anxiety about sparring, especially contact sparring. Simply by developing a new attitude toward sparring, your speed, endurance and abilities will increase tremendously. You will then be able to begin improving many areas of fighting reserved for advanced martial artists.

The more you spar, the more you begin to enjoy it. Spar as much as you can. Have fun with it. Do not approach it to win or to avoid getting hit. That only increases your anxiety. Have fun. Go slowly at first if necessary. Wear plenty of padding until you become used to getting hit. Put the pads on and go all out. This way you learn that getting hit can be fun, not something to be afraid of. Keep sparring and you will develop this attitude. Sparring becomes a form of stress relief, not a stress inducer. Look forward to it. Ask others to spar as much as possible. When you go against an expert fighter, look forward to how much you can learn. By developing this attitude, your speed, abilities and enjoyment of training increase substantially. You wind up sparring more, and this in turn lowers your anxiety and increases your abilities even more.

Emotions and The Athlete

Emotions directly and indirectly affect an athlete's performance. The following is a brief discussion of negative emotions and how they affect the body. The brain, triggered by thoughts and feelings, affects physical changes through three mechanisms:

- · It transmits impulses through the bulboreticular area to the muscles. This occurs through conscious or unconscious stimulation.
- · It sends impulses to the autonomic nervous system. This can result in an increase in heart rate and capillary contraction.
- · It also regulates and controls endocrine glands. This includes the release of adrenaline, also called epinephrine.

Negative emotions or emotional stresses such as worry, anxiety and self-doubt, can be detrimental to your speed. These emotions affect the autonomic nervous system, causing, among many other things, a restriction of blood flow to the brain. This decrease in nutrients and oxygen tends to result in the brain focusing on the last error, or loss, rather than focusing on the present.

Psychologists Dr. James Loehr and Dr. Charles Garfield have interviewed many hundreds of elite athletes for their mental training research. Neither observed evidence of peak performance when negative thoughts were present. They did note short bursts of high energy and optimal performance brought on by an adrenaline rush that was associated with the fight or flight response. As explained later in this chapter, strategy stops at that point because the fight or flight response precludes the use of conscious thought. They also noted that the adrenaline rush is highly unpredictable and that it frequently was followed by a sense of confusion and sometimes fatigue. (29)

In another study involving a non-athletic population, psyching up proved more effective in strength tasks than did using relaxation/focus techniques and imagery. It is not known what level of competency the test subjects had with the relaxation/focus techniques and mental imagery. In this same study, psyching up techniques were not found to be effective on motor tasks requiring more skill and timing. (31)

A study of the U.S. skiers training for the Olympic team revealed that the physical abilities of the skiers were equal, as best as could be determined. Those who made the team had one difference that separated them from the others. They consistently expressed positive attitudes about their abilities, whereas those who did not make the team tended to be more negative or tentative about their abilities. Attitudes and expectations play a significant role in performance.

Winning Thoughts & Feelings

Common sense dictates that stresses should be avoided and inspirations should be cultivated. Ninety-eight percent of the expert Korean judoka studied performed worse with their mothers watching. In Eastern culture, this is a stressor because if they lose, they lose face, whereas, in the United States, American judoka perform better with their inspirational mothers watching. (35)

1996 Olympic non-medalists tended to develop negative thoughts and worries and this was attributed to their lack of focus and/or confidence. Medalists on the other hand, felt relaxed, focused in the present, confident, and did not have anxiety or fear. (35)

Among the elite judoka, the athletes described their best matches as having the following factors:
· they had no negative feelings or thoughts
· they had a heightened sense of effort and commitment
· they focused on technique, strategies and motivation

When asked to describe their mental state before and during their worst matches, they had the following factors in common:
· most had negative feelings
· most had a lack of focus on technique, strategies and motivation
· they suffered from too much intensity
· they had no pre-match mental plan or opponent information
· they had a lack of feelings that seemed to be related to too loose a mental state

· their loose mental state resulted in their being overly aggressive, or lacking in intensity, or lacking discipline in following the plan. (35)

The above examples illustrate how emotions and frame of mind affect performance. It's important to have a positive attitude. Do not worry about mistakes or losses. Instead, focus on improving. Determine that today you will overcome yourself of yesterday, tomorrow you will overcome those of lesser skill, and later you will overcome those of greater skill. Don't let yourself get sidetracked. Keep your goals in sight and work toward achieving them. (56)

Altering the Mindset of Your Opponent

Be relaxed in mind and body and look relaxed in mind and body. Like a yawn, this can be infectious to your opponent. When you notice a moment of slackening, quickly strike. You are trying to catch your opponent off guard. Do you remember the feeling and lack of any possible response when you were suddenly caught off guard and surprised? For instance, you walk around a corner and someone is standing right there. For a fraction of a second, you panic, jump back in shock, gasp and then start laughing. This is the response you are trying to elicit from your opponent. Obviously, you will not be able to shock him to this degree. If you are successful in eliciting this response to any degree, it will slow him down just a little, and in effect, speed you up. A shout can have a similar effect, causing a temporary shock effect, disrupting your opponent's concentration while possibly boosting your confidence and aggression. (Refer to *Chapter 7* for more information on shouting. There you will find information on how to use the shout tactically, and how shouting affects the psychology of both yourself and your opponent.)

Emotions are like yawns, they are contagious. You can affect your opponent's emotions through the display of your emotions. A display of pity or a lack of emotion for example, can irritate him, deceive him, and weaken his motivation. (32)

Humans are capable of hundreds of facial expressions. Fortunately for fighters, the most common of these are also some of the most powerful. Many are genetic and therefore evoke automatic responses that you can use to your advantage. Smiling is one of these. Just before attacking, smile at your opponent. Unless he has trained and prepared for this, he will automatically lose his concentration and relax. It's a genetically programmed response. It is wise to train yourself to avoid this reaction.

One method of training to overcome this is stimulus/response training. Whenever your opponent smiles, attack. Or, you could train yourself to step back. A learned facial expression is winking. What do you think would happen if you winked at your opponent half a second before you attacked him? You have possibly, completely interrupted his thought process and changed his frame of mind. Laughing works well also. Chances are, he will be thinking, what's so funny? For more tactics on altering the mindset of your opponent, and for more information how these tactics accomplish the goal of altering his mind set, refer to *Chapter 7*, subsection, *Interruptions*.

Using Psychology to Boost Your Performance

Brain Washing

If you are going to move quickly, you have to feel fast. Have you ever seen an inspiring movie or fighter and had an overwhelming urge to immediately spar with a new found feeling of incredible speed? If so, remember that feeling. Seek out that movie or song, warm up and play it. To further enhance the feeling, throw your techniques with practically no power, placing all effort in speed. Only extend your punches and kicks half way, further increasing the speed of the technique by decreasing the distance traveled. Remember this feeling and bring it back up from time to time to ensure that you are training at your top speed. You may want to place yourself in this mental state, reliving this feeling, before every match or round.

Mental Focus

The mind is like a computer in many ways. Best of all, it is programmable. The next time you or your student has trouble side kicking the heavy bag with the heel instead of the entire sole of the foot, try this. For the next kick, think of nothing else but the heel. Do not think of speed, power or technique. Your mind is focusing on the heel, feeling it impact with the bag as you prepare for and execute the kick. Your percentage of contacting with the heel should have increased by 200 percent or more. Your mind is just as programmable for speed. When shadow boxing or training on the bag, think of nothing else but speed. Forget power, technique and combinations for now. Your only concern is speed. Once you have increased your speed and developed a feeling for it, then you can be concerned with technique and combinations. Throughout this book, you will find different methods of training for speed. With each of the methods, incorporate some of this focus into your training. Remember this focus is to the exclusion of everything else. Whenever you think you may have slowed down, revert to this training for a few techniques to insure your continued performance at top speed.

Superstition or Preparation?

Why do many people perform the same routine before an important event? For example, before a bench press competition, a competitor may wear his lucky sweats and slap his hands together as he approaches the bar in the same way that he always does. He then grips the bar with his index fingers first, pulls his torso off the bench toward the bar two times and takes a deep breath as he tightens his grip. He goes through the same routine every time. Take the example of a surgeon. Dr. Robert Patterson would drive to work via the same route, park in the same slot and check into the hospital in the same manner as always on surgery days. Following his same old routine he continued with getting dressed and scrubbing. Dr. Patterson is not a superstitious man. By following the same routine, he frees his mind, allowing it to focus on the pending surgery. By the time the operation begins, not only has he already reviewed the operation once or twice in his mind, but he is in his zone of peak performance.

Another example would include perhaps the most famous scientist of all time, Albert Einstein. Einstein kept five identical suits in his closet, all with identical matching accessories (shirts, socks, ties, etc..) His reasoning for this was that he would not have to devote any time or energy deciding what to wear each day. This form of habitual behavior makes it easier to devote your undivided attention to the challenge ahead and ultimately to enter your zone of peak performance. Once you have entered your zone, remain focused on the present task, don't start to wander into the future. (42)

Reward vs. Punishment

The evidence is hard to ignore. More and more studies are concluding that punishing children is not as effective as rewarding them when attempting to change their behavior. This rule does not change for adults. Training has its drawbacks. It's difficult to maintain discipline and it can be painful at times. But for every drawback, there is a benefit. Routinely remind yourself of the advantages and gains. Allow yourself time to enjoy the benefits as well. Reward yourself. When you finish a hard day's schedule, watch a movie or treat yourself to something you enjoy doing. If you meet or exceed your training goals for the month, buy a pair of new running shoes. Such a reward system inspires you to work even harder. (2)

Survival Situations

The level of stress often met with under survival situations is greater than stress levels generally created during intense training or competition. When someone has reached such a high level of stress, they have entered what has been termed the fight or flight response. When someone suddenly encounters a life-threatening assailant, the body prepares the person to fight or flee, by making almost instantaneous changes. These include an increase in heart rate, breathing, blood flow to the major muscles, metabolism and the secretions of the hormones adrenaline and noradrenaline. The secretion of these hormones is part of the cause for the above noted increases. As a result, hand dexterity and coordination suffer from the vascular occlusion of the extremities because the blood has been re-routed to the major muscles. In addition, the contour of the lens of the eyes changes. In an attempt to take in more information, the pupils dilate, resulting in a loss of ability to focus on close objects, such as gun sights, and in the narrowing of the peripheral field of view. (69) The loss of peripheral vision can slow reaction time (refer to *Chapter 7* for more information.) The increased blood flow to the major muscles helps increase speed and power, however, the loss of dexterity and coordination in the hands negatively affects the use of weapons, including knives, sticks, nunchucks and firearms. The adrenaline may help by boosting aggression and decreasing the sensation of pain, however, it has the adverse effects of reducing the cognitive functioning of the brain.

If the victim has no training, then the effects of survival stress may benefit him in his fight or flight for survival. If the victim has training and wishes to put that training to good use, he needs to minimize the level of stress placed upon the body. Otherwise, what he has learned will not be available because his subconscious mind takes over, prohibiting him from applying what he has learned to resolving the problem. Factors that affect the level of stress perceived and created by the victim include: confidence, personality, training and life experiences. Of these, confidence, training and life experiences are all factors that can be greatly influenced through proper training.

Boosting Your Confidence

One of the surest ways to slow your attack is to be intimidated. Not only does a lack of confidence slow you down, but it increases the speed of your opponent by boosting his confidence. One method of building confidence is through mental programming. If you tell yourself enough times that you are capable of a certain goal, you mind will begin to believe it. The most effective means of mental training is based around visualizations. The clarity of your visualization, the degree of detail involved and the frequency of the visualization training are the primary factors that determine to what degree you will change your mind set. Each part is connected to the other. The more detail you incorporate, the clearer the image you can visualize. The clearer the image, the more completely your mind believes what it sees is real. Moreover, the more visualizations you engage in, the more detail you can incorporate.

Determine what situations you lack confidence in. If you notice that you tire more easily when sparring with someone larger than you, perhaps this is not because you are trying harder, but because you tense up more. Work on developing more confidence in defeating large opponents with the following visualization method.

The next time you are in a public place, look for the largest, strongest and most intimidating person there. Weight gyms are great for this. Now, knowing that you are going to have to take this person out, analyze how you could best accomplish this. Once you have determined which techniques you will use, visualize yourself dropping him like a rock. See your techniques explode into his body. All of your moves are lightning fast. Do this while he is there. If you can see him at the time, your visualization will be clearer. Remember the more detail the better. Include not only the sound and feeling of your strikes, but also the surroundings and the sounds of his gasps for air, his vocalizations and even his odor.

Take your visualization to any extreme, whatever is necessary to help build your confidence. You can start by believing that he severely injured a loved one and you attack him by surprise. As you develop more confidence in yourself and as your visualizations become better, you can have him confront you. Perhaps try to avoid the confrontation at first and attempt to walk away, just as you would in reality. Work on staying focused in your detailed, movie like, visualizations.

Paralysis

If you or one of your students has the tendency to freeze when suddenly surprised or accosted by someone, you need to realize that this occurs when the victim feels overwhelmed by the severity of the threat and by the lack of time to respond. He feels incapable of controlling the threat or the situation and therefore, loses control of himself. Thinking about this analytically, this results from the perception of a threat and the lack of confidence in his ability to control it. The solution to this is to realize that stress is a matter of perception and both perception and confidence can be changed through training. (69)

A common scenario that involves freezing can be found in the following example. You walk around a corner and are suddenly surprised by someone standing there, resulting in a lack of response until your heart settles back into place. This problem is not necessarily a result of a lack of confidence, nor it is a result of a lack of high repetition training. It is a result of a lack of stimulus training. Research has shown that recall and automatic responses are not the result of high-repetition training. For a response to be conditioned as an automatic response, there must be a stimulus associated with the response to trigger that response. To resolve this problem, you need to train in responding instantly to this or a similar stimulus. Then you would develop an instant response when you encounter this situation or a similar one. (69)

Continuing with the above theme, a portion of all survival training should include simulation training. Simulation training is training that places the student in a situation he may come across and wishes to be prepared for. The training must be as realistic as possible. If the training includes handguns, then simunition rounds (actual rounds firing dyed soap) could be used. If it involves knives, ink markers or stun guns should take the place of the knife. If it involves hand-to-hand combat, then all-out fighting under the protection of adequate padding is necessary.

Incorporating simulation training into your program accomplishes two goals. First, the simulation associates a survival skill with an assault that you feel you may encounter. Second, the training reduces anxiety levels about meeting with such a situation by giving you experience in successfully dealing with these situations. This in turn increases your confidence level. Confidence minimizes both the physiological and psychological effects of stress, as well as the overall stress level experienced, thus helping you maintain a physical parameter for optimum combat performance. This all causes the heart rate to remain at a lower level when such a situation is encountered, thus increasing reaction speed and effectiveness. (69)

Few vs. Many Options

An age old argument revolves around the number to techniques to teach. One philosophy argues that many techniques should be taught, increasing the number of options available to the student, making him more prepared to face the varying problems he may encounter. The other side of the argument states that it is best to teach students only a limited number of techniques, making their skill level with those techniques greater and increasing their confidence in performing those skills and techniques.

Hick's Law states that an increase in options directly correlates to an increase in reaction time. If speed were the primary factor in determining which philosophy you were to choose, then the choice would be the school that teaches a few techniques for many situations. Several studies have determined that there is a direct correlation between the number of options available and reaction time. The more options available, the longer it takes to react. A study as early as 1885 demonstrated that by increasing the number of options from one to two, the reaction time increased by 35%. (69) Hick, in 1952, demonstrated that by increasing the number of choices available from one to two increased reaction time from 190 milliseconds to 300 milliseconds, a 58% increase. (69) Also, the more complex the response, the more time required for the response. This holds true for both mental and physical parameters.

In 1993 Joe Ferrera measured the reaction time of a block to a punch at 183 milliseconds. He then increased the number of options available to four (four blocking techniques could be used against the punch) and the response time increased to 481 milliseconds. (69)

Myelination

The adult human brain consists of 12 to 15 billion nerve cells. Each nerve cell, a neuron, can make thousands of connections with other neurons. The more connections there are, the more capable, or intelligent, the brain is. Many of the connections are made automatically during fetal development. When the brain is exposed to a new stimulus or experience, a complex pattern of neurons is activated. This pattern is referred to as a program. When a new learning experience, or program, occurs, the impulse has a difficult time bridging the synaptic gap from one neuron to another. As the new program is reintroduced through repetition, the ability of the impulse to cross the gap becomes easier. (69)

Responding to an attack, an opening or a telegraphed movement, involves memory. Even if the response is automatic, the program that you conditioned into your automatic response is run on the memory of your stimulus/response training. When new information, a program, is learned, the brain releases a fatty substance called myelin. Myelin coats the connections between the parts of the neurons that send and receive impulses from each other. These parts are called dendrites. The first time a program is created and the connections are initially made, myelin is secreted. Each time thereafter the program is run, myelin is secreted and the coat becomes thicker. The thicker the coat, the easier the impulses bridge the gaps between the neurons. Eventually, with sufficient repetition, the dendrites become sufficiently coated so that the program operates without effort. The connections have then become 'myelinated'.

The more often a program is repeated, the stronger the neural program becomes due to the increased myelination of the dendrites. As the myelination increases, so does the speed and fluidity of the response or technique. (69) Professor Michael Posner of the University of Oregon confirmed that this holds true for tasks involving concentration as well. Through the use of positron emission transaxial tomagraphy (PET) and electroencephalograms, Posner demonstrated that performing a task for the first time substantially increased blood flow and electrical activity in the brain. However, the more the subject practiced the task, the less blood flow and electrical stimulation in the brain were needed to accomplish the task. Posner believes the more that concentration is practiced, the less brain activity is needed to remain focused in one particular area, i.e., remaining relaxed and light on your feet. This allows you to focus on another aspect of the activity, perhaps perception. (42)

A badly executed move is the result of impulses being sent to the wrong muscles, sent out of sequence or sent too strongly or weakly. This occurs because of stress, trying to go too fast, being tired, or other factors. Myelination makes it hard for your body to perform the technique incorrectly. Take advantage of the myelination process. Through precision repetition, your body performs the technique more smoothly. It also develops the ability to perform the technique perfectly on its own, without thought other than the initial command by your conscious or, better yet, your subconscious mind. Your neuromuscular system begins to resist poor technique because this not only feels foreign to it, it is more difficult because these pathways are not myelinated. Just as learning to walk and run require your neuromuscular system to develop the coordination to send out precisely timed, targeted and powered impulses so that you may walk or run efficiently, effortlessly and automatically, so does repetition training. Properly performed repetition training coordinates your neuromuscular system to punch and kick as effortlessly as you walk and run.

In addition to myelination, memory is affected by the number of associations that may stimulate the program. In other words, if you automatically condition yourself to respond with a technique upon a certain visual stimulus, the conditioning of this response will be more complete if you include other senses in your stimulus/response training. These would include touch, smell and sound. Incorporate into the stimulus/response training as many sensory associations as possible. Using a scenario where your training partner grabs you, have him say something as he reaches his hands out. Next time have him make the sound of his clothing scraping against the wall just before he grabs you or have him pull something from behind his back so that you can become aware of the sound and body mechanics when someone reaches for that weapon. Use your imagination. (69)

Stress

Stress has many effects upon the body. Some of the major factors fighters need to be concerned with include increases in heart rate, breathing rate, muscular tension and a decrease in cognitive functioning. Hyperventilation, which is often associated with stress, especially if the stress is fear or anxiety induced, can lead to the following:

· Lowering of CO2 levels in the blood stream with a concomitant lowering of blood acid levels
· Several sympathetic nervous system alterations including changes in renal function
· Increased risk of cardiac dysrhythmias, increased heart rate, decreased O2 supply to the brain and heightened cerebral vasoconstriction

The last group of factors could potentially affect your speed. Numerous studies have concluded that voluntary control of breathing helps cope with pain by increasing the threshold of tolerance and helps cope with situations that invoke fear. Training fighters in scenarios that help them cope with fear-provoking situations results in the following when one meets with such a situation:

· Lowering of the heart rate, the benefits of which are explained below
· Enhanced mental abilities involved in the acquisition and processing of new information
· Reduction in the overall experience of anxiety (69)

Stress and Heart Rate

As the level of stress increases, the heart rate increases. As the heart rate increases, so does the level of performance in physical and mental functioning. This is only true up to a point, however. As the heart rate climbs past a certain point, mental and fine motor-skill functioning begin to suffer. With an even higher heart rate, performance of complex, and lastly, gross-motor skills, decline as well. Examples of these skills include the following: typing is a fine-motor skill, drawing a pistol and firing using the weaver stance is a complex motor skill, and jumping or bench pressing is a gross-motor skill.

You may have heard that it is good to get a little exercise before taking an exam because the increased heart rate supplies more oxygen to the brain, thus improving mental functioning. Think about when you first wake up. Your body temperature is slightly lower and your heart rate is significantly lower, in part due to the lower body temperature. You are not in any condition to ace a test then, are you? You first have to get the body going. For some it may take a morning jog, for others a cup of coffee or hot shower and for others it may take a hectic ride to work. The result is the same however, each of these activities significantly increases the heart rate.

Levitt, referenced in (69), studied the effects of exercise-induced stress on varying tasks involving information processing. Tests were conducted at heart rates of 80, 115, 145 and 175 beats per minute (BPM.) The test subjects clearly performed best with a heart rate between 115 and 145 BPM. Subjects consistently performed poorly at 80 and 175 BPM in comparison. Another study testing performance in the areas of concentration, judgment and discrimination concluded that the best performance occurred when the heart rate was at, or slightly higher than, 115 BPM.

Factors that affect reaction time include visual perception, mental alertness, training, life experiences and stress levels. Mental alertness, like mental functioning, is optimal at this moderate range of heart rate. Visual perception is also affected by heart rate. When the heart rate increases above 145 BPM, the peripheral field of vision decreases. This loss of peripheral vision may decrease your effectiveness in picking up telegraphing movements by your opponent or by additional assailants. (69)

For fine-motor skills and motor skills that require a high degree of cognitive decision making, research indicates that optimal performance occurs during low levels of stress, when the heart rate is between 95 and 115 BPM. For motor skills involving a moderate level of coordinated control or cognitive complexity, optimal performance occurs as the heart approaches 145 BPM. For gross-motor skills, those involving large muscle masses and little decision making, optimal performance occurs during high levels of stress. (69)

It's no secret to any athlete that psyching up improves performance in gross-motor skills, be it running with a football, bench pressing or broad jumping. This has been confirmed in numerous research studies. However, Weinberg, Gould and Jackson, referenced in (69), concluded that while psyching up helped increase simple dynamic strength events, it had no effect on balance, or speed of arm movements. From this it can be concluded that psyching up will increase the speed of your lunge, however, it will not increase the speed of your punches or kicks. The only way it could increase the speed of your punches, other than having faster lunges, would be through the indirect benefit of boosting your confidence, diminishing a common tendency to hold back.

Focus & Concentration

The ability to think clearly is just as important as the ability to kick smoothly and powerfully. Stress, whether caused by surprise, fear, or other internal or external pressures, can prevent an athlete from performing a skill that, under normal conditions, could be accomplished easily. In 1992, decathlon star, Dan O'Brien, was setting a record pace at the Olympic trials. His position on the team seemed assured. Then he relaxed and stumbled on the pole vault, failing to clear a height that he had cleared hundreds of times before. He later stated that he was unable to get his head together as he tried two more attempts and failed. Despite having physical abilities that should have easily qualified him for the team, his Olympic hopes were shattered by a mental lapse. (42) The ability to remain focused during both stressful and routine training sessions, and competition, is usually what determines the winner when skill levels are near equal.

Recall from above that mental skills, like physical skills, increase through practice and that by repeating the mental or physical task, the brain pathways involved in the task become myelinated. This results in greater speed and ease of transfer of information through electrical stimulation. There are several methods you can employ that can help you concentrate better. Some of these you may already employ. For the others that are new to you, try incorporating them into your routine in the future. Here are some ideas.

Even the best athletes are affected by atmosphere. That's why home court advantage makes such a difference. When a player on the opposing team attempts to make a foul shot, his shooting average drops significantly. The shouting and waiving of arms and banners by the fans distracts most players, causing them to miss a greater percentage of free throws. Interference, whether external or internal, must be overcome in order for you to be successful under such circumstances. To develop the skill of tuning out audible and visual disturbances, attempt to recreate the situation as closely as possible.

Like physical adaptations, mental adaptations are very specific as well. The more realistic the training, the better. If you are a basketball player, you could put up a background behind the net. This background could be a large drawing of waiving fans, or a picture designed to create an optical illusion. You could add to this by recording some scenes of fans attempting to interfere with a player's concentration. Then place the television in front of your background. Now you have the background, the movement of the fans in the TV screen and the noise of the fans to contend with. This will help you develop the focus to see the hoop and block out the rest.

To train your ears in these skills, try listening to music, hearing only one instrument. Attempt to ignore the others. You could also record a conversation with background noise from the stereo or television. Then play the recording, hearing only the conversation. For sparring, tell your training partners to routinely attack you while you are sparring someone else. The punches, kicks and strikes with sticks from the training partners are not designed to hit you. You know that they will not hit you, therefore, you do not have to be concerned with them. All of your concentration should be on fighting your opponent. You could also have your training partners shout things at you to try to distract you. Attempt to completely block out all stimuli other than those of your opponent.

Self-Regulation Training

Training aimed at controlling the heart rate, body temperature, muscle tension and stress, began many centuries ago in India and China. In the 1950s, Soviet Cosmonauts were taught self-regulation training to develop their abilities in controlling the same factors. It was also the Soviets that developed self-regulation techniques into a science and applied them to sports training. Soviet youths are taught to look upon a competitor as an equal. Therefore, to beat him or her, it is necessary to draw upon resources usually considered to be outside the normal range of capabilities. (29)

In 1979-1980, Soviet researchers studied the effects of four different training regimens on world class athletes. Group 1 trained 100% physically. Group 2 performed 75% physical and 25% mental training. Group 3 split their training 50/50. Group 4 performed 25% physical and 75% mental training. Group 4 showed the greatest improvements. They were followed by Group 3, then Group 2 and last by Group 1. These results do not mean that you should follow the regimen of Group 4. These athletes had already, nearly reached their physical capabilities. If the study subjects had never trained before, the expected results would be different, possibly the reverse. Remember beginning athletes have an incredible strength surge in the first six to eight weeks that is mostly attributed to improvements in the neuromuscular wiring. The majority of athletes would benefit the most from regimens closer to those of Groups 2 or 3, depending on their present level. In the 1976 Olympics, Russia won more gold medals than any other country. East Germany was second in this competition, followed by the United States. Initially, it was suspected that these results were attributable to steroid usage. It is now believed that it was mostly due to their unique training methods. (29)

Neurophysiologists have proven that mental and physical relaxation are the same thing. If you relax the muscles, you relax the mind and vice versa. On the other hand, tension in either arena stimulates its counterpart. With this knowledge, techniques have been developed to relax both mind and body to enhance not only performance, but the effectiveness of the many types of mental training employed by elite athletes and by the people of the Far East hundreds of years ago. These types of self-regulation training decrease your mental tension, increase your confidence, decrease your reaction time, increase your motivation, increase the effectiveness of your training, and directly and indirectly increase your speed through these and other factors. (29) Of the 42 studies incorporating a variety of biofeedback techniques, 83% reported improvements in arousal control, performance, or both. (31)

Stress Reduction

Both mental and physical fatigue will slow your perceptual, mental and physical reactions. Stress is a common element in today's hectic environment and everyone has had days where they were mentally and or physically exhausted from a stressful day at work. There are numerous methods of reducing stress levels, some of which can be employed at almost any time and location, others are more appropriate at home or before a competition. The following sections explain several different methods of stress reduction through mental and physical relaxation.

You can also reduce your stress levels through consistent training. Practice daily if possible so that fighting becomes ordinary. Then your mental state can remain unchanged in a real fight without stressing out. (56) Every move you perform, be it a punch, block, slip, tie up, etc., must be thought of as an opportunity to strike down your opponent. Don't think of blocking, slipping, etc., per se, rather, think of everything as an opportunity to drop your opponent. Otherwise, you will miss your opportunity and possibly lose control of your stress level. (56)

Fear, Anger, Anxiety & Relaxation

If your mind is preoccupied with anger, fear and anxiety, you are obviously not devoting 100% to fighting. You are less able to perceive and immediately recognize the very subtle cues your opponent is giving away about his intentions. Also, these mental stressors usually manifest themselves through physical tension. Most people carry some of this tension in their shoulders and the back of their neck, others in their lower back. This physical tension prevents the muscles from being relaxed and loose, slowing down the speed of movement. It also causes you to tire more quickly and to telegraph your technique. These factors further slow you down. Remaining relaxed while you fight enhances your speed, power, endurance, balance and reflexes.

The two primary methods of dealing with this problem are to: 1) work on lowering the levels of fear, anger and anxiety; and 2) reduce the amount of tension held within the muscles. A method for reducing the level of fear and anxiety is learning to think of sparring as fun. If you develop an attitude of seeking out the best fighter because you find the challenge exciting, your stress will diminish if not altogether disappear.

For reducing these emotions, visualizations and self-hypnosis also work well. Below you will find several methods for reducing the levels of muscular tension. This chapter also includes techniques for visualizations and self-hypnosis.

Relaxation Exercises

Find a comfortable, quiet, place where you can relax without being disturbed for a while. You should be in loose, comfortable clothing and the room should be warm. Most people find that lying down on a bed with a pillow under the knees or in a recliner is most comfortable. If this tends to put you to sleep, either do the drill when you are wide awake or in a different position.

All relaxation exercises involve deep breathing. Deep, slow breathing causes a slowing of the pulse rate and prepares the body for further relaxation by releasing chemicals frequently released during sleep. Rapid, shallow breathing on the other hand has the opposite effect. If you are skeptical, place earplugs in your ears so that you can hear your heart rate. If necessary, you may have to place earmuffs over your ears as well. Listen to your heart rate. Breathe rapidly and shallowly as if you were scared. Notice how your heart rate increases. Now breathe deeply and slowly. Your heart rate almost immediately begins to slow. As your heart rate continues to slow, notice that it momentarily speeds up when you inhale and then it slows down again as you hold your breath and slowly exhale.

Breathe deeply from the lower abdomen, not the chest. Your entire abdomen should rise and fall, not just your rib cage. Inhale for a slow count of 5 to 6 seconds, hold for 3 to 4, and exhale to a count of 5 to 6 seconds. Many people teach that you should inhale through the nose and exhale through the nose or mouth. It doesn't really matter. There is no physiological difference between the two. Do whichever feels easiest for you or whichever way feels most comfortable. After a while, you will be able to feel your heart rate without having to listen to it with the earplugs in. You will be able to feel it under your skin in different parts of your body and you may be able to feel the changes in pressure in your head with each beat.

Below are some common and effective methods of relaxation.

Taking a warm bath and stretching beforehand can improve the effectiveness of the relaxation training. However, doing so also increases the likelihood of falling asleep during the relaxation exercises. Another effective time to perform a relaxation drill is immediately after a strenuous workout. Even though your heart may still be racing, the intense, focused concentration involved in your workout prepares your mind by forgetting everyday problems and helps it settle into the relaxation exercise.

Relaxation exercises are very effective when trying to make your mind more receptive to visualizations. Consider making a habit of performing both each night when you go to bed. They can be especially effective at that time because your conscious mind is shutting down and your subconscious is taking over. Another benefit is that it can help you get a good restful night's sleep.

Progressive Muscle Relaxation

Begin relaxing using the same techniques as outlined previously, i.e., a comfortable position, the deep breathing, lowering of the heart rate and possibly a warm bath or a vigorous workout beforehand. The idea behind this method is to tightly tense up one part of the body at a time, then relax the muscles as completely as possible. Then tense up again, only to a lesser degree than before. Relax again, striving to feel the muscles relax more than the previous time. Repeat the procedure again if necessary before moving on to the next muscle group. Again, the degree of contraction and relaxation should be a little less and more than the previous time. Tense as you inhale and continue tensing for about 2 to 3 seconds while you hold your breath. Then relax as you exhale. Feel your body and limbs sink into the bed as the muscles relax. Continue your exhaling as you feel and visualize the muscles relaxing. It does not matter if you start at your head or your feet, however, it does help if you are systematic, moving up or down your body working one muscle group at a time. Remember to include all your body parts, including your toes, thighs, buttocks, hands, forearms and face.

This drill helps build awareness of muscles holding tension. Discover the different feelings of holding muscular tension and of being relaxed. Learn to invoke this relaxed feeling at will, feeling the tension dissipate from the tense muscle or muscles. Finally, strive to develop this feeling during tension provoking situations. This takes practice. The more experience you gain, the more proficient you become. Therefore, practice this in various situations. Tournaments, dates, job interviews, tough and aggressive sparring partners, and even during movies are all situations where you can practice.

Blue Fog

Loren Christensen, author of *Speed Training*, (11) has added color to this standard technique. The addition of color helps with visualization. As explained above, get comfortable and begin your deep breathing. Close your eyes and listen to your heartbeat. When your heart rate lowers, after one to several minutes, depending on the level of your stress and your skill with these relaxation techniques, begin to visualize each breath you take as a cool, blue fog that you are inhaling. Feel the cool, moist air move down your windpipe and expand your lungs. Feel every part of your lungs come into contact with the fog. Visualize the fog moving through your veins and into your muscles. As the fog moves through your muscles, feel them relax. Feel each part of your body sinking into the bed. Then, toward the end of the holding period, visualize that the fog has moved throughout your body and is now on its way back up, only now it is red. Visualize that the hot breath you are exhaling contains the stresses and worries that are on your mind. Continue with this technique, progressively feeling yourself sink deeper and deeper into the bed as you become more and more relaxed.

Bouncing

Another easy way to develop awareness of your tension level and learn to relax throughout the day is to bounce. When walking downstairs, walk quickly, allowing your shoulder and chest muscles to relax completely. Feel your shoulders and chest bounce with each step. Allow them to float up and then come crashing down. If you are holding tension in the upper body, this is a great way of releasing it. You can do the same thing without stairs. Jump rope in place, but without the rope. Bounce lightly off your toes, striving for the same feeling of having your shoulders and chest float up and crash down. Whenever walking down stairs, allow yourself to do this, at least for a few steps, just to insure that you are not carrying tension.

Deep Relaxation

Researched by the Russian sports psychologist, Dr. Romen, deep relaxation is achieved by learning to produce four stages of feelings. These stages are identified as:

- Rhythmic breathing along with an inner calm and muscular relaxation throughout the body. Sensations of heaviness and immobility accompany the feeling of relaxation.
- Feelings of warmth in the arms, legs, torso and head.
- Feelings of coolness in one area of the body with the ability to produce feelings of warmth in another. Different researchers have reported that their subjects can produce temperature changes in their hands of up to 10 degrees Fahrenheit during a two minute period. (29)
- Feelings of a calm heart with a strong, steady beat.

Such control over the body can provide tremendous advantages to a competing athlete. The author is aware of the time commitment required to mentally train as suggested in this book. Many of the less comprehensive regimens fail to produce any lasting benefits to the athletes, however. It is necessary to continue training until you cause a change within you. You must develop the ability to induce a state of deep relaxation at will. Otherwise, you will not be able to make the necessary adjustments to your mindset or physiology when you need it most, for example, between matches or even between rounds.

Recall from the previous discussion in this book how the "fight or flight" response activates a branch of the autonomic nervous system, the sympathetic nervous system and how this automatic response obscures and even prevents an individual from executing the learned program that would serve him best. Also remember that although the response is automatic, the perception that triggers the response is not. Not only can mental and physical training change one's perceptions to such stimuli, but deep relaxation training can cause a decreased activation of the sympathetic nervous system through another mechanism. In the same way that relaxation training helps someone maintain a reduced level of stress throughout the day, this training can reduce the level of activation of the sympathetic nervous system when encountering a stress invoking situation.

Deep Relaxation Exercise

Begin with your deep breathing. Now clench your fist tightly. Describe to yourself how it feels. Use single words. Do not allow yourself to explain the feelings. Write the words down afterwards if you wish. Do the words tight, pain, tension, hard, strong, cold or warm, come to mind? Now make a mental note of any emotions that come to mind while you are clenching your fist. Finally, relax your hand and observe how this feels. Again, mentally note how your relaxed hand feels using single words. Now that you are in tune with the feelings and emotions of tension and relaxation, try the following exercise until you can produce the feelings routinely and easily. Continue working on this exercise.

After a minute of your usual deep breathing, take three deep breaths. Hold each breath for ten seconds and feel the release when you exhale. Next, follow this routine.

1. Relaxation mask. Starting with the eyes, see and feel them relax. Continue relaxing every part of the face.
2. Now relax your right arm. Say to yourself "my right arm is getting limp and heavy." Repeat four times.
3. Now tell yourself that your right arm is becoming relaxed and warm. Repeat four times as you feel these sensations.
4. Tell yourself that you feel supremely calm and warm. Repeat one time. Now repeat steps 2 through 4 for your other arm and then your legs. As you become proficient with this, add and mix the limbs using any combination.
5. Tell yourself that your chest feels warm and relaxed. Repeat four

to six times.

6. Feeling your heartbeat, repeat four to six times, "My heartbeat is calm and steady." If you have trouble feeling your heartbeat, use ear plugs.
7. Repeat, "I feel supremely calm and relaxed."
8. Feeling the sensations, repeat, "my stomach is getting warm and soft," four to six times. Repeat Step 7 once.
9. Continuing, repeat "my forehead is cool," four to six times.
10. Finish with Step 7.

It is not necessary to go through all steps. After completing the relaxation breathing and the mask, you may wish to only work on your limbs and your forehead sensations. Once you have mastered this exercise, you can induce a deeply relaxed state by simply sitting down, taking the three breaths and thinking the following thoughts. Mask in place. Facial muscles smooth. Arms and legs heavy and warm. Heart calm and steady. Stomach warm. Forehead cool. Supremely calm and relaxed.

Mental Imagery

The placebo effect is a scientifically proven fact that the mind, based on a person's belief that a particular substance or 'practice', can create physiological effects in the body, even if the substance is physiologically inert. This most frequently occurs when people take an inert pill, believing that the pill is actual medicine designed to help them, and they go on to get better. It is the BELIEF that they will now start getting better that affects the change. A belief can be extremely powerful, both positively and negatively.

The power of mental imagery should not be overlooked. Through the same mechanisms by which the placebo effect creates physiological changes, mental imagery can cause desired physiological changes when you believe in and work toward your goals. As with all other mental training, the more specific the images, the more realistic they are and the more frequently you imagine that you are as fast as you want to be, the better the chance of realizing your goals. When it comes to specificity, there has probably never been anyone with excessively specific visualizations or too highly defined goals. Make your visualizations as detailed as possible, incorporating all of your senses.

Visualizations

Begin with the standard deep breathing relaxation techniques. After you have slowed your heart rate and felt your muscles relax, begin a visualization. You may find it helpful to first go through the progressive muscle relaxation or the blue fog techniques to ensure that you have relaxed enough to begin a visualization.

See yourself sparring. Don't forget about detail. What is on the walls? How is the lighting? Does the room have an odor? When first training with this technique, imagine you are sparring someone you can easily beat. Someone who generates no anxiety for you and hopefully, makes you feel fast. See yourself as a bullet. Visualize your lunges exploding forward. Feel the lightness of your limbs. See your movements as quick and sudden flashes. See and feel the excitement as you immediately begin to dominate the match. To further increase the speed of your visualized techniques, create the feeling of relaxation of the antagonist muscles. Feel your toes grip the floor as you lunge forward. Most importantly, feel how relaxed you are as you are sparring. Try not to leave any detail out. Visualizations can focus on improving any number of skills.

Self Suggestion

Self suggestion is an effective means of altering your mind set. You have most likely heard and experienced first hand how you can talk yourself into or out of something. It is for this reason that some parents teach a child faced with a difficult decision to make a list of the pros and cons of both sides. The child then goes to bed and observes how he feels in the morning, before he has the chance to talk his way over to either side. This little trick actually helps.

Self suggestion is also an effective method of creating a positive, or negative attitude about yourself, your confidence and your abilities. Which lifter has a better chance of bench pressing a new maximum of 250 pounds? Lifter A who told his friends earlier in the day that he was going to set a new record? Now there he is with his friends, he has just ripped off the headset that was playing his most inspirational song, he slaps his hands together as he tells the bar, "You are going down!" He slides under the bar, telling himself that he can do this, that the bar is light as he wraps his hands around the bar and gives it his all.

Or on the other hand, lifter B who didn't tell his friends because he wasn't sure if he could do it. He has a couple of friends there and they recognize that this will be his max. They try to psyche him up, but he tells them to be ready for the spot because he doesn't think that he can do it. Obviously Lifter A has a greater chance of attaining his goal. The second lifter has defeated himself before he's even begun. Even if Lifter A doesn't achieve his goal the first time, he knows that with persistence he will, because he believes in himself. There is no greater power that an individual can possess.

By repeatedly thinking positive thoughts, your mind will begin to believe what it keeps hearing. It begins to think that you ARE fast. Not only does this provide a tremendous psychological increase to your speed, such as increased confidence, but it can also increase your physical speed. Your mind begins to direct your body to do what it has been programmed to do, to move explosively. It's similar to the placebo effect.

To make self-suggestion work for you, it should be frequent and specific. The more your mind hears the message, the faster and more thoroughly it begins to believe it. Place sticky notes up as a reminder to tell yourself how fast you are. Place these reminders on your calendar. You could take a pen and write the word 'fast' on your wrist. Then every time you look at your watch, you see the word and are reminded to tell yourself how fast you are. This next point is important also. The more specific you are, the easier it is for the mind to understand and conceptualize its new programming. Tell yourself statements like, "my back-fist is like Bruce Lee's" as you see yourself hitting Bob Wall as Lee did, or "my jab is devastatingly fast" as you visualize yourself lunging and jabbing into your opponent's attack, causing him to begrudgingly change from attack to defense.

Self-Suggestion via Head Swapping

If there is someone whose speed you admire, obtain a picture of him. Preferably one where he is performing a technique that involves speed. Place this picture on your refrigerator. Every time you open the refrigerator door or walk by it, visualize that the person in the picture is you. To help with the visualization, glue a cut-out picture of your face over his face. If you take a second to perform this visualization every time you walk by, the result of all of this self-suggestion can be a very effective means of increasing your speed. Self-suggestion also works well during relaxation drills.

Self-Hypnosis

A common form of self-hypnosis is nothing more than entering into a very relaxed state for the purpose of performing self suggestion. The mind is more receptive to suggestion in this relaxed state. Begin with the standard deep breathing exercise. Find a dot on the ceiling if you are in bed. If you are in a recliner, pick a dot on a wall. An uncluttered wall is more helpful. If you prefer, a candle just beyond your feet works great as well. When you are at the point where you would start visualizing the fog, start looking at the dot or candle. Look at the dot, or flame, continuously, but do not stare. The eyes should be relaxed. Try to focus on the object to the exclusion of everything else around you, as if you find it mesmerizing, but do not forcefully concentrate on it. Look at nothing else as you continue your breathing.

Begin telling yourself you are becoming more and more relaxed. As with the other techniques, feel your muscles relax as you sink into the recliner. As you continue, your eyes should become tired. You may want to close your eyelids. They may start watering. At this point, if your eyes haven't become tired yet, begin telling yourself that your eyes are becoming more and more tired. Tell yourself that your eyelids are growing heavy and that you can't keep them open. Allow your eyes to slowly close. Yes, this is a conscious decision to close them, but it is not like normal. It feels like it does when you are falling asleep. You are obviously awake, only very relaxed.

You can now begin self-suggestion or you can test yourself further while simultaneously practicing self-suggestion. This additional test involves imagining a tingling feeling in your hand or a feeling that your arm is either especially light or heavy. Whichever one you choose, begin a very slow count to ten. As you count one, tell yourself that your hand feels a little numb or tingly, or that your arm is beginning to feel light. Continue with your count. As you progress to ten, the sensations should become more pronounced. With practice, the sensations will become more and more real. Your arm may float up as you have convinced yourself that it is lighter than air. The more you can feel these sensations, the more susceptible your mind is to self-suggestion and the more you benefit from the hypnosis.

Once you are relaxed and prepared to begin self-suggestion, begin telling yourself that your hands are as fast as lightning. Tell yourself that you can snatch flies from the air. See yourself snatching them from the air with first your right hand and then your left. Continue with the suggestions, telling your mind exactly how fast you are in regard to punches, blocks, kicks and lunges. The more specific the better. When you have finished the self-suggestion, tell yourself that by the count of ten, you will feel awake and refreshed. Start with one, telling yourself that you are beginning to feel as you have a lot of energy. By the time you have reached the count of ten, your eyes should be open and you ought to feel ready to go. If not, stand, stretch and move about a little to help yourself become completely alert.

*In the final moments before competition,
successful athletes self-induce, either consciously
or subconsciously, a mental state where they lose
all conscious thought of what has been learned
about how to use the mind and body. Players
describe this state as letting go, or going on
automatic pilot, or being in the cocoon.*

Chapter 6
MENTAL TRAINING

Letting go is described by those who achieve it as a release from conscious thought. The athlete lets go of all concerns and outside stimuli. He is in the "here and now", where nothing other than the task at hand presents any stimulus to him. Athletes frequently remember feeling joyful, powerful and highly energized during times of peak performance. In his book, Peak Performance, (29) Dr. Garfield wrote a composite from the hundreds of statements of peak performers describing how letting go looks and feels.

"All at once it seems as though everything is working for me. There is no sense of needing to do anything. My actions unfold as they do in pleasant dreams, though my body may be putting out great efforts. I have no thoughts about what I should do or how I should do it. Everything is happening automatically, as though I have tuned myself in on a radio beam that directs my nervous system so that it works in synchronization with everything in and around me. I feel insulated from all distractions. Time disappears, and even though I know the speed of actions taking place around me, I feel I have all the time I need to respond accurately and well. I am so completely involved in the action that there is not even a question of confidence or the lack of it. There are no issues such as worries about failure or feelings of fatigue. Even such feelings as momentary fear appear to serve me, changing automatically into positive forces. Success is not an issue, though at the same time it seems natural and easy to achieve. I feel strangely detached from what I am doing even while I am completely in touch with everything, at one with my actions.

The whole issue around mind and body separation seems to dissolve, really, as I feel as though both are responding perfectly to my own wishes and inner prompting. I am acutely aware of colors, sounds, the presence of people around me, the feeling of being a source of power and energy in this moment in time. It is a trance-like state, but I feel totally in touch with everything around me, with everything within me, as though the usual barriers between me and the outside world have been pulled away, and I am completely at one with myself and the physical world with which I am interacting. It is a wonderful feeling, crisp, full of joy, more real than the everyday world, going very deep, an experience that rewards me many times over for all the effort I have put into my sport."

To achieve this state of release at will during competition it is necessary to develop skills in other areas of mental training. These skills will be presented in an order in which the skills learned from one session are used to build a foundation upon which the next level of skills is based. Having studied many forms of mental training and having put those methods to the test, in the author's opinion, Dr. Garfield's book, *Peak Performance*, is the most thorough, well-written book on the subject. In addition, the methods employed have been backed up by numerous physiological studies and hundreds, if not thousands, of interviews. The author highly recommends the book. It is well worth the investment of time.

The following assignments, aimed at building your skills to increase your potential and to develop control over letting go, are found in Garfield's book. The exercises have been greatly condensed to save you time and for the sake of space. The author has found this shorter version to be very effective. However, he still recommends Garfield's book to those ready to put in the extra effort.

In the final moments before competition, successful athletes self-induce, either consciously or subconsciously, a mental state where they lose all conscious thought of what has been learned about how to use the mind and body. Players describe this state as letting go, or going on automatic pilot, or being in the cocoon. The athlete who thinks too much while playing inhibits himself. Actions must be automatic, natural and spontaneous. Four steps have been identified for achieving this performance state. They are:

1) Relaxing the mind and body.

2) Discovering the power of mental pictures.

3) Improving concentration by holding a mental picture of the desired end result for a few seconds.

4) Learning to let it happen rather than trying to make it happen.

In a five year study by the Association for the Advancement of Sports Potential, it was determined that the more an athlete could achieve a state of relaxed attentiveness through exercises corresponding with the above four points, the more efficient their movements became. (29)

What is letting go? Before learning to achieve this state, it is first necessary to understand what it is and how it looks and feels. Most people perform with the left side of the brain. The left side is responsible for analysis, logic and verbalization. Many athletes suffer from paralysis by analysis. It is not paralysis per se, yet it interferes with performance because the individual analyzes something that the brain is capable of handling without analysis. The right side of the brain has great potential in recognizing and manipulating complex patterns and making split second decisions in sports. To achieve this state, it is necessary to refrain from focusing on the past or the future (left brain dominance). Therefore, all focus is on the present (right brain dominance). This also defines the state of Zen. Refer to the previous composite writing by Garfield of how letting go looks and feels. (29)

Letting Go/How to Let Go

Negative thoughts are the worst impediment to focusing on the present. Negative thoughts, in this context, are any thoughts that stimulate memories about the past or provoke concerns of the future. The leading causes for stiff performance, the opposite of letting go, fall into the following four categories:

1. Trying too hard. Don't think that the harder you try, the better or faster you'll be.

2. Worrying about past mistakes. Anxiety over repeating past errors causes muscles to tighten up and actions to become tentative and unsure.

3. Being overly concerned about the outcome of the play or match. This causes movements to be cautious, anxious and mechanical.

4. Being overly worked up and excited, forgetting that the best performances are spontaneous and natural. Being excessively keyed up becomes a source of stress. Each action should not feel that it is of the utmost importance, otherwise the athlete becomes anxious and overly conscious of every move.

These four areas are the result of left brain activity or concerns. The following directions help you turn off cerebral activity in the left hemisphere, allowing you to use the right hemisphere to dominate athletic performance through imagery and other intuitive processes. Fifteen to sixty minutes before training or competition, sit down, relax, and create a mental image of the activity you will be performing. If the competition involves sparring or katas, begin with a detailed image of the competition floor.

Next, imagine how it feels while you're competing. Mentally rehearse the positive feelings you wish to feel during the activity. As unrelated thoughts, feelings or ideas enter your mind, as they frequently will, brush them aside by creating a new detail for the mental rehearsal. As you continue focusing on your activity, your concentration will improve. After a few minutes, those unrelated thoughts and feelings will disappear. At the point when you are completely focused on your action, stop the mental imagery. Trust that your mind is prepared and that your images were complete. (29)

If you are at a location where it is difficult to find a quiet place, lay a towel over your head. Not only will this help you relax, but it will signal to others that you don't want to be disturbed. As stated above, while you are quieting your mind, discard all thoughts, feelings or ideas. If a new strategy comes to mind, let it go as well. If it is worth remembering, trust yourself to remember it later. If you just can't do this, try writing it on an imagery sheet of paper and placing it in your imagery notebook. Then get back to your mental rehearsal.

Remember that your number one detriment to achieving this automatic state is negative thoughts. Discard all negative thoughts immediately. Use any type of mental imagery that works for you. The image of a Pac-Man gobbling up the negative thought may work if you are familiar with the game. Bruce Lee used to visualize himself writing the negative thought on a piece of paper, wadding the paper up into a tiny ball and then burning it, never to be bothered by that thought again.

Finally, as your mind becomes increasingly clear, allow your attention to turn toward the reality of the present. Focus on your senses. Don't focus on the meaning of the stimulus, focus on the quality of it. Notice the volume, the rhythm, or the pleasant tones of a sound. With light, notice the brightness, colors, textures, etc. Continue with the senses of smell and touch. If you use equipment in your training and competition, pick up the equipment. Notice it's weight, how it feels in your hand and how the light reflects off it. Dr. Garfield summed up the essence of letting go with the following. "The key to successfully focusing on the present is learning to be attentive to your senses, to the quality of what you are sensing rather than your interpretation of the meaning." (29)

Another way to develop your abilities to enter the zone is to practice while at work, or during any number of activities. The zone of optimum performance occurs when your skills perfectly match those required for the challenge at hand. Therefore, to increase your performance and zone experience, make a simple job harder. Not only will the experience of performing at a higher level benefit you, but the task may be accomplished more easily because you are performing in or near your zone. Attempt to turn a boring task into a challenging game by inventing rules, setting goals and pacing yourself against the clock. Consider this. You fight best when going against a challenging opponent don't you? You also improve more during those challenging sparring sessions. Take advantage of this fact. Turn an easy sparring partner into a challenging one by placing rules and restrictions on yourself. Make yourself rise to the occasion.

Peak Performance Scale Exercise

The zone is a multidimensional state of arousal. It is affected by how nervous and worried an athlete is. It is also affected by one's perception of his or her physiological activation, as well as by a host of physiological assessments including heart rate and brain wave activity. When someone is in their zone, the amount of activation in each of the above areas is a unique equation. One person may need less physiological arousal and more cognitive stress to be in their zone than another person would. (31) In order to become aware of and determine your optimal recipe of physiological activation and arousal cognition that leads to peak performance, sports psychology specialists suggest that you retrospectively rate your performances.

This exercise provides you with a basis to evaluate your peak performance state for eight peak performance feelings. Rate your most recent performance, and then your worst and best performances for each of the eight feelings.

From this you will learn to judge your mental state before performance, competition or training, so that you can consciously change any state necessary before you're 'up'. The eight peak performance feelings are:

1) Mentally relaxed.

2) Physically relaxed.

3) Confident/Optimistic.

4) Focused on the present.

5) Highly energized.

6) Extraordinary awareness.

7) In control.

8) Letting go.

Use the following scale:

Below average performance ranges from 0 to 3.
Average ranges from 4 to 7.
Peak performance ranges from 8 to 10.

Now rate the three performances. Begin with the most recent. For all three, go through the relaxation exercises already explained and relive the experience to its fullest. Allow yourself to feel the sensations associated with the eight performance feelings. For example, when focused on mental relaxation, do you feel an inner calm? Do you feel that the sense of time slowed down, or do you have an ability to calmly focus on details? Do you feel anxiety? Do you feel pressure from having to succeed? Rate the criteria. Then continue with 2 through 8. Do the same for your worst and best performances. Make a chart with the ratings. From this you can determine what areas need work. If your ratings for confidence/optimism and letting go average, say for example, 5 or 6, then you know that you need to continue your mental training in those two areas.

__Volition__

Volition, also known as will power, is the desire necessary to succeed. Volition has determined the winner in many competitions. With closely matched opponents, the contestant with the strongest will to win frequently prevails. Not only can will power keep a fighter from dropping after receiving a hook to the chin, but it can provide motivation for your training, helping to push you to the next level. The following four-part exercise teaches you different sources of volition from which you may already consciously and subconsciously draw.

Step One

Recall a moment or an event when you performed exceptionally well. It could involve sports, school, hobbies or personal relationships. The only thing that matters is that you were very excited and pleased with your performance. First or second place is irrelevant. You need to have been fully satisfied and there should have been a great investment of effort on your part. Recall three such events. On a blank sheet of paper, write a short title or sentence for the event in the center of the page. Circle it. Do the same for the other two events on another sheet of paper.

Step Two

Sit comfortably, close your eyes and relax. After fully relaxing, perhaps through the blue fog method, recall the event as clearly as you can. After remembering as many details as possible, concentrate on the thoughts and feelings you had at the time. Were you proud? Excited? Ecstatic? Highly energized? Did you feel powerful? Did you think that you could accomplish anything you set your mind to? Write down the word or words that come to mind. Draw a circle around each set. These circled words should surround the event title from Step One.

Step Three

Now ask yourself what things you associate with this peak experience. Write these down and circle them. Connect any of the groups that are related. A solid line signifies a strong relationship while a dotted line denotes a weak one. The associated elements may include a motivational statement from a friend, a movie or book, or perhaps the performance of a mentor. Anything that significantly contributed to the experience, you should write down.

Step Four

Continue by writing down and including in the diagram those things you did that directly contributed to your accomplishment. This could include your diet, sleep patterns, training discipline, etc. If your event involved acceptance of employment, what aspects of your education or interview preparation contributed. Repeat this procedure for the other two events.

By studying the diagrams, you can learn what your mind and heart need to help you become a peak performer. Instead of simply following someone else's training prescription, you will identify the experiences, thoughts and feelings that spur you on and increase your will power. Perhaps you work best alone. Maybe you perform best when outclassed or when someone doubts your ability. By learning what suits you best and incorporating these factors into your regular training, you will increase the effectiveness of your training substantially. Garfield writes that most peak performers attribute this individualized training as a key ingredient to their success.

VOLITION

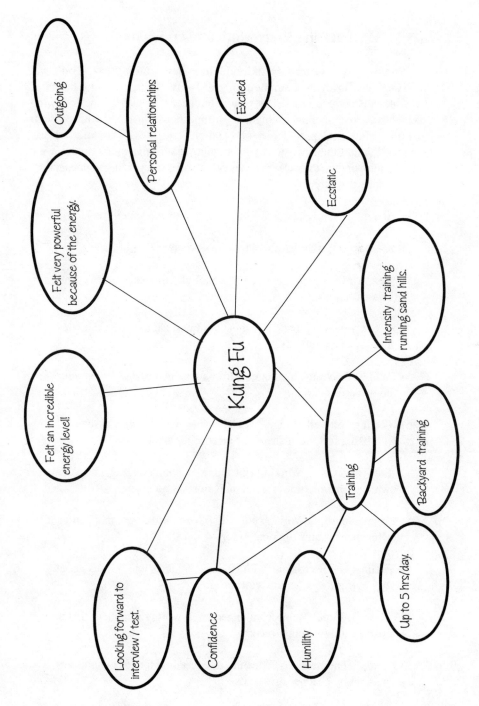

Rating Your Motivational Factors

Another exercise to help individualize your training based on what motivates you involves a simple rating of twelve factors. Using the three separate clusters you created as your reference, rate each of the following elements as low, medium or high, regarding their impact on you and your volition. For example, if one of your clusters involved a martial arts competition, did the activity of your training and/or the competition have a low, medium or high impact on you and your volition regarding your excellent performance that day?

1) Action. Actively partaking in training and/or competition.

2) Spectator. Watching others train or compete.

3) Coaching. Learning from coaches, books, videos and demonstrations.

4) Past experiences. Thinking about your past triumphs, hard battles or enjoyable moments.

5) Future. Thinking about or constructing mental images about your future performances.

6) Feelings of well being. Mental or physical feelings associated with being fast, or in shape, or performing well.

7) Solo workouts. Working out alone or competing against your own personal record rather than against an opponent.

8) Companionship. Working out with others for support, motivation, or for the stimulus of competition.

9) Feedback. Discussions with coaches, athletes and friends about your performance and/or your progress.

10) Competition. Being challenged by a worthy opponent or the prospect of breaking a record.

11) External motivations. Meeting or exceeding the expectations or goals set by coaches or friends.

12) Other. Anything else that motivates you.

Based on the information learned from the above two exercises, create a picture of your training regimen that now incorporates your own personal motivational factors. Choose a goal that you want to accomplish soon. It can be a small and private goal, but it must be important to you. It could be anything from learning to shadow box smoothly to benching 200 pounds six times.

Write a brief description of your goal in the center of a sheet of paper and circle it. Go through each of the above twelve factors you rated. Think about each one that you rated as having a high impact on your volition. If you rated competition and feelings of well being high, develop clusters on the paper, articulating what it is that motivates you. Perhaps it is sparring against the best fighter. Or the memory of how proud and confident you were when you were in great shape two years ago. Another example would include watching videos of your sparring with a coach or training partner if you rated coaching and feedback as high volitional factors for you. These clusters might each read, "always looking forward to fighting the best," or "1998 and 175 pounds, felt so strong and fast."

Also use the volition clusters created earlier to develop your highly motivational workouts. If a song always psyches you up, include this in your diagram and consider listening to it before attempting your goal. If specific events give you pride and motivation, include them. When completed, your goal will be surrounded by feelings, specific training memories or events, important reminders such as keeping relaxed, scenes from movies, etc.

Goal Setting

Write down your goals and what you believe you need to do to reach them. Then keep a daily log of your training. Many people are surprised at how little time they actually put into training, or how little they actually accomplish during training after they review their log. This is an excellent method of ensuring that you keep on track in your efforts to achieve your goals. Initially, you may be disappointed by how all those bad days or busy days add up to an inconsistent or overly abridged training regimen. Turn the situation around and use the information to provide yourself with additional motivation and/or discipline.

Unfortunately, humans have a tendency toward comfort. This tendency must be fought. The truly committed never take it easy. They apply their will power, backed by the strong desire to achieve their goals, to rise above this tendency toward weakness. Dieting offers a perfect example. You are on a diet combined with training to lose fat. Of course you're performing resistance training to prevent, or at least reduce, the loss of muscle mass while dieting, right? Someone offers to treat you to a small pastry. You say to yourself, "It's okay, I'll need the few extra carbohydrates for my workout and this little snack won't make a difference on my physique." There's the temptation. There is the weakness within your mind. Don't give in. Rise above this weakness. When you have made a goal, give yourself credit and stick to it. Never give in to an offer, impulse or temptation. (63)

When you do make a mistake of some kind, don't fret about it. Act aggressively to limit the damage. Remind yourself of your goals and move on. Soon you'll have forgotten all about it.

Goals

Don't create an unreasonably large goal and set your sights on it. You have a better chance of realizing your ultimate goal if you make smaller milestone goals along the way. These milestones, or short term goals, help you better plan your training strategy, provide more realistic goals that you can make soon, and therefore, help maintain your motivation. Strategies for developing and maintaining motivation are thoroughly discussed later in this chapter.

Humans tend to strive for a goal and then stop when it is reached. Tom Morris has an excellent analogy in his book, *Make Your Own Breaks.* Morris compares people to the furnace in his old house. Whenever he turned up the thermostat on a cold day, the furnace worked hard heating the house until the inside temperature reached the new setting. Upon reaching its goal, it stopped. The temperature of the house would start to drop again. Don't allow yourself to fall into this trap. Rather, reward yourself, enjoy the moment, and continue working toward a higher goal.

The One-Percent Rule

Don't try to reach the top immediately and don't try everything at once. Attempt to improve by one percent over the session before. Consistent efforts, combined with smart training, produce consistent gains, although not necessarily steady gains. The body seems to adapt this way. Increases in strength and skill usually come in spurts. It is the result of consistent training during the highs AND lows that produces results. You may have heard that you improve the most on your 'off' days. Or perhaps, that the days when you don't feel well, or you feel tired, are the most important days to train. These sayings were designed to provide motivation when you need it most. No, you won't improve the most when you are fighting a cold. However, the most important factors concerning success are time and effort. The best way to rack up training time is through consistency. (2)

Performance Plans

The following section on goals and performance plans is based on the program found within Dr. Garfield's book, *Peak Performance*. Goal setting is used to develop a blueprint of your peak performance training program. The goals should be as detailed and precise as possible. Not only does a highly defined goal help in the development of a plan of action, it also aids in generating mental images and auto-suggestion phrases that affect your performance. To more accurately develop a specific goal, first articulate why it is you are training in your sport. This is referred to as a mission statement.

Mission Statement

Make a list of your thoughts and feelings relating to the following areas:

1) What feelings do you experience when you are enjoying your sport the most? Are they of confidence, victory, intensity, complete absorption, etc.?

2) If any mentors have influenced you in your sport, what do these people or their accomplishments mean to you?

3) What do you most admire about these people and have you changed in any way because of them?

4) Do you have a personal philosophy that you express in your life outside of sports that can be expressed athletically?

Take your time with these questions. Within the answers is the foundation of your personal mission. This is the internal fuel for your volition. The answers are also the basis of your mission statement. Consolidate them into a single, clear statement that goes beyond any numerical goal.

Long Term Goal

Defining your long term goal is the next step. In developing a long-term goal, you should feel that accomplishing this goal will greatly contribute to actualizing your mission. If your mission statement read, "I want the incredible feeling that comes from being able to control my opponents, hitting them at will," then perhaps your long-term goal might read as follows. "After having allowed sparring partner Joe to attack first, or to prepare to attack, I quickly, confidently and aggressively strike him, completely overwhelming his attack."

If your mission statement involved weight training, your long term goal could specify a specific weight and percentage of body fat. Psychologist Dimitrova published the results of his study in the January, 1970 issue of International Journal of Sports Psychology. Dimitrova concluded that the more clear and detailed an athlete's goal, the greater his tolerance of fatigue and distractions. It's also necessary to develop a time table for achieving your goal. An example of a time table and a specific training program to accomplish your goal follows this section.

The next two steps are not absolutely necessary. If you are growing tired of the homework assignments, these would be the two to skip. It is recommended that you not skip them, however. These short exercises will help solidify why you are striving toward your goals and why they are important to achieving your mission. These two exercises are termed Goal Embodiment and Associated Rewards.

Goal Embodiment

Create a sentence explaining why you are striving toward your goal or goals. The sentence may be similar to the following examples. "These goals embody my mission because mastery of the skills necessary to attain my goals will invoke the personal feelings that are my mission." Or perhaps, "These goals embody my mission because the attainment of my goals will result in the psychological rewards that are my mission."

Associated Rewards

What are the inherent rewards associated with your goal? Feeling stronger, faster, confident, superior or proud? Perhaps winning is important or making a team that many of your friends are on. List your personal rewards in order of the most important to the least important.

Now decide when you will begin working toward your goal and when you will reach it. Be careful to be realistic when estimating the time you expect to take to achieve your goal.

Goal Training Plan

Here is where you develop a training regimen designed to methodically increase your abilities toward your goal. It is assumed that you know your current performance level. If you are not sure, think about it and devise a way to test it while assigning quantitative figures to the results. Model your goal training plan after the following chart.

Long Term Goal: Write in your long term goal. For the sake of simplicity, the goal of attaining a specified weight and percentage of body fat has been used.

Associated Rewards: List the most important first:

1st: Become faster & stronger

2nd: Look & Feel better

3rd: Learn more

Segments: These are the various aspects of your training that are necessary to achieve your goal. In this example, they include: diet, weights, aerobics and stretching. Note: stretching is not a necessary aspect of this goal. It has been included for illustration purposes.

GOAL TRAINING PLAN

Start	Segment	Step	Present Perform. Level	Goal/Changes in Program	End	Result
1/1	Diet	1	Lots of fat & junk food. 3 pieces of candy/day	More rice & chicken. Only 1 bad meal per day	1/18	Accomplished
1/18	Diet	2	More rice & chicken. Only 1 bad meal/day, still eat candy	< 4pieces candy/week No cookies	1/25	Accomplished
1/25	Diet	3	< 4 pieces candy/week.	1 bad meal/every 3 days	2/10	Accomplished
2/10	Diet	4	Continue in this manner.			

GOAL TRAINING PLAN

Start	Segment	Step	Present Perform. Levrl	Changes in Program	End	Result
1/1	Weights	1	Bench, 3 sets of 6 @ 190#	Bench, 3 sets of 8 @ 190#	1/22	Accomplished
1/22	Weights	2	Bench, 3 sets of 8 @ 190#	Bench, 3 sets of 6 @ 200#	2/10	Too much; 3 of 195#
2/10	Weights	3	Bench, 3 sets of 6 @ 195#	Continue in this manner.		
1/1	Aerobics	1	None.	2/week for 15 min.	1/20	Hurt ankle. Repeat.
1/20	Aerobics	2	None.	2/week for 15 min.	2/10	Accomplished
2/10	Aerobics	3	Continue in this manner.			
1/15	Stretching	1	None.	2/week for 15 min.	2/1	Feels good.
2/1	Stretching	2	2/week for 15 min.	Before & after workouts.	2/25	>3 workouts/week.
2/25	Stretching	3	Continue in this manner.			

Living Your Long-term Goal

The following visualization exercises help provide motivation for you on a recurring basis and help you prepare yourself mentally before each event.

The focus of this exercise is to experience the achievement of your long-term goal. Review your goal, relax and begin visualizations in a setting where you will not be disturbed. See yourself achieving your goal. Where are you? Who are you with? What did you do to achieve it? Do not limit yourself to the memories of your past peak performances. Use your thoughts and feelings as a basis, but this is your long-term goal. You are triumphant. How do you feel? Focus on this. This is the backbone of the exercise. Feel the excitement, the wide smile, the pride. After completing your visualization, write a description of it for future reference. This record should trigger your full recollection of the visualization. Make a point of recalling your goal and reliving your visualization at least once per day. Also, do this just before you warm up before a workout or competition.

Living Your Short-term Goal

Continuing with the same process, visualize yourself achieving your short-term goal(s). Do not jump too far ahead, skipping steps. Remember that each goal must have a high probability of success. Otherwise, this could lead to imprecise images, poor gains and discouragement. In study after study, athletes with the complete, highly detailed and vivid visualizations performed the best. (29) Visualize achieving your short-term goal and successfully making gains that are steps to achieving that goal.

For example, if your short-term goal is to bench 250 lbs. six times and your present level is 225 lbs. six times, visualize yourself pressing 230 lbs. six times. Do this not only whenever you can find the time, but also just prior to attempting 230 lbs. for six repetitions. The visualization should include the sights, sounds and odors of the gym. See your partner place the weights on the other side of the barbell. See the bar. Feel how relaxed and confident you are. Feel yourself take a deep breath and then slide along the bench. Grip the bar as you always do, take a deep breath as you feel your pectoral muscles stretching. Hear yourself count aloud to three as your see your partner give you a lift off. Feel how light the bar seems to be. Lower the bar as you inhale, feel your chest stretch and press it up smoothly as you exhale. Hear yourself count aloud or silently as you normally do. Continue with all six repetitions. What the mind can conceive, the body will achieve. The trick is that the visualization must be precisely the same as the actual achievement of the goal. Train the body and the subconscious through this form of auto-suggestion.

Scientists, including Bulgarian psychiatrist Georgi Lozanov, have demonstrated that self-spoken suggestions can program the mind to respond automatically to a specific stimulus. Russian scientist Alexander Romen took these tests one step farther. Using an electromyogram, a device used for measuring the electrical impulses that occur in muscles just before contraction, Roman revealed that muscles perform the physical activity imagined or suggested by words. Romen also showed that psychoneurological training, mental imagery and auto-suggestion, can program specific muscular responses to a stimulus before the subject ever attempted to program the responses under physical training. (29) Further tests have demonstrated that stimulus/response training is best developed through a training program incorporating both mental and physical arenas.

How to Create an Expectation for Success

This exercise is similar to the one under the heading "volition", but it differs in that it helps you focus specifically on the feelings of success. First you must identify the feelings. Then you will develop the skill to activate those feelings while under pressure. This imbues you with athletic poise, the ability of some athletes to perform at their best even while under intense pressure.

As with many of the other exercises, through deep relaxation go back in time to a point when you did something extraordinarily well. It does not have to be an athletic event. What you are focusing on here are the intense feelings of accomplishment. What were you feeling at the time? What did you want to do? Who did you want to rush over to and kiss or tell? What were the sights, sounds or smells at the moment of success?

Experience your emotions again. Take a deep breath, hold it, and exhale slowly and deeply. Now focus on your feelings some more. Continue until you are reliving the experience again. When you are done, write down your thoughts and feelings of the experience.

Most people tend to look for their errors more than they give themselves credit for their accomplishments. Yet, as we know, success comes from having a positive mental attitude. It comes from building upon successes, becoming energized from one accomplishment and turning this energy toward the next goal. To develop the habit of thinking in terms of success rather than dwelling on past errors, focus your attention on those feelings you just wrote down at least twice a day. Begin to expect success.

Visualization Training

Visualization training is an integral part of virtually every Olympic gold medal winner's training. Every elite athlete the author has interviewed or read about integrates visualization into his or her training program. Visualization provides numerous benefits for the athlete. These cover the realms of physiological, (both physical and mental), technical, practical and numerical benefits. Numerical benefits means that going through a kata or stimulus/response drill in your mind counts as one training repetition. The more times your body does the routine, the better your body learns it.

Recall from above that visualizing yourself performing an activity does more than stimulate neurons in your brain. It actually sends impulses through your nervous system to the muscles that would be involved in the movement. Up to this point, your neuromuscular system does not distinguish the difference between visualized movement and actual movement. Therefore, recalling the process of myelination, each time you visualize yourself performing a technique, you are laying down another coat of myelin. Remember, as the myelin coat becomes thicker, the action becomes smoother and faster. Your actions become better balanced and more powerful. Because of this, it is of the utmost importance to visualize the movement with perfect technique. Based on the theory of myelination, you want to make it easier to perform the technique correctly and harder to perform it incorrectly. Garfield quoted the Russian researcher V.M. Melnikov as saying, "The smaller the difference between imagery and actual movement, the lower the probability of errors in performance and the greater the opportunity to influence the process of learning."

Visualization training also builds confidence and helps program the mind for success. For example, if you are going to compete against Joe Karate in an upcoming tournament, visualization will do more than increase the speed of your movements. Through visualization, you can see yourself defeating

Joe many times over. You can see yourself slipping his kick or punch and countering with a cross to his solar plexus. This will increase your confidence in beating him when you fight. Your anxiety level will be lower, thus conserving energy and decreasing the onset of fatigue. The decreased muscular tension will also increase your speed and power. By repeatedly programming your mind for success, you will expect to win. Not only will you consciously feel more confident, but your subconscious will take the steps necessary, through its actions and reactions, to win.

Mental imagery must include movement. Visualizing still shots is not effective. You must visualize the movement with flawless execution. In this way, you will be laying the proper neurological tracks for optimal performance, overriding previously laid faulty tracks. Electromyograms taken of athletes during visualization training showed that the muscles performed the exact motions imagined, subliminally taking the athletes through the movement. In addition, numerous studies have demonstrated that mental rehearsal is as effective and beneficial as the actual physical training. Alexander Romen concluded that mental rehearsal, self-regulation and relaxation training are invaluable in improving and enhancing just about any human function or ability desired, including reaction times. (29)

Visualization is also a practical method of training. You can engage in it any place where you can relax enough to visualize yourself overcoming your opponent with lightning speed.

Visualizations work well for just about any sport. They are especially great for katas. You can run through the movements of a kata in seconds. An effective method of using visualization for katas is to first use them to learn the pattern. You will save significant amounts of time by going through the katas mentally as you are learning them. After you have memorized the pattern, the next step is to work on the finer elements of the kata. Your visualizations should now reflect the mental image of you performing the kata with perfect execution of the finer details. After this, use your mental imagery to perform the kata in its entirety, at normal speed with perfect execution. Using this method, you can have a flawless kata down faster than simply by practicing it physically.

Conditioned Response Visualization

Visualization training can also be used to enhance stimulus/response training. As always, this can be done practically anywhere and it does not require a training partner. To develop your instantaneous responses, find a place where you can relax and use your mental imagery to place yourself in a sparring session. Remember to include as much detail as possible. Visualize the size of the ring and room, the lighting, the smell of sweat, the feel of the floor, etc. The more detail you include in your visualization, the more effective your training will be. Next, allow yourself to 'let go.' Perceive the stimulus and see yourself responding instantly and effectively.

Mentally recreate your best performance, reliving every detail, feeling it in your body as you recreate it. Rehearse this repeatedly as often as you can until you can easily recall it in its entirety whenever you wish. When you can create a clear picture at will, take this visualization into the field. A few minutes before performing, recall the visualization. If at first you do not notice any benefits from this, continue with the training. It should not be too long before you do. Once the visualization comes to life effortlessly, assign a trigger word to it. Choose one word that describes the event. Hit, counter, slip, or any word that feels appropriate to you will work. Then, at the beginning and end of the visualization, say the word. After a short while, just repeating the word will elicit a replay of the visualization. Once you are at this stage of self-suggestion, such a trigger word can be used during actual competition.

If you become restless during your mental rehearsal, don't worry or fight it. It's not a sign that your concentration is waning. The visualization should be sending impulses to the muscles. Also, a vivid visualization evokes emotions. If restlessness occurs, get up and walk around for a minute or begin acting out the visualization.

When performing a mental rehearsal, you have all the time necessary to visualize every detail of the movement. The rehearsal elongates the action from what might take a few seconds into a few minutes. Then, in competition, the reverse happens. The mind flashes back to the mental rehearsal and creates an illusion that there is all the time in the world to execute the action. Not only does this reduce stress by reducing the sense of being rushed, but it increases perception and allows the athlete to pay attention to the finer details of the technique. For time alteration to occur, it is necessary to rehearse each increment of the movement. With practice, the mental rehearsals will occur in real time, while the perception of real time remains slower.

*The better you are able to articulate to yourself
and to others what the cues are and how they
provide clues as to a fighter's intentions, the
more capable you are of perceiving and
correctly interpreting the cues of your opponent.
This holds true on both the conscious and
subconscious levels.*

Chapter 7
PERCEPTIVE SPEED

If your level of perception is keen, then you will see an attack coming before it is launched. Your speed will seem incredibly swift, even in the face of a fast attack. Consider the old adage used in western movies about a gun fighter focusing on his opponents' eyes, rather than on his gun hand. The point is, if you focus on reading your opponent, then you could know the instant he decides to strike, even before he begins to move. Keen perception of this type can be incredibly demoralizing to your opponent, especially if you launch your counter assault while your opponent is still preparing to attack. This state of demoralization affects all four P-NR-A-NR-D-NR-A areas of your opponent's speed.

Psychology also plays a role in your perception. The mind must be well focused to perceive the minute bits of information that all opponents give out. Psychology factors into how quickly and effectively that information is used in the analysis and decision phases. This chapter focuses mostly on the various techniques you can use for strategy, touching only briefly on their psychological effects when it is helpful in understanding their value.

To have great skills at perception, you must be able to feel what your opponent is going to do. OK, perhaps in Wing Chun, judo and wrestling, but what if you are not touching your opponent. None of us can truly read the thoughts of others. So how do the best competitors do it? They pick up on subtle cues, mostly by sight, sometimes by sound. Even if they do not consciously know what the cues are themselves, they exist and they are perceivable. The better you are able to articulate to yourself and to others what the cues are and how they provide clues as to a fighter's intentions, the more capable you are of perceiving and correctly interpreting the cues of your opponent. This holds true on both the conscious and subconscious levels. Later in this chapter, you will find training drills designed to improve your skills in perceiving and articulating cues.

A study by the Department of Human Movement Studies at the University of Queensland, Australia, found that expert racquetball players often begin to move to intercept the opponent's ball even before the opponent hits it. Slow motion video demonstrated that expert players consistently initiate their response before casual players. Further investigation, through interviews and testing players watching a video of others in slow motion, revealed that these expert players pick up on smaller, more subtle cues than the casual players. For example, an expert player may notice how an elbow moved and then deduce how the player was going to hit the ball, whereas, the casual player would not make the deduction until the entire arm moved and the racquet was about to strike the ball. (1)

Fighters should have an easier time than racquetball players with this since they are looking directly at their opponent. Some of the cues you should train yourself to pick up on include: foot movements, including readjustments and twisting; knee movements; tensing of the legs, hip and/or shoulders; movements of the hands and arms; leaning of the body; eye and head movements; and changes in facial expression and tension. These cues may indicate a plan to attack, an outside distraction, hesitation, loss of concentration, change in determination, frustration, fear, confusion, anger, impatience, etc. Regularly remind yourself of these cues, look for others and remember that your opponent is looking for cues from you.

In many sports, early perception and decision making are more important in affecting performance than the technical aspects of the athletic movement. (1) Both perception and decision making skills can be improved through training. There is no difference between experts and novices in visual perception speed when it comes to a general task, such as hitting a buzzer when a green light is perceived. It takes approximately .25 of a second for everyone to receive and process the stimulus of the green light and then to send the preprogrammed response down the arm, stimulating the muscle, causing the hand to hit the light. Visual acuity, stereopsis (binocular ability), and phoria (a turning of the visual axis) are all the same in experts and novices.

The only exception involves visual defects and usually these are easily corrected. (1)

However, experts are faster and more accurate in recognizing and recalling patterns in their specific area of expertise. (1) Tests have shown that experts can decipher information from less stimuli than can non-experts. For example, they might recognize what move is foreshadowed by a slight movement of the elbow where a non-expert would not recognize the pending attack until the entire arm moved. (1) Tests have also shown that experts initiate a response earlier than non-experts. (1) This is most likely the result of the earlier recognition as noted above and from a faster decision response. You can significantly develop these skills through training.

Decision Speed

Experts can make a more advanced and more accurate prediction of their opponent's actions partly because of their superior observation skills and partly because they have reduced their opponent's probable responses and/or actions. Studies have proven that as the knowledge of action probabilities increases, so does the speed of decision making. (1) Experts are more familiar with the foreshadowing movements of techniques and what techniques potentially and naturally flow from one to another. Furthermore, they are more familiar with typical responses to different types of attacks. For all the above reasons and for many more, nothing beats experience in the ring. Research confirms what common sense suggests, that perception and decision making skills are trainable. (1)

The sooner you notice your opponent initiating his attack, the faster your response will be. Also, the sooner you observe an opening, the faster your attack will be toward that opening. How can you increase your abilities to observe and interpret the cues your opponent gives out? Don't think that an expert can have a flawless match, not giving out any cues. Just as we all give out some form of body language warning others that we are lying, expert fighters cannot hide all of their body language all the time. However, they may only give out occasional and very subtle clues.

There is no substitute for hours spent in the ring. You learn faster if you enjoy sparring. Don't fear it, look forward to it. This change in attitude does wonders for your relaxation in the ring. It also significantly increases your skills in perception. To further enhance the training of your perception abilities, try the following training methods which are very effective for increasing your skills in observation and interpretation. While training, keep in mind that your opponent is looking for your body language.

Before every match, or round, pick one or two cues that you are going to look for. Your objective for this round is not to win, but to observe as many of those cues as possible, as early as possible. This is an effective method for training any skill you wish to work on, be it perception, keeping your crosses straight, relaxing, footwork, etc. Continue practicing your perception skills while sitting on the sideline observing others. Pick a fighter and look for those tell tale hints he is expressing. If you find this difficult, spar with a novice fighter or watch a beginner spar. They give out cues with a great deal of exaggeration.

A more advanced training method is to video tape yourself and your partners sparring. Then watch the rounds in slow motion. While watching, play a game. The object is to be the first to call out what a fighter is going to do and articulate how you know. To play the game, everyone should watch the same fighter and one person should pause the tape whenever someone says stop. Then he must articulate what is happening. This helps instill observation skills and it helps you learn to prevent telegraphing.

This is a great method of training. Along with learning about your partners' weaknesses, you can learn about your mistakes. Not only do you gain information about what cues you give out, but you learn about all aspects of your fighting. Do you drop your hands, spread your feet too wide, fail to put your body behind your hooks, fail to take advantage of an opportunity, tense up, overcommit, lose balance? After viewing the video, choose one aspect you wish to improve. Then spar another round while concentrating on that one element only. Watch how much you improve. You can make a list of techniques to work on or skills to improve. Before every round, read one of your lists, programming your mind to address those areas.

Research indicates that the best approach to learning the links between early, advanced information such as the raising of a shoulder or a facial expression, and the ultimate outcome, is to do so through progressive stages. In other words, do not jump in the ring with the idea of improving your perception skills in general. Work on observing one type of cue, or one body part at a time. When you have increased your skills in that particular area, begin working on another cue or body part. (1)

If using the previously mentioned game to train your acute observation skills, focus the camera on one body part. Have only the lower body of one fighter in the field of view. The camera operator or another person should verbally announce the techniques of each fighter. Then watch the video in slow motion. Assume that each movement or tensing has a purpose and attempt to determine what it was for. If there was no justifiable reason for it, then it was wasted energy. If you cannot figure it out, play the part again at regular speed to include the audio. The announcer will provide the answer.

A variation to this type of training is to have a third person shout stop while you are sparring. Then, stop and think about what you believed your opponent was going to do. Tell him. He should then tell you what he really was planning and what his mind set was. He should then tell you what he thought you were thinking. You reciprocate by telling him what you were planning to do, why you were planning to do it and what your frame of mind was. Both fighters can learn a lot about their own body language and about the body language of their opponent from this drill. Tests have clearly shown that experts can not only recognize patterns better than non-experts, but they can also recall those patterns better. This drill also helps you to recall and articulate the cues that your opponent gives out.

Another effective and fun way to conduct the same training is to spar with a beginner. Beginners make every telegraphing error possible and they do it with a great deal of exaggeration. In round one, look at the beginner's feet; round two, his hips; round three, his elbows; round four, his shoulders; round five, his eyes; and round six, his facial expressions.

Additional exercises to increase your abilities of perception can be found in *Chapter 11*.

<u>Sense of Time</u>

Recall from *Chapter 5* that highly stressful situations frequently cause people to have time distortions. Generally, those who feel overwhelmed by the situation or are unprepared for it have difficulty remembering what happened. For these individuals, time seems to speed up. This loss of time increases the stress because of the perceived lack of time available to deal with the situation.

For others, time seems to slow down. These people can remember every detail of the situation and every thought that went through their mind. This feeling of time moving in slow motion can provide five advantages in survival situations.

1. With time passing slowly, the individual does not feel as rushed to respond. This helps reduce the stress level because the person does not feel as overwhelmed.

2. Being conscious of his thoughts, the person is able to evaluate the situation and put his training to good use.

3. Viewing the situation unfolding in slow motion, the person is better able to perceive the actions of others.

4. He is also less likely to develop tunnel vision that causes a loss of peripheral vision.

5. The individual is better able to remember what happened later.

Anticipating Your Opponent's Moves

Anticipating your opponent's attack can save tremendous amounts of time. Not only can you perceive it earlier if you know what the pending attack will be, but you can choose a response before he begins to attack. You can also attack when he steps in, thus thwarting his attack, damaging his confidence, and appearing incredibly fast. Knowing when the attack will come and what it will be helps you act sooner and more effectively. Your speed appears unbeatable. Remember that you can move an arm or a leg, especially an arm, much faster than you can lunge your entire body forward.

If you attack when he attacks, either because you know what he is going to do, or because you have been working on your avoidance techniques and you decide to slip and counter, you will not have to lunge forward. He will perform the slow part, the lunge. Your technique will most likely be a slip and jab, or a bob and cross, or slip and hook. Not only will it appear that you closed the gap and hit him in only the amount of time it takes to throw a jab, but your opponent had the advantage of moving first and you still beat him. There are a few ways of impressing everyone with your speed. This is one of them.

Often the difference between experts and non-experts is their ability to anticipate. If you anticipate the wrong attack by your opponent however, don't completely change your response. It's better if you can modify it. You can modify your response faster than you can scrap it and initiate a different one. If you anticipate the correct attack, it can be a tremendous advantage. Be wary though, you can be fooled. Changing or modifying your response may be a longer and less effective response than if you had never anticipated the attack.

Peripheral Vision vs. Binocular Vision

The author has read two sources stating that humans respond more quickly from peripheral vision than binocular vision and from close auditory cues than from visual cues. The author has not been able to verify these claims through medical literature. Both seem plausible when thought of from the perspective of a biological adaptation for survival. If a threat is within binocular vision, then it has most likely already been recognized. The issue of having to respond instantaneously is a mute point. A threat perceived by peripheral vision or by auditory means most likely has not already been recognized. There is a biological advantage in responding faster through these modes than with binocular vision.

With this in mind, do not rely exclusively on your binocular vision. Use your peripheral vision and your sense of hearing as well. Listen for the footsteps, breathing and clothing rubbing together. One excellent method of practicing this is to spar in darkness. Your sense of hearing begins to feel as if it extends beyond your ears. This training is also great for your balance. Since you always want to be ready to respond immediately, you learn to move while maintaining your balance.

To take advantage of the speed at which you perceive movement through peripheral vision, work on improving your peripheral vision skills with the training drills discussed in this chapter and in *Chapter 11*. Increasing your peripheral observation skills increases your ability to observe movement while not looking directly at that specific area. This increases your speed through two mechanisms. First, you perceive the movement at an earlier moment. Second, by observing the movement through your peripheral vision versus your binocular vision, your brain may process it more quickly. This is only true if the above neurological theory is correct.

Eyes

Where should you look? There are almost as many answers as there are schools. Different experts recommend different areas of focus. This is partly due to the reality that it depends on the level of expertise of the individual. A beginner is better off looking in one area and an expert in another.

Take for example, a knife wielding assailant. The knife is the primary danger. If forced to fight someone with a knife, a beginner should look at the knife, accept the probability that he will be cut and attempt to gain control of the knife hand. An expert fighter should not change his techniques. He should continue looking at the face of the assailant, knowing that he can see every move of the knife hand without looking at it. An expert tournament fighter faced with this life-threatening situation may not have full control of his emotional state. In this case, he should also look at the knife hand. If he reacts to the situation emotionally, he loses some of his peripheral vision, thereby reducing the effectiveness of his awareness. An emotional fighter and a beginning fighter will automatically look at the knife in most cases. They will develop tunnel vision, focusing on the knife to the point of exclusion of everything else.

The reason an expert fighter should look at the face is that he should focus on the heart and mind of the opponent. (56) He should not look at the knife, a hand, or focus on any item. With practice, he can see everything, including the feet, while looking at the face. A juggler can ride a unicycle and juggle bowling pins without looking at the pins. In fact, if he looks at any individual pin, he looses awareness of the other pins. When a fighter develops the ability to see the hands and feet without looking at them, he can then look into the heart and mind of the opponent to determine his state of determination, confidence and intentions.

The eyes have been said to be the window into the soul and thoughts of everyone. However, more than just the eyes give away one's thoughts and intentions. The lips, eyebrows, neck, hands and shoulders do as well. Look at the eyes, but not to the exclusion of everything else. Remember that peripheral vision must be used to see everything. Otherwise, the eyes, or another body part for that matter, could be used to fool you. If someone is attempting to fool you, know that it is impossible to conceal all body language. By observing everything, you may be able to notice an inconsistency and become aware of the deception.

To develop the skills necessary for this, you must learn to immediately recognize the subtle telegraphing hints made by the feet, hands, hips and shoulders of your opponent. Spar while looking at the feet, looking for a turning of the heel, raising or lowering of the foot, shift of balance, etc. First become proficient at detecting them. Then practice observing them without focusing on them. Next, move on to another area of the body. When you can do this for various areas of the body, start looking at the face. Look for telegraphing hints in the face. If he does not telegraph with the body, perhaps he does so by glancing at the target area, clenching his teeth, lowering his eye brows, developing an intense look, etc.

When you become skilled at recognizing the movements and conditions of your opponent, you are one step closer to attaining that sixth sense that many of the best fighters seem to have. You have developed a significantly faster response time that gives you a definite edge.

Another point on perception and eye focus: Some experts consciously look for stimuli, be it a slight movement of the hips, or what ever, while other experts do not. For those that do not, it's done subconsciously for them. For those experts that do make a conscious effort to search for stimuli, there is substantial, individual variation of how they do it. Therefore, do not automatically subscribe to one individual expert's techniques. Do what comes naturally to you in your efforts to be quick in perceiving what your opponent is going to do. Try different approaches. If you find a sure winner, stick with that technique. If not, keep working on it consciously for a while. The better your conscious mind can perceive a cue from your opponent and recognize it for what it indicates, the better your subconscious mind can do it as well.

Openings on your opponent are cues as well. Train yourself to see these openings subconsciously. Watch others spar. Look for the lowered hand, an exposed rib or an extended leg. Learn to recognize these openings to such an intimate degree that your peripheral vision and subconscious mind spot them the instant they appear.

When attacking, see your opponent where he will be. Aim your strikes at the distance he will be at. If your strike is executed in a manner where it is at its maximum reach when it reaches your opponent, then if your opponent moves back a little, the strike will miss. If you take his movement into account, then you have the option of continuing the attack to hit him if desired.

Intuition - The Sixth Sense

What is intuition? Does it exist? Is it magical? Can it help a fighter? Intuition is a form of prediction. It is a feeling about the actions or reactions that something or someone is about to take. A storm chaser feels that the team should head west for the best chance to see a tornado form. A mother calls her daughter and senses that something is wrong even before she says anything.

Intuition does exist, but it is not magical. It is a form of prediction based on perceptions. The storm chaser, based on his training and experience, makes the best deduction he can from the information at hand. He bases his decision on his knowledge of how supercells tend to form tornadoes in the area, his observations of the current wind and cloud patterns, etc. Through this information he either consciously or subconsciously forms an opinion as to where the best location will be to see a tornado. If he can articulate why he feels this way, then he consciously came to his conclusion.

Many people perceive subtle bits of information subconsciously and develop a feeling. This process would then come under intuition. The mother may have felt that something was wrong and asked her daughter, 'What's wrong honey?', without being able to articulate how she knew something was wrong. She used her intuition. If this same mother sat down and pondered how she knew something was wrong, she might have put one or more of the following factors together so that she could articulate to someone else just how she knew.

1) Her daughter did not call after her test as she usually does.
2) It took her daughter longer than normal to pick up the phone.
3) The phone was picked up lazily, not in the clean and crisp fashion that her daughter normally uses.
4) It took her longer than usual after picking up the phone to say hello.

The better you understand how you knew your opponent was about to make a certain move, or react in a particular manner, the more developed your sense of intuition will become. Attempt to be aware of the times when you are intuitive. Whenever you experience intuition, be it in the ring, or in another aspect of your life, stop and ask yourself how you knew. The better you can explain how you knew, to yourself or to someone else, the better you understand it. If you notice someone else seems to perceive the actions, or the state of mind of another, ask him what it was that he perceived.

You can increase your skills in intuition through the perception training techniques explained above. You can enhance these abilities by entering a certain frame of mind when sparring or fighting. Below you will find two methods of entering this state of consciousness. Along with helping you develop a superior mental state for fighting, these methods also help you maintain a peak performance frame of mind when encountering a stressful situation.

Zen

Can intuition help a fighter? The samurai of Japan religiously studied a particular philosophy because they believed that this philosophy developed their abilities of intuition to the utmost. The philosophy they studied is Zen. The aim of Zen is enlightenment. Defined more objectively, it is the immediate, unreflective grasp of all reality, without logic and intellectualization. The follower of Zen hopes that it will turn his mind back in time, back before it was clouded with biases, logic and intellect.

Psychologists have plenty of examples where they show a picture of something to a child and the child instantly recognizes it for what it is. When shown to an adult, the adult will scratch his head endlessly until the image is pointed out to him. Then the standard, "Oh, yeah" comes out and he wonders how he did not perceive it earlier. Zen followers believe that enlightenment helps them to break this barrier of logic. True perception can only be achieved when the mind is allowed to act on intuition, without the restrictions of logic. When one reaches this state of openness, he is in tune with his sixth sense. This training was also incorporated into their martial arts training. The act of drawing the sword provided stimulus for the mind to enter this state. (60)

Zen also helped the samurai transcend the fear of death. They accepted death or the possibility of it, at any moment. The samurai knew that fear of defeat in battle, which would mean death, interfered with achieving his full potential. To better his chance of beating death, he had to dissolve any concerns for it. (60)

To summarize Zen, if what you are doing at the moment is exactly what you are doing at that moment and nothing else, you are one with yourself and with what you are doing. There are no extraneous thoughts. No one and no thing, internal or external, causes your focus to waver. Sounds a lot like the zone of peak performance, doesn't it?

Awareness/Relaxation Programming

In his book, *Speed Fighting*, (47) John La Tourrette has an excellent drill for developing awareness in your surroundings and for placing yourself in a relaxed, fully aware state when you desire. This training can prove to be especially beneficial in situations where your stress level rises and your awareness suffers. The initial part of the training increases your awareness of your surroundings.

Find a place where you can sit or walk without being disturbed. First work on visual awareness. Using both your peripheral vision and your detailed binocular vision. Observe every detail possible. Notice the colors, shapes, textures and movements of every object. Close your eyes and make a mental picture of what you saw. Open your eyes and do it again.

Now work on the sense of touch. Feel the breeze over your skin. Observe the temperature of the air and its humidity level. Feel your clothes touch your skin. Observe the state of your muscles. Feel your pulse beating in your chest, wrist, or neck.

Do the same for your sense of hearing. Extend your ears as if they were limbs. Allow your ears to search out all sounds, the more distant and faint the better. Notice any changes in the tone or pitch of voices. Notice the Doppler effect (the change in pitch) as cars change from moving toward you to moving away.

Finally, concentrate on your sense of smell. Your sense of smell is better than you think. With practice, you will begin to notice more and more aromas. The best time to practice this is just after it rains.

After a few times practicing this drill, begin to work on all senses at the same time. When you do, feel as if your senses are projectable extensions. In addition to extending your senses, imagine that you can feel anyone within five feet of you. As you do this, choose a trigger that you will use to place yourself in this state of mind on command. It may be a loosely closed fist with the thumb on top of the index finger. (If you use this position frequently, choose another trigger.)

Now, as you begin the drill, place your hands in this position. Squeeze your thumb into your fingers very tightly. As you relax and begin to increase your awareness, relax the hand. With practice, you will be able to fully relax the hand almost immediately after beginning. With continued training with this stimulus/response drill, you will be able to put your new skills to good use. When you find yourself in a situation where remaining relaxed while increasing your awareness would benefit you, simply apply your trigger. (47)

The number and variety of awareness drills are limited only by your imagination. To increase your ability of perceiving movement, perhaps imagine you are a hunter; try sitting on a roof, or other advantageous position and observe the ants walking on the sidewalk below. If you want to work on your senses of smell and hearing, sit in a mall with your eyes closed. Better yet, have a friend walk you around blindfolded. You will be amazed how much you can perceive without your eyes. You will know what type of store you just walked past. You will be able to describe the people who just walked by in the other direction. If you don't feel too embarrassed, try it. It's fun. This drill also helps you with your balance. Balance is maintained in large part by sight. To demonstrate, stand on one leg, close your eyes and put your shoe on.

This leads to another drill. Many people look at the ground when walking. One of the reasons they do this is to avoid objects. This must detract from the enjoyment of hiking if they cannot walk with their head up, observing the wildlife. It is not necessary. The mind can be trained to memorize the terrain for many feet in front of you, allowing you to keep your head up. You can work on this skill any time you walk. Next time you are walking down a sidewalk, observe a crack in the sidewalk or a tree 20 feet ahead. Close your eyes and keep walking. Open your eyes when you think you are at the crack or the tree. As you get better, you can look at a street, close your eyes and walk across it. As you approach the curb, you know that with the next step you must pick your foot up to step onto the sidewalk. Now open your eyes. This type of training also builds confidence as your awareness increases. The next level of this training takes place in the woods. As you are hiking, routinely close your eyes and avoid the rocks, roots and leaves in your path. Do not stop or slow down to memorize the trail ahead.

Zone vs. Awareness Training

A quick review from *Chapter 6* of the zone of peak performance follows. When you are in the zone, 100% of your mental capability is focused on the task at hand. You are not aware of the passage of time, you are not concerned with the outcome and you are not concentrating on the task. You have let go and your abilities flow from within you. You are aware of, yet completely detached from, the outside world. This mental state is where you want to be for optimal sports performance.

However, it's not necessarily the best mental state when involved in a fight for survival on the street. In a survival situation, you may have to be concerned with obstacles, other assailants coming up behind you or help from a friend coming to your aid. These are two different situations and they require a different frame of mind to perform your best. For this reason, two types of sparring have been designed to help you develop the skills necessary for you to perform at your best in each type of environment.

Getting into the zone, or flow state, as it is referred to at the U.S. Olympic Training Center, is not easy. In fact, there is no sure method of training to have absolute control of it. However, for the sake of illustration, permit the idea that it can be turned on and off. If fighting an opponent in a boxing or kick boxing bout, or if fighting during a martial arts competition, you want to be in the zone in order to do your best. Recall from *Chapter 6* that the zone is active when the right side of the brain takes over. Most people perform with the left side in control. The left side controls analysis, logic and verbalizations. If you are in the awareness state, then the left side of your brain is in control. When in the ring, you do not have to worry about someone coming up behind you, or about avoiding a curb or a slippery surface. You do not need to extend your senses out beyond your opponent. If you were conscious of all of these factors, your reactions would be slower. Not only would part of your thoughts be focused away from your opponent, but being controlled by the left side of the brain, you would not be able to use the right side's capability of making incredibly quick reactions.

If fighting on the street however, you want to be a thinking fighter. You want to tell yourself to check your surroundings. You want to improvise a weapon if possible and appropriate. You want to position your opponent on a slippery surface or facing the sun. You may want to use dialogue to your advantage, catching the person off guard with a comment like, "Isn't that your mother?" Yes, in the awareness state, you are giving up the instantaneous reactions produced while in the zone, but you increase your speed through other mechanisms. You are more aware of your surroundings, therefore, you can perceive another threat earlier. You can distract your opponent with a cleverly improvised tool and tactic. In a perfect world, you could switch back and forth between the two, turning on the zone during a fight against one or two people, and turning it off when the situation requires you to think on your feet.

To increase your awareness skills while sparring, make the situation more complex. Add obstacles that must be avoided. Place some kicking shields on the floor. Use whatever you like, just consider the safety factor. Have a heavy bag or two hanging in the area. Point a bright light, placed at eye height, into one side of the sparring area. Spar in a wooded area where the trees are thin and short. Have your training partners drop rubber knives that can be taken advantage of. This ensures that you maintain your awareness of the surroundings. In reality, an area that you deemed safe can become a dangerous area very quickly. You could even go as far as making a tape with voices and perhaps music on it. The tape could say, softly as if there was other noise in the area, "John, kick his butt, I'm coming". You might then step back, glance in the direction of the speaker and attempt to position your opponent between you and the speaker.

To increase your ability to enter the zone, create a sparring situation vastly different to the one described above. Impose different types of stimuli on the two fighters. However, the stimuli are of the type that they do not need to respond to. One method of doing this is to have two training partners make fake attacks on you and your opponent. The training partners can pretend to strike you two with a shinai or a wiffleball bat. The strike must not hit either of you nor can the attacks impede you in any way. You both know what the rules are and that you should attempt to completely ignore the training partners. The goal is to maintain 100% of your focus on your opponent, not allowing any outside stimuli to interfere with your concentration. You do not want to know when the round is about up. You are not aware of the passage of time. You do not want to be aware of any extraneous stimuli, including a ringing phone, arriving students, comments of spectators, etc.

As stated above, being in the zone is different from concentrating. You know you entered the zone when you were not aware of the stimuli created by your partners and other factors, yet this extreme focus occurred without a conscious effort of concentration. The goal is to attain this level of focus without cognitively trying to attain it. This method of training improves your skills of concentration and this in turn improves your fighting abilities.

As you are able to focus on your opponent without being interrupted, you will hopefully end a round realizing that you were completely engrossed in what you were doing, yet there was no mental effort telling yourself to concentrate. You do not remember the passage of time and you may not remember the attempts by your training partners to interrupt your concentration. You have then entered the zone. Stop. How did it feel? What were the sensations, your emotions? What was your energy level then and now? Write down your impressions.

Draw upon your skills learned from *Chapter 6* and relive the experience. The sooner you do this, the more detailed your mental training will be. The more thoroughly you learn what it is like to be in the zone, the better your chances of entering it again. Immediately before your next sparring session, visualize your experience. Relive the feelings. Hopefully, you will repeat it. However, remember that trying to enter the zone can impede your chances.

The following is a list of factors that affect both your and your opponent's reaction times. Some of these factors also affect the speed of your movements:

- The number of possible reactions you have to choose from.
- Your and your opponent's skills in perception.
- Your fatigue levels.
- A lack of concentration.
- Your levels of physical fitness.
- Your present state of health.
- Your emotional mindsets, i.e.: are you prepared, unprepared, angry, scared, etc.
- Your psychological state including motivation and confidence.
- Your physical and physiological state, i.e.: are you warmed up, stretched, nourished, etc.,
- Your physical positioning, including balance and stance.

Even if your movements are quite rapid, if the opponent can see your attack from its inception, he can take action against your technique.

Chapter 8
DECEPTION

If you can deceive your opponent by hiding your actions, then you will increase your speed, by lengthening your opponent's perception time. To repeat, if he does not see your attack coming, then it was effectively, very fast, regardless of the rate of movement at which it traveled. Conversely, even if your movements are quite rapid, if the person can see your attack from its inception, he can take action against your technique even before it is initiated. Remember the phrase *He never saw it coming.*? Chances are, it was not because it was so fast, but because it was so cleverly deceptive.

Fundamental Principles of Deception:

1) Hide movement within movement.

By remaining mobile, your movements are faster and their initiation harder to perceive. You are also a much harder target to hit.

2) Cause distractions.

Distractions are designed to either change your opponent's mind set or to cause a delay in perceiving your actions and/or your intentions.

Distractions

If you distract your opponent just before, or when you begin your attack, this slows him down considerably. Not only does your attack appear to be fast, but it seems overwhelming as well. There are many types of distractions, although they generally fall into one of two categories. As with most techniques, one works well on one person and not very well on another. One type attempts to misdirect the opponent's attention so that he does not observe your attack until after it is well under way. The other type is designed to interrupt the opponent's concentration, changing his frame of mind from preparedness to confusion.

Misdirection

Most misdirection tactics are visual. In *Chapter 13*, it is recommended that you always throw a punch when kicking. One of the benefits of this involves distraction. The opponent hopefully reacts to the punch, thereby increasing the odds of your kick successfully landing on its target. Your opponent's attention is misdirected from your actual attack (the kick) to your fake (the punch). Some other distraction tactics include the following:

1) Looking at one body part and then attacking another to fool your opponent about your intended target.

2) Looking away. If he falls for this one, he's yours. He won't fall for this twice, however. It is a good idea to vary your distraction tactics. Otherwise, they lose their effectiveness.

3) Using techniques incorporating either high/low, or hand/foot combinations.

For example, a common tactic of boxers is a hook the ribs followed by a second hook to the head in anticipation of the opponent lowering his guard to protect his ribs. This principle works when switching sides of the body, or from feet to hands. Faking combinations also work well, for example, fake high and strike low.

The tricks you can play on your opponent are bound only by your imagination. Try stomping your foot. If he looks down, strike. You could look at your gloves as if one came untied or you could point at his foot. If you consider this cheating, first consider this. Your training partners learn not to fall for them. Their level of concentration benefits from this. It also teaches all of you not to fall for these tactics when facing strangers.

The other types of distractions are targeted toward your opponent's frame of mind. Shouting, smiling, winking, mumbling something, etc., all serve to cause an interruption of concentration within your opponent.

Deception for Altering Distance

Learn to use deception to appear to change the distance between yourself and your opponent. The following are several examples of ways to do this:

1) Hands stretched outward make it appear to your opponent that you are closer than you actually are.

2) Hands kept close to your body make you appear farther away from your opponent.

3) Leaning your torso forward makes you appear closer than you actually are.

4) Leaning your upper body backward makes you appear further away from him.

You can use any of these techniques to fool your opponent about the actual distance between the two of you.

For instance, you could appear to retreat by bringing your arms in and leaning your torso back to lure your opponent in closer to you. When he steps in to readjust the distance, attack before he has the opportunity to realize his mistake or before he uses the short distance against you.

Rear Foot Forward through Illusion

Another deception technique is to lean backward while sliding your rear foot forward. It does not appear that you have closed the distance, but in reality you have. You may not even have to lean back if the opponent does not recognize that you are closer. Chances are, he did not notice your rear foot inch forward at all. Sliding the rear foot forward does not give the appearance of moving closer in the way that sliding the front foot forward does. Remember, do not allow the torso to move forward when sliding the rear foot up.

Moving the rear foot four inches forward moves you closer to your opponent than moving your front foot four inches forward because it's the rear foot that pushes you forward toward your opponent. When you slide your rear foot forward four inches, you will not have to lunge as far. If you slide your front foot forward, all you have really done is spread your feet. It is true that if your opponent is very close, you may be able to hit him because you are a little closer. However, under most circumstances, you have decreased your mobility and you have not decreased the lunging distance needed for your attack.

More Illusions

As stated previously, by leaning back and withdrawing your arms so they are closer to your body, it appears that you are farther away. In doing so, your opponent may step closer to maintain the stand-off distance, not knowing that it's an illusion. When he moves closer, he is within your range without knowing it, or without knowing that you are in his. Your attack seems fast because of the short distance traveled. Bending your forward knee also makes you look closer, and bending your rear knee can make you look farther away. This is safer than leaning back because by leaning back you lose mobility, stability and an aggressive posture. Also, strikes that you receive may do more damage when you are leaning back.

By sliding your front foot backward, closer to your back foot, it looks as if you have moved back. Obviously, you haven't. It only appears that you have. Strike as he moves to correct the distance. By sliding your back foot up, closer to your front foot, you have actually moved closer. Your opponent may not have noticed, though. The proximity to your opponent of your upper body, arms or front leg, has not changed. Now all you need to do is to 'reach out and touch someone'. When your opponent becomes aware of your trick of sliding your rear foot forward, you can still accomplish this by hiding the movement. Slide the rear foot up when the forward foot is directly in front of it.

Rear Foot Forward via Camouflage

This strategy requires that you temporarily move your front foot directly in front of your rear foot. The front leg blocks the view of your rear leg so you can slide your rear foot forward without being observed. If he doesn't see it moving, he won't notice the change. Be careful not to cross your legs. For information of the physics and biomechanics on placement of the rear foot, refer to the section, *Weight Distribution When Lunging, Chapter 18*.

Hide Movement within Movement

Another method to close the distance between yourself and your opponent without being observed is to slide your rear foot forward while distracting your opponent with hand or body movements. This movement could consist of a glance, jab, bob and weave, or an unorthodox movement that causes him to miss your actual movement and intentions. Every magician knows that humans are attracted to movement. You should take advantage of this trait.

Perhaps a little closing of the forward fist with a 1,2,3,4 movement of the fingers will do the trick.

You can also attempt to slide your front foot forward using the same distractions. Hide this movement with hand actions while leaning the shoulders back a little. This is harder to pull off without being noticed.

The benefit of these techniques is that closing the distance between yourself and your opponent means that you will not have to lunge as far to attack. By moving your rear foot six inches closer, you have added six inches to your reach. Now you will not have to lunge as far. Since your opponent will not realize that you have closed the gap, your shorter lunge translates to a faster attack because of:

1) Shorter distance to travel.

2) Less work to be performed, therefore more speed. Remember the

basic rules stated earlier. The more body weight behind a technique, the slower the technique. A shorter lunge can allow you to perform the technique without having to put as much body weight into motion.

3) Less work usually means less telegraphing.

Continual Movement

Another technique of closing the distance between yourself and your opponent is to bob your body up and down as you inch forward. This up and down movement can mask your forward movement. By the time your opponent realizes his mistake, you can be within striking range, again, creating the illusion of speed.

Maintain continuous movement during sparring. Your opponent will not be able to recognize the initial movement of your attack because it is hidden within the movement of your fighting style. You are a much harder target to hit if you continually move around the ring. This can have psychological effects on your opponent that serve to slow him down.

Interruptions

There are many forms of distraction that target the opponent's concentration. You may already be familiar with many of these. Shouting is the most common. Shouting can have many effects. A sudden loud noise can shock someone, causing a moment of confusion and hesitation. If he was totally unprepared for it, it can cause him to react emotionally, resulting in a sudden influx of chemicals that prevent him from thinking and responding effectively. You will not find this level of reaction in tournaments where it is commonly used and expected.

A shout can divert his attention from his pending attack to your actions, thus interrupting his concentration on attacking. A shout is another stimulus that he must process in conjunction with the other stimuli of your attack. This additional task placed upon your opponent's mind helps to slow his reaction. The shout can also help you overcome any fear that may be present, thus increasing the speed and effectiveness of your attack. Additionally, the shout causes you to tighten your abdominal section, better preparing you for a counter strike to that area. If you wish to add this to your response in survival situations, you must practice this and all other aspects of your desired response. Otherwise, the shout will not come out when you want it to. When you include shouting as one of your techniques, first feint and shout, then attack. Give a fraction of a second for the feint and shout to take effect.

A smile works well also. Humans have a genetic and learned response to facial expressions. One of the most powerful is the smile. It is also the most appropriate for fighting situations because of the effect it has on the mind of the observer. It is difficult to resist the automatic response of friendship and relaxation when someone smiles. Even if your opponent does resist this powerful mental stimulus, it interrupts his concentration, providing you with an opportunity to attack. It could also be used when you are in a disadvantaged position and he is about to attack. Used in this way, it interrupts his attack, providing you with a moment to better position yourself.

A laugh works in a similar fashion. Think about it. If your opponent laughed at you, at the least wouldn't you wonder what he is laughing about? Wouldn't it cause a momentary interruption in your concentration?

You can also say something. "Ouch!" can be very effective. Perhaps mumble something that he cannot understand. He will most likely attempt to figure out what it was you said. Winking at him can also work to disrupt his concentration. Point at something, perhaps as if his shoelace is untied. Again, use your imagination. Whenever you are distracted, made a mental note of what it was that distracted you. This has two benefits. First, it helps you maintain your concentration by increasing your awareness of this human weakness. Second, it might give you ideas for additional methods of distraction.

Recall from *Chapter 5* that emotions are contagious. Use your imagination to take advantage of this mammalian trait. Here's an example. You feint, your opponent moves back or parries. Then, you relax. Your opponent may then relax, thinking the attack is over. Now strike.

*Fifteen minutes of training each day results in
faster improvement than one hour and forty-five
minutes of training once a week.*

Chapter 9:
SPEED TRAINING METHODS

The frequency of training is a more important factor than the length of the training. This is especially true for the development of skills and flexibility. Fifteen minutes of training each day results in faster improvement than one hour and forty-five minutes of training once a week. Perhaps you have been told that the most important training days are those days when you feel sick, weak or unmotivated. In reality, you are not going to increase your muscular strength more those days. What happens though, besides increasing your mental strength and determination, is that you ensure that your training is consistent and uninterrupted. This is the single most important factor to success. Therefore, train often, even if it's just a short workout. Keep your neuromuscular system, flexibility and/or strength, honed.

Review Your Techniques

The following training technique works well with or without videotaping yourself. Review your training frequently and make written notes about what you need to do to correct your mistakes. If you do not have a video, as soon as possible after your training, sit down and think about how you felt. What felt effective? Did you feel fast at any one particular point? Why? Did you feel slow at any time, and why was that? Conduct this evaluation for each aspect of your training, including sparring, speed, power, techniques, concentration, etc.

In 1995, San Diego Padres outfielder Tony Gwynn won the National League Batting Championship for the sixth time. One of the reasons for his success is his attention to detail. He has all of his at-bats videotaped. After batting, he reviews the tape and works on overcoming any problems he saw during his next practice. (2)

Muscular Training

It's easy to see how possessing large, powerful quadriceps and calf muscles can benefit a fighter. Strong quadriceps and calves help drive a fighter forward for a quick lunge. They also help push him backwards quickly when he wants to move out of range. Strong quads help develop speed and power in front kicks and traditional style roundhouse kicks, in other words, for snapping techniques.

Do not neglect the hamstrings and the gluteus muscles, however. If the quadriceps and calves do the driving, then why do sprinters have such strong hamstrings and gluteus muscles? The answer is two-fold. It involves a pulling on the ground and an extending of the hips. When a sprinter moves down the track, each time his foot hits the pavement, both his quadriceps and hamstrings are working. The quadriceps pushes the leg up off the ground with a straightening action of the leg. True, the hamstrings pull the foot up toward the buttocks so that the quads can extend the leg out again. But very important for the production of speed is the action of the hamstrings while the foot is still on the ground. While the foot is on the ground the hamstring muscles are exerting force, attempting to pull the foot backward. This adds force to the action of the quadriceps.

An easy way to examine how much pulling the hamstrings can perform in this manner is to refer to the long distance lunge explained in *Chapter 18*. During the long distance lunge, the front foot starts the lunge with a pulling action. When the forward foot initiates the action, this action is generated by the hamstring muscles. The stronger your hamstring muscles are, the faster and farther you can lunge using this technique. The same holds true for standard rear-foot lunges, only the contribution of the hamstring muscles is significantly less. The farther forward the foot is in relation to your body weight, the more the hamstring muscles contribute to the action in this manner.

The other reason sprinters and jumpers, have strong hamstrings and gluteus muscles involves hip extension. Think of dunking a ball. You run toward the basket and leap up off your foot, your left in this example, as your right knee drives upward. Since your left foot is moving up instead of forward on this last step, the pulling action of the hamstrings is significantly less. But what happens to your hips and thighs? They go from a bent position to a straight position. The quadriceps have nothing to do with this. All they do is straighten, or extend, the knee. The straightening action of the hips provides much of the lifting of the body upward. Strong hamstrings and gluteus muscles actually play a major role in any jump.

Now consider the broad jump. Again, the quadriceps performs a portion of the drive forward, pushing off the ground by extending the knees. However, the hamstrings and gluteus muscles also push off the ground by straightening (extending) the hips. The hamstrings also contribute with a pulling action of the feet along the ground. Why are your hamstrings and gluteus muscles sore after doing squats? It's because when you are in the squatted position, they do much of the work in getting you to an upright position. They straighten the hips. For these reasons, having strong hamstring and gluteus muscles makes your lunge faster and more explosive. It also makes your jumping techniques more explosive. Therefore, train your hamstrings and glutes at least as hard as you train your quads.

Adaptation Training

Ever notice that professional baseball players swing weighted bats before stepping up to the plate? What about how light your feet feel and how high you can jump after you take off heavy boots or a backpack?

If you want to go for your maximum on the bench, try doing half of a negative rep with 20 pounds more than your max. Then rest a couple of minutes and do it. You will be surprised how light it feels. What is happening here is that you are pre-conditioning your muscles to recruit more fibers than what they usually recruit. The neuromuscular system is used to swinging a normal bat and it knows how many fibers are necessary to accomplish the job. When you add weights to the bat, the neuromuscular system must change its programming to compensate for the additional weight. This compensation is temporary, lasting only a few minutes at the most, however, it is still in effect when the players step to the plate. The neuromuscular system fires more fibers, still thinking that the player is using a heavier bat. The additional fiber recruitment causes the bat to swing faster, translating to more force being delivered to the ball. (19)

How can all this help you increase your speed? You simply need to increase the resistance to your punches and kicks. The preceding paragraphs explain how this temporarily increases your speed. Holding weights in your hands does not really increase the resistance to the muscles used for driving your hand forward. It's great training for boxers in developing the deltoid muscles, helping them keep their hands up when they become tired. But weights used in this manner are not very beneficial in terms of providing the proper resistance needed to increase your speed.

Springs and elastic bands work well for providing the resistance necessary. One method is to attach an exercise spring (such as the kind used for chest pulls) or an elastic band, to a wall. Stand facing away from the wall in your fighting stance. Grab the other end and bring the spring or band over your shoulder. The exercise works best if you have two springs or bands set up so that you can work combinations instead of having to do ten reps with one hand and then switch. Brace the heel of your rear foot against the wall. Throw your jabs, crosses, back-fists and combinations as desired.

Remember this is not a strength building exercise. This is only to temporarily recruit more fibers for the purpose of increasing your speed and power. This increases your speed for the reasons stated above. As previously stated though, the increase is only temporary. Within the first 30 seconds of your round, your speed has most likely returned to normal. Not very useful unless you are involved in some kind of speed contest or smokers' tournament with 30 second rounds.

This training is more useful when combined with speed shadow boxing. Speed shadow boxing involves punching using one-half to two-thirds of the normal range of movement while concentrating on nothing but the speed of movement. Because the hands are moving in and out so much faster than normal, you are reprogramming your neuromuscular system to fire more rapidly. Perform the resistance training, stopping frequently to speed shadow box, or kick. The combination of the resistance training with the speed shadow boxing increases the stimulus for adaptation by the neuromuscular system even greater.

Having to frequently stop to perform the resistance training is a nuisance if using a device attached to a wall. A more useful method is to take a short piece of bungee cord, make a handle at each end and stretch it across your back. Get in your fighting stance and throw your punches. To further clarify this idea, the cord runs from the left hand, which is near the left cheekbone, across the back, around the right shoulder to the right hand. When you throw a right cross, the left hand does not move. This training tool is much more convenient and practical, especially when incorporating it with speed shadow boxing.

This also works with weapons training, including swords and staffs. A barbell makes an effective weighted staff. Do your kata with the barbell and then pick up your staff. Your moves will never have felt so fast and crisp. Use caution when using weighted staffs and swords because this can be stressful on the wrists and shoulders.

This training can also be used with kicks. It is not recommended that you add weights to your feet, however. This can place a dangerous amount of stress on your knees. Even heavy boots can be dangerous. Using bungee cords is a safer method. As with the punches, attach one end to the ground and the other to your ankle. Only front and back kicks should be trained this way. Kicks that cause the knee to roll over are too risky.

There is a safe method of training your kicks that incorporates using weights. Wearing heavy boots or ankle weights, perform front kicks, roundhouse kicks, side and back kicks, crescent kicks and any other kick that you can execute in slow motion. Perform the kick slowly. Increasing the speed only increases the risk of injury. Develop a training routine to suit your needs. Three to four sets of 10 kicks for each leg and each kick is an effective routine to gain strength. Like weight training, this training increases your speed by increasing your strength.

Water Training

Another way to practice kicks and punches with increased resistance is to train in water. This training allows you to punch and kick, exerting one hundred percent, without risking injury. Standing in chest high water, throw your techniques as fast as you can. This training has the same benefits as training with bungee cords. Like training with the bungee cords, it becomes more effective if you frequently get out of the pool and execute some partial rep punches and kicks. After you have shadow boxed at full speed using partial reps, get back into the pool and start over.

High Repetition Technique Training

High repetition training is like a power sander moving back and forth across a piece of raw wood, with each run making the wood smoother and smoother. High rep training smooths the bumps, imbalances, rough spots (flaws in your technique) and the neuromuscular wiring for the technique. An improvement in any one area increases the speed of the technique.

Stretching

Increasing your flexibility has a direct, positive impact on your speed. This is especially true where high kicks are concerned. There are four types of stretches. Each type benefits you through different mechanisms. All increase your speed by helping you learn to relax your antagonistic muscles more fully. The four types are explained below.

Dynamic Stretching

Dynamic stretches involve moving your limbs, almost as if swinging them, in a manner similar to the motion that you use to train. For example, if you want to increase the flexibility of your front kick, dynamic stretches require sets of 10 to 20 repetitions of raising your leg up as high as you can to the front, similar to that of a front kick. This it is not an actual swinging of the limb. It requires a lifting of the leg and you are in control of the movement along the entire path. However, the movement should be loose and relaxed, as opposed to focused and concentrated, as in muscular conditioning. Dynamic stretches are used to program your neuromuscular system to be capable of performing movements near your maximal range of flexibility without any warm up. Each morning, about ten minutes after getting up, perform dynamic stretches. Do these for front kicks, side kicks, back kicks, crescent kicks and shoulder movements. In time it will take fewer sets to reach your maximal range of movement.

To perform the dynamic stretch for the front kick, hold your right hand out in front of you. Keeping your back straight and your left heel on the ground, raise your right leg up to your hand. Kick your hand. Start low and slow. Continue to raise your hand and the speed at which you kick your hand. Never attempt to kick your hand as fast as possible. Remember to maintain control of your leg at all times. You are lifting it more than you are

Maintain good body positioning and remain relaxed as you lift your leg up. You can hold out your hand as a guide if you prefer. Do not go for your maximum level on your first lift. Start low and go a little higher with every repetition.

swinging it. Initially it may take four or five sets of 20 repetitions to reach your maximum level. After a couple of months, you may be able to reach your maximum level in one set of 10. When you have reached your maximum level for the day, move to the other leg and then to the next technique, such as side raises.

Dynamic stretches have two functions. First, they are the most appropriate type of stretching before kicking high, as in sparring. Isometric and static active stretching tire your muscles. Relaxed stretching prepares your muscles for stretching, but not specifically for the dynamic type of movements that occur in kicking. That is best accomplished with dynamic stretches. Dynamic stretches, if done every morning shortly after rising, program your muscles to your maximum range of flexibility for the entire day. (You should not stretch immediately after waking because your muscles may be too stiff and there is a risk of injury. Walk around for a few minutes first or begin your morning routine.) Through dynamic stretching you can attain your full flexibility without having to warm up. Dynamic stretching should not be performed when your muscles are tired. You will not be able to obtain your maximum level, thus, you will not be rewiring your neuromuscular system to its full potential. Dynamic and relaxed stretching can be performed daily. In fact, the more frequently they are done, the faster you realize results. (46)

Relaxed Stretching

You are most likely familiar with relaxed stretches. Most of us have performed relaxed stretches in sports, gym class, physical therapy or for any number of reasons. The hurdler's stretch is an example of a relaxed stretch. Relaxed stretches use gravity, your effort or the gentle pushing of a friend, to increase the range of movement. You may have been told in the past to bounce slightly when at the end of your reach in an attempt to gain extra length. Bouncing can be harmful and can cause tears in your muscles, ligaments and tendons. It is better to hold the stretch at your maximum position for 15 to 60 seconds.

When you feel resistance during relaxed stretching, hold that position. After holding for 15 to 20 seconds you may notice that you can ease into a new range. When you have reached your maximum length, hold it for 30 to 60 seconds. Then, when your muscles have relaxed slightly, try for a few centimeters more. Do not continue if your muscles start to spasm.

Relaxed stretches use gravity, your effort or the gentle pushing of a friend, to increase the range of movement.   Bouncing, however, can be harmful and can cause tears in your muscles, ligaments and tendons. It is better to hold the stretch at your

Relaxed stretches increase your speed by increasing your flexibility and by decreasing the stimulation of the antagonist muscles. You get better results if you do them while on the ground as opposed to standing. Standing requires some activation of the muscles and this reduces the stretching potential.

Static Active Stretching

Static active stretching is more like an exercise than a stretch. It requires holding a leg up as high as you can for up to 15 seconds. Weights can also be added to the ankle. Balance yourself with a chair, keep your knee straight and raise your leg up to the front, side, back and diagonal front (a little to the outside.) Hold your leg as high as your can, maintaining good posture, for 5 to 15 seconds. Keep your hips straight, facing forward. Perform another set allowing your hips to move with the stretch. These two hip positions change the exercise significantly. Work on them both.

Static active stretching is the safest form of stretching. It does not increase the maximum range of your flexibility. It does however, increase the speed of your kicks by:

1) decreasing the stimulation of the antagonist muscles
2) increasing the strength of the muscles involved in lifting the leg up
3) through the benefits of the first two factors, multiple kicking capabilities increase

An example of a static active stretch would include the following. Brace yourself against a chair or wall. Raise your leg, in the side kick position, as high as possible. Hold this position for up to 15 seconds. As your strength increases, add weights to your ankle. Hold the top position and perform raises, slowly lowering the leg and raising it. Static active stretches should be done after a workout.

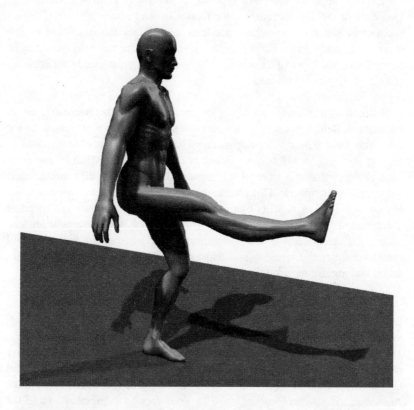

Keeping the knee of the raised leg straight, hold the leg up at your maximum level for up to 15 seconds. Maintain good posture.

Isometric Stretching

Isometric stretching involves moving into the position of your maximal range and then forcibly contracting the very muscles that are being stretched. Next, relax your muscles and gently come out of the stretch.

By far, the most effective type of stretching is isometric stretching. Isometric stretching increases your flexibility and strength more in a few weeks than what you may have accomplished during the last six to twelve months. In addition to increasing your flexibility, and therefore your speed, faster than other types of stretching, it also increases your speed by increasing the speed of your withdrawal.

Isometric stretching strengthens the antagonist muscles while they are in the fully stretched position. These are the same muscles that retract the leg after you have struck your opponent. Therefore, the muscles involved in pulling your leg back into your stance are strengthened. What is important about this is that the strength of these muscles while fully stretched is substantially increased. This affects the speed at which you can retract your leg when it is at or near its maximum range, which increases the speed of combinations. This is true because the sooner you withdraw your leg, the sooner you can go to your next technique. Also, by increasing the strength of the fully stretched muscle, your chances of injuring the antagonist muscles when kicking are reduced.

Isometric stretches can be performed with or without a partner. After you are thoroughly warmed up, begin stretching. The stretch in this example is the side split. From a standing position, spread your legs, toes pointed forward. Do not bend forward. Keep your shoulders over your hips. When you have reached approximately 70% of your range, pinch the floor using the muscles on the inside of your thighs. In other words, contract the inner, upper thigh muscles as if you were trying to slide your feet back together. Hold the contraction for about five seconds and relax. Spread your legs farther and repeat. Continue the process of tension and relaxation until you can not lower yourself any farther. At this point, hold the contraction for as long as 30 seconds. Do not lean forward and do not support yourself with your arms.

You can do the same stretch with a partner. Extend a leg out to your side. Your partner holds your foot in his cupped hands. Brace yourself by holding onto something. With each relaxation phase, your partner should raise your

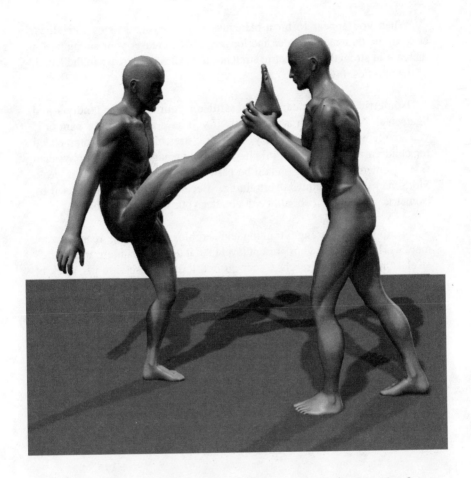

In this example the hamstring muscles are stretched in the front kick position. Forcibly contract the hamstring muscles, pushing your heel into the palms of your partner. Relax and ask your partner to raise your leg higher. Forcibly contract the hamstring muscles, relax and repeat. Perform this exercise keeping the hips facing forward for one set and allow them to twist to the side for the second set.

leg a little higher. Again, when you have reached your maximum height, hold a maximal contraction for 10 to 30 seconds.

When you appear to hit a plateau and your progress slows or stops, concentrate on tensing harder and longer. This increases your strength. An increase in strength in isometric stretches translates to increase in the length of the muscles. (46)

Isometric stretches can be stressful on your muscles, tendons and ligaments. Never stretch isometrically if you have any localized pain or if you are recovering from an injury. Isometric stretching is not recommended for children and teenagers. (46) If you are a teenager, consult a physician first. Isometric stretching should be performed three to four times a week. More than that constitutes overtraining. Because of the fatigue caused by isometric stretching, it should be done after your workout, not before.

Flexibility, like strength training and aerobic conditioning, requires a lot more work to increase your present level than it does to maintain an acquired level. Once you have reached your desired level, one session per week of static active and isometric stretching should suffice. You may have to experiment with how much dynamic and relaxed stretching, to be used in conjunction with static active and isometric stretching, is required to maintain that level.

Chapter 10:
PLYOMETRICS

As previously stated, plyometrics are dynamic, explosive muscular contractions. Therefore, plyometric training involves inherent risks associated with the exercises. It is more important to be thoroughly warmed up before conducting plyometric training than it is with any other type of training. The warm up also increases the sensitivity of the muscle spindle, which houses the fibers that register the amount of stretch within a muscle. These fibers are called intrafusal fibers. The intrafusal fibers are wrapped with nerve cells. When the intrafusal fiber is stretched quickly, the nerve cells send a signal to the central nervous system (CNS.) The CNS triggers a muscle reflex (referred to as the stretch reflex) that generates a fast, powerful contraction. The purpose of the contraction is to stop the stretching and hopefully prevent injury. The more sensitive a muscle spindle is due to having been warmed up, the more stimulation the CNS receives from the intrafusal fiber and its adhering nerve cells. The more stimulation the CNS receives, the more forceful the contraction is. Therefore, warm up thoroughly to decrease the risk of injury and to increase the effectiveness of the training. After a general warm up has been performed, warm up the specific body parts about to be engaged in the training. This warm up should include the same movements that constitute the plyometric exercises.

When the intrafusal fibers are stretched, they store energy, ready to assist the muscle in contracting back to a safer length. This stored energy increases both the speed and power of your movements because it is like having a bungee cord contract along with the muscle. Plyometric training increases the strength of the intrafusal fibers. This in turn increases the amount of energy they can store. An increase in stored energy directly increases the speed and power of the contraction. The intensity of the training of the stretch reflex is a factor of the speed and depth of the muscle stretch. The faster the muscle is stretched and the degree to which it is stretched, determine the amount of training stimulus placed upon the intrafusal fibers. Do not sacrifice speed for degree of stretch. Speed is the most important factor in determining the intensity of the stretch reflex training. (15)

The sequence of your training should be as follows. First, warm up and stretch thoroughly. Then perform any speed training drills you wish to for the day. The speed drills must be performed before you become fatigued. Otherwise, you will not be moving at your maximum speed and, therefore, you will not be adapting your neuromuscular system to perform at top speed. Next, perform your techniques and sparring. Follow this up with plyometric training. End the training with resistance training if you include it in your workout. Relaxed stretching is an effective method of cooling down following a workout. This is also a perfect way to lead into any type of meditative training that you may employ.

The sequence of your plyometric training should be as follows. Start with rhythm plyos, followed by speed plyos and conclude with power plyos. Rhythm plyos are good for making sure you are thoroughly prepared for the upcoming exercises and they help build coordination and balance. The speed plyos should be performed before the power plyos because the speed of execution is the key. If you are too tired to perform them at a sufficient speed, you will not realize the desired results. It is of utmost importance to perform the speed plyos with the fastest possible movements. By forcing your muscles to contract in a shorter period of time in which they are accustomed to, you increase your overall capacity for speed and power. (15)

Upper-Body Plyometrics

Speed Push-Up Plyometrics

Pushing plyos are easily learned and they do not require a training partner. Push-ups are the basic pectoral, deltoid and triceps plyometric exercise. They also have an obvious and direct benefit to fighting applications. Push-ups can be both speed and power plyometric exercises.

For speed plyo push-ups, start in the basic push-up position. Push upward as fast as you can, lifting your upper body off the ground. Remember to keep the body straight. As the upper body starts falling back to the ground, keep the elbows bent, prepared for contact. As the palms contact the ground, the elbows are already bent. They should be bent for two reasons: to reduce the force that your skeletal system has to absorb and to increase the necessity for speed in the plyometric movement. Do not go down all the way. Reverse direction as quickly as possible and explode off the ground again. Remember, the effectiveness of this exercise is directly related to how quickly you force your muscles to absorb the eccentric force, stop, and explosively reverse direction with a concentric movement.

If you do not have the strength to properly perform this exercise, place you knees on the ground instead of your toes. You can also switch to this position for your second or third set. Only push off the ground a little bit. Otherwise you may go too high, forcing your palms to be in contact with the ground for too long. When performing speed plyos, the shorter the period of time you take to switch from an eccentric contraction to a concentric contraction and finish, the better. The duration of the time your hands are in contact with the ground is the primary factor in the exercise's effectiveness.

The more bent your elbows are when the hands hit the ground, the harder it is to keep moving quickly enough to effectively perform the exercise. You can perform the first set with the elbows fully bent and/or wider apart as you may have more strength to explode quickly from this position. Again, when you do a set with the elbows bent a bit more, you can do it from your knees. This makes the exercise easier which helps guarantee that it is performed quickly enough. The exercise should be performed with the arms in different positions. Complete three to four sets of ten repetitions.

Power Push-Up Plyometrics

This is the same exercise as the speed push-up plyos, except that the emphasis is on the amount of force your muscles must quickly, eccentrically absorb and reverse, and not so much on the speed with which they are performed. Again, your contraction is at 100% and it should be as fast as possible. However, since the amount of force placed on the muscles is greater, it takes longer for you to absorb, stop and explode back off the ground again.

Just as with speed push-up plyos, you should vary the position of your hands and arms, i.e.: hands under the shoulders versus wide grip, elbows out versus parallel to the body and elbows bent at 20 degrees versus 90 degrees when the hands hit the ground. If these exercises bother your wrists, it helps reduce the stress on them if you turn the hands out a little instead of keeping the fingers facing forward. Wrist braces may also be beneficial.

When doing the power push-up plyos, push up off the ground as high as possible. This helps overload your body when your hands hit the ground. Obviously, the higher your upper body is off the ground, the more force your muscles must absorb when your hands hit the ground. Similarly, the more your elbows are bent, the more force placed on your muscles when your hands hit the ground. This is because by bending your elbows and thus, delaying the moment when your hands hit the ground, your upper body increases its speed of falling because it has more time to fall. If initially you do not have the strength to perform the exercise with the elbows fully bent, try the exercise from your knees. Perform two or three sets of ten repetitions.

As you become stronger, fall from a kneeling position, absorb and explode back up. A very advanced method of this exercise is to fall from a standing position. The straighter you keep your body while falling, the more force created at impact, therefore, the greater the training stimulus. Be very conscious of wrist and shoulder injuries when doing these exercises.

The elbows should not be bent any more than this when you hit
the ground. For most people, the arm position illustrated is
most appropriate for power push-up plyos. Only exceptionally
strong athletes could push off the ground quickly enough from
this position to meet the time requirements of speed
plyometrics. For speed plyos, straighten the arms more or
perform the exercise from the knees.

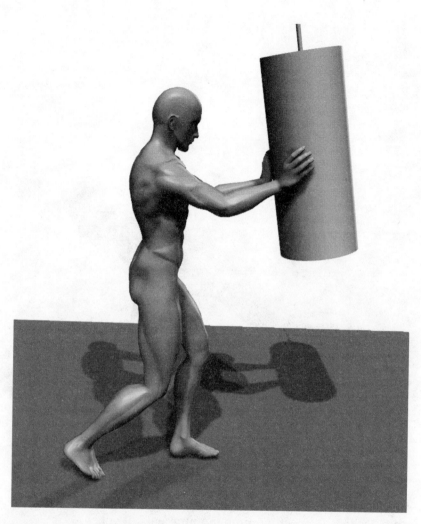

Your elbows should not bend any more than those illustrated above. Maintain your fighting stance.

Two-Handed Speed Plyos on The Heavy Bag

Get in your fighting stance and swing the bag to set it in motion. When the bag is in the vertical position, on its way back to you, it should be making contact with your hands. Your arms and hands should be in a basic boxer's position, elbows down and in, hands at about shoulder height and your shoulders should be squared off, facing the bag. When the bag contacts your hands, absorb the momentum and push it back as quickly and explosively as you can. Do not anticipate the bag and reach out for it. It may help to close your eyes. Let it hit your hands, then explosively push back, almost as if hitting it. Always attempt to have your hands in contact with the bag for as little time as possible. This should be just a fraction of a second. It may help to have a partner hold the bag up and delay its fall so that you do not anticipate it.

One-Handed Power Plyos on The Heavy Bag

Perform the same exercise as above, using only one hand. There is no need to square the shoulders for this exercise. This becomes a power plyometric exercise because it takes considerably more time to explode the bag back in the other direction. While contact with the bag should still be less than one second, it will not be fast enough to cause an adaptation for increased speed. However, it can increase your speed by increasing your strength. As you know, increased strength can translate to increased speed. The drill is otherwise identical to the two-handed drill above. You can work on your jab and cross with each hand. Perform three sets of eight for right hand jabs and three sets of eight for right crosses. Repeat with the left hand.

Pulling Plyos

To train pulling plyos, i.e. the biceps, lats and traps, you will need a partner. The easiest method to use is to stand facing your partner. Bend your arms at the elbows, forearms horizontal, palms facing up. Have your partner drop or throw a medicine ball down at your outstretched arms. Remember the feeling when someone unexpectedly drops something in your arms? You instinctively catch it. That is a plyometric movement and that is what you are duplicating in this drill. Close your eyes, keep your elbows in near your sides and place your forearms in a horizontal position extending outward and parallel to each other. Depending on the weight of the medicine ball, have your partner drop or throw it straight down into your forearms. Catch it and explosively toss it back up into the air. There does not need to be any follow through. Remember, you want to have as little contact with it as possible. This exercise can be potentially dangerous to the lower back. If you have any lower back problems, you should either avoid this exercise or use a light weight ball. To help stabilize the back, you may find it helpful to perform this exercise while in a horse stance.

Lower Body Plyometrics

There are many ways to perform plyometric exercises for the lower body. To help reduce compression shock on the lower back, knees and ankles, they should be done on a soft surface. Pads, grass or sand work well. The basic plyometric exercise can be used to train for rhythm, speed and power plyos. This is the hop jog. As with any plyometric exercise, first do rhythm plyos until you develop the coordination and neuromuscular adaptations necessary to train at a more intense level. If you are a highly conditioned and coordinated athlete, you may be ready to try some speed and power plyos on your second training day. It is not recommended that you move on during the first day.

Rhythm Hop Jog

This exercise is basically a slow jog, except that every time a foot contacts the ground, you leap off it as quickly as possible. The hop jog is distinctly different for speed and power plyos. Perform hop jog plyos slowly in both speed and power fashion until you feel comfortable with both techniques. With rhythm plyos, do not strive for speed or power. Your goal is to execute the exercise in a smooth, coordinated and rhythmic fashion. These should be performed as a warm up before speed and power plyos.

Spring off the ground striving for a smooth, coordinated rhythm.

Power Hop Jog Plyometrics

First perform rhythm plyos to ensure that you are fully warmed up. When ready to begin with power hop jogs, start from a very slow jog. After three or four steps, hop off the right foot as high as possible. When the left foot contacts the ground, reduce the amount of time that it is in contact with the ground as much as you can. Spring off the left foot explosively, attaining as much height as you can. Continue until each leg has made eight to ten hops. The two important factors are height (determining the amount of force your muscles must quickly generate) and the length of time that the foot is in contact with the ground.

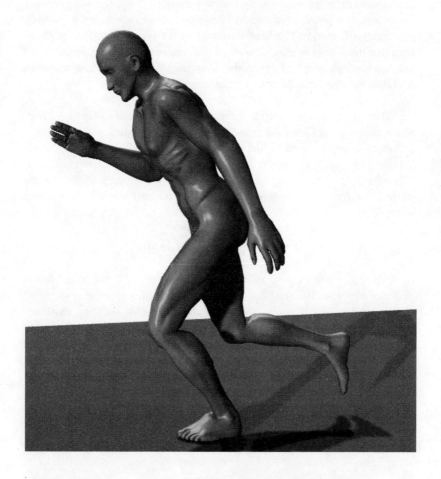

Your landing leg should not bend much more than shown above. Attempt to gain as much height as possible with each jump.

Speed Hop Jog Plyometrics

First conduct the exercise in the rhythm mode until fully accustomed to it and as a warm up before each plyometric workout. Speed hop jog plyos are the same as the power plyo exercise described above except that it has only one emphasis, speed. The height attained is not important. The length of time that the foot is in contact with the ground is of utmost importance. If you hop too high, you will not be able to spring off the ground fast enough to stimulate the neuromuscular system to adapt.

When performed properly, this exercise feels more like a skip than a hop. Since hopping up slows the muscular contractions down too much, it is necessary to hop forward. If the right foot is driving off the ground, the left leg swings forward, almost straight. When the left leg contacts the ground, it drives forward with a strong pulling action of the hamstring muscles. In this method, the foot is in contact with the ground for only a small fraction of a second.

Two-Legged Speed Hops

The basic movement of the two-legged hop plyos is the broad jump, performed repeatedly. For two-legged speed hops, this exercise is the same as the standard broad jump except that all movements are kept short and quick. The legs do not bend much and the arms do not have time to swing fully. Hop forward ten times, each time making sure that the feet are in contact with the ground for as little time as possible. Attaining approximately a two-foot distance while not bending the legs much should help you avoid having too long of a muscular contraction. This provides sufficient stimulus for adaptation. Attaining more distance frequently leads to losing your balance.

In order to maintain a coordinated rhythm while only contacting the ground for a small fraction of a second, you will find
that it works best if your legs remain fairly straight and the
front leg kicks out almost as if punting a ball.

Two-Legged Power Hops

Two-legged power hops require that you drive up as much as possible, only moving forward about 18 to 24 inches. Compared to two-legged speed hops, the knees bend considerably more, the arms drive up much more, and the legs handle considerably more force. Think of two-legged power hops as a kangaroo hopping at full speed and two-legged speed hops as your attempt to hop across a hot lava field without burning your bare feet.

If this exercise feels awkward, try performing the same exercise on one leg. Use the same principles outlined above for both speed and power one-legged hops. Unlike the hop jog, there is no changing of legs. The same leg that begins the exercise continues for the set of eight to ten repetitions.

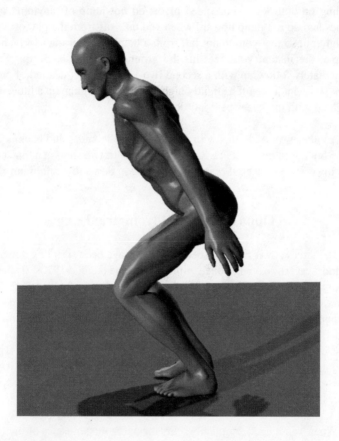

Your knees should not bend any more than this. Your waist should not bend more than illustrated or your run the risk of injuring your back. Keep your back straight and look forward.

Box/Platform Hops

Another more advanced exercise is to jump off a one or two foot high platform. This should only be done on a soft surface as this exercise can be especially hard on the knees and back. Jump off a chair or other platform, landing on both legs. For speed plyos, do not jump off anything over 18 inches and do not jump upward when you take off from the platform. Jump straight out so that you do not fall from a height greater than 18 inches. Of course, the instant your feet hit the ground, explode back up. You can immediately follow up with a second two-legged hop if desired. For power plyos, you can jump off a slightly higher platform or jump up a little. Or you can land with the knees bent a little more.

Another way to do this with less stress on the knees and back is to hop, using both legs, up the stairs. Only hop up one or two steps at a time because it is imperative to keep the time of contraction down to a minimum.

Opposing Force Plyometric Lunges

To increase their running speed, athletes have been sprinting down hill or behind a car while being pulled with a rope since the mid 1970s. This type of maximal speed training, where the body is forced to work at a rate faster than it can unassisted, is called overspeed training. Fighters can augment their plyometric training with the same strategy to increase their lunging speed. Attach a bungee cord to a wall. Attach the other end to your waist in the front. Step back, stretching the cord. Assume your fighting stance and prepare to lunge forward as fast as possible. To remain in this position, it will be necessary to push backward with the front leg as if doing a regular Opposing Forces Lunge as described in *Chapter 18*.

When you lunge, completely relax the antagonist muscles of the forward leg while driving forward with the appropriate muscles of the rear leg. When beginning this exercise, you may observe how your antagonist muscles prefer to relax slowly. With a little training, you quickly retrain them to relax more fully and more quickly. This training can improve your speed in three ways. First, this is a specific fighting stance. This training helps increase your effectiveness with this particular type of lunge. Second, it helps you develop your relaxation of the antagonist muscles, increasing the speed of contraction of the driving muscles. Third, it stimulates adaptation of the neuromuscular system by training it at a speed that it is not presently accustomed to.

This illustration depicts an athlete at the point when he has reached his maximum level of absorption and begins to jump up. You should not bend your knees any lower than illustrated.

Front Thrust Kick Plyometric Training on the Heavy Bag

The most effective and safest kicking plyometric exercise is the front thrust kick. Stand facing the bag with the right leg in the air, primed to execute a front thrust kick. The knee has already been raised. Push the bag with the leg. Executing the drill in a similar manner as with the upper body, the instant the bag contacts your foot, explosively thrust your leg out. To increase the depth of the stretch, begin with the leg bent more. Because of the length of time the bag is in contact with your leg, even though it is kept at a minimum, this is a power plyo exercise. Complete three sets of ten thrusts for each leg.

Plyometric Training Regimen

You will not feel fatigued while performing these exercises. They may not even make your muscles sore the following day. Do not think, however, that they are too easy, that in order for them to be effective, you must train plyometrically until you are fatigued, or that you must train every day. Plyometric training can be very stressful on your musculature. Train each body section plyometrically no more than twice a week. After you have conditioned and accustomed yourself to plyometric training, the following is an effective and safe regimen. If your muscles do become fatigued while training plyometrically, it is time to stop. Always remember the potential hazards involved with plyometric training. If your muscles are sore for any reason, be it a lactic acid buildup from a previous workout or from a minor muscle strain, do not train plyometrically until fully recovered.

Upper Body

Speed Plyo push-ups:	3-4 sets of 10
Power Plyo push-ups:	2-3 sets of 10
Plyo bag drills:	3 sets of 8-10 two-handed drills

3 sets of 8-10 for both jabs and crosses, performed for each arm

Lower Body

Speed Hop Jog:	3 sets of 10 speed hops for each leg.
Power Hop Jog:	3 sets of 10 power hops for each leg
Two-legged Speed Hop:	3 sets of 10
Two-legged Power Hop:	3 sets of 10

The two-legged hops can be substituted with speed and power box hops or with the stair hops.

Front Thrust Kick:	3 sets of 10 for each leg

*A one hundred percent, all-out effort causes
mental and physical tension. Slowing down
to a ninety-eight percent effort actually
speeds you up.*

Chapter 11
SKILL TRAINING

Like fitness, the element of skill is very specific. If a beginning athlete switches from tennis to racquetball, the general concepts and gross skill pattern elements he developed from tennis would help him perform at a higher level in racquetball than someone with no experience in either sport. In high level athletes however, this is not true. Skill development is neurologically based and therefore, is specific to every minor variation of activity. If a tennis pro decides to start playing racquetball with his friends once a week, this would adversely affect his tennis game. Ergo, the training of skills must be specific if you want to reach your full potential. The closer your training matches competition, the better prepared you are. Once the quality and technical features of a skill have been maximized, the repetition of these skills at the same intensity as competition is the best method to reach full potential. (68)

Sparring

Sparring causes anxiety for most people. The best way to overcome that is to spar as much as you can. Not only does this increase your speed by increasing your sparring skills, but it erodes your anxiety. Keep sparring until it becomes fun. Think of it as fun. Do not think of it with a kill or be killed mentality. This does not mean don't try. Try to beat your opponent. Give 100% at a 98% level. (See *Chapter 14*, subsection *Give it a 98% Effort* for an explanation of the 98% rule.) Do not think that you must attempt to 'kill' your opponent. Think of it as a challenge that you really enjoy. Some days choose two or three techniques or skills that you want to work on. Make it a game to work on them until they become effective for you.

If you have a classmate weighing over 250 pounds or taller than 6'5", ask him to spar. Beg if necessary. Think of him as a new challenge and learning experience. After a while, you will notice that you no longer have anxiety toward sparring. You will look forward to sparring and sparring will be all you want to do. In fact, you most likely will become addicted to it. It will make you feel better when you feel sick, frustrated or lethargic. Once you have reached this level of peace with sparring, then it's time to engage in some of those all out, try to kill your opponent sessions. You will notice that these are fun also.

Spar with people faster than you are. Humans have the tendency to rise to the occasion. Take advantage of this most noble human trait. This alone can help increase your speed tremendously. If you are already the fastest, great. If that's the case, spar with people better than you are. This has the same effect in increasing your speed and skill. What you are looking for are situations that require you to use your speed to be effective.

Other effective sparring situations include sparring big, tall guys. Don't be afraid of them. Seek them out! You will have to work hard to overcome the disadvantage in reach but this will boost your confidence and skill when sparring or fighting someone your size. A similar sized opponent will seem small to you. At that point, your level of confidence is so high against an equally sized opponent that you can feel a level of relaxation that you have been striving for in your attempt to reach optimum performance.

Footwork

What action is performed more than any other in the martial arts? Lunges and footwork, depending on what fighting style you choose. Martial artists, boxers and wrestlers lunge on almost every attack. In martial arts, the athletes also lunge backwards. Of course, you always side step after one step back, right? *Chapter 18* thoroughly discusses proper technique for lunging quickly.

You also need neuromuscular skill and strength to propel yourself across the ground. One hundred lunges a day should be a minimum. That is only 25 forward and 25 back with each leg. Three hundred would be better. Or better yet, two hundred a day, right leg one day and then the left leg the next.

After six to eight weeks of this, you could start to add resistance to increase strength. This could be accomplished with bungee cords, a weight vest or lunging up hill. Lunges should also be practiced with socks on from time to time in case you ever have to compete on a slippery surface. If this is not likely, then do not train this way because this changes the biomechanics of the lunge and therefore decreases the neuromuscular gains realized from doing the activity on a surface with good traction. Remember, make your training as specific as possible, striving for conditions that equal those you will be competing or fighting under.

You can also practice side stepping. Side stepping can be hard on the knees, therefore, if you have bad knees, it's not advisable to add very many of these to your lunge training. Adding resistance to side stepping only aggravates an existing knee problem. When side stepping your opponent's attack, you can move your body out of the way a little faster if you snap your torso over just before side stepping. This snap is similar to how a runner crosses the finish line. Quickly bend your torso to the side as if slipping a punch to your head. Do not delay the side step for this. In fact, it will appear to others, and perhaps yourself, that it occurs simultaneously with the side step. Realize that this advantage only lasts for that initial movement. It does not provide an increase in speed for a second step and it may actually slow a second step down because of a disturbance in your balance. As a result, only use this when it does not interfere with your counter and when it is appropriate for the technique you are avoiding.

Many fighters have a tendency to step back too often and too far. Stepping back should be an option, not the rule. Side stepping or standing your ground is often best. There are only two attacks that routinely require you to step back. These are the rear leg front thrust kick and the rear leg side kick. Of course it's possible to side step these or to brush them to the side at times, but some situations require you to step back. With all other techniques, you can stand your ground.

To learn how to fight without moving back, begin sparring every other round without moving your rear foot. At times, move it while attacking so that your opponent does not become excessively confident with your apparent lack of aggression or figure out what you are doing. For the most part however, refrain from moving the rear foot. Bob, weave and slip his hand attacks. Block his roundhouse kicks. Pick up your front leg against sweeps and leg kicks. The majority of your attacks should be counter strikes. If it helps, place a piece of tape on the floor. Keep your rear foot over the tape for the entire round. This training technique is an excellent confidence booster. It also helps you develop a better understanding of how to manipulate the movement of your opponent while avoiding being manipulated yourself. This prevents the opponent from using his aggression to get you moving backward.

Similarly, if you do not cause your opponent to move back, then you will appear very slow. Your opponent's confidence will increase because he will not fear your attacks. Instead of moving back, he will stand his ground and counter your attack. His counter will be very quick because there is no gap to close. If his skills are high, he may counter you as you are closing with your initial attack. The surest way to move an opponent back is with straight attacks. The front and side kicks mentioned above are two. An aggressive, highly committed jab and cross are two more. It's important to make sure your opponent respects your attacks. If that requires taking a good shot yourself while delivering one of your own, that's OK. Just make sure you get a powerful strike in from time to time. If your opponent does not respect your attacks, it's very difficult to get him moving backward.

Dancing

Boxers are great at dancing around the ring. They have excellent footwork and their right calves have great stamina, assuming that they are not south paws. Fast footwork is essential for quickness. Not only does it help you move in and out of range quickly, but it can distract your opponent. Fast footwork training develops balance during fast, abbreviated actions of the feet and legs. An increase in balance translates to an increase in speed. Dancing around also increases speed because it is easier to initiate movement from movement than it is from a stationary position. One defensive point to remember is not to develop a pattern that could be predicted by your opponent.

Jumping Rope

Jumping rope develops fast foot work, balance, strong calves and endurance. It's an excellent exercise. To avoid changing your muscle fibers to slow contraction properties, either jump at no more than 50% VO2 Max or jump at a high intensity for a minute or less. Take a break and then jump again.

If you maintain a correct stance, one in which you are fully mobile with the heel of the back foot raised, your calf muscles will tire when sparring and training. When the muscle becomes fatigued, your speed decreases because it lacks the energy to drive you forward and because you can not maintain the heel-raised stance. Jumping rope is an excellent way to increase the endurance of your calf muscles.

Hand Speed

Coin Drill

This exercise is an excellent drill for observing the effects of trying too hard. It also helps build hand-eye coordination, fluidity of movement and speed of movement. Hold a penny in your palm. Toss the coin into the air and catch it in the same hand in a striking method, similar to how a cat swats at a fly. Now place two pennies in the palm. Toss them so that they separate in the air. Catch them with two separate strikes.

Move up to three. Lay the three out in a line in your palm. Toss them into the air. Catch all three with the same hand, using three separate striking grabs. Two separate strikes and letting the third coin drop into your palm does not count. With each successful series, add another penny.

As you reach the limits of you current abilities (for the sake of this example, four), you will notice that you only catch two, maybe only one and perhaps none, when attempting to go for four. How is this possible? If you only toss two coins up, you can catch them both very easily. This is a perfect example of what happens when you try at 100 percent. Don't try so hard. Slow down to about 98% and relax. Do not think about getting the third, fourth or fifth. Catch one, then another and so on. This 98% rule applies to mental aspects as well. Let yourself get into game. React without thought. Put your mind simply into responding, not into winning. You will be much more successful this way.

To work both hands at the same time, toss the coins up in your right hand. Grab one coin at a time, alternating between right hand catches and left hand catches. Using this method you can increase the number of coins successfully caught.

Fast Hands

This is a fun game that helps you develop fast reflexes. It requires two people. Stand in a shallow horse stance, a fighting stance or in an ordinary standing posture, upright with your feet shoulder width apart. It does not matter which stance you choose or if you vary them. Bring your hands up to your shoulders with your elbows tucked in. Close your eyes. Your partner should hold out his palm. You will not know where or how far out it will be, but it should be between 12 and 18 inches from your hands so that you do not hyperextend your elbow when attempting to hit it. Your partner should then make a sound, any sound, as long as it starts and ends quickly. The instant you hear the sound, open your eyes and strike his palm quickly. Close your eyes again. Your partner will move his hand and make the same or a different sound again. Open and strike!

Initially, do it with only your right hand. Then only your left hand. Next, hit his palm with the most appropriate hand. If his palm is on your left side, hit it with the closer hand, the left hand. Finally, use both hands. Your partner holds both palms out. Upon hearing the sound, open your eyes and simultaneously explode with both hands toward the targets. Continue this game until you can simultaneously strike with both hands the instant you open your eyes. You should be amazed at the speed with which you move. When you can do all of this instantly, that's great. Do it again!

If there is a pause between opening your eyes and striking with your hands, you are thinking about it. Don't. This game is designed to help you react instinctively, without conscious thought. If you have trouble with this, continue practicing. It may help to switch to two hands. Some people react faster during the two-handed phase of this game. One would think that they would be slower because there is twice as much information to perceive, calculate and send. But they're faster. Why? Because the extra information requires that they forget about thinking about it, otherwise they would be embarrassingly slow. This extra information overloads what they can quickly process consciously, causing them to put intentional thought aside and allow the right hemisphere of their brain to take over. After you have the feel of this process, or lack thereof, go back to the one-handed drill. Hopefully there will be no pause after opening your eyes.

Peripheral Vision Drill

Stand with your feet parallel, hands at your sides, or up near your chest. Your training partner should be 8 or 10 feet off to your side. Stand relaxed and look straight ahead. Your training partner will toss balls in front of you, crossing your path at a ninety degree angle to where you are looking. Punch or grab the ball as quickly as possible. If this drill is too difficult at first, your training partner can take a step forward so that he is a little in front of you. This gives you a little more time to see the ball coming. He can also toss the balls at knee level for you to kick them. This drill helps develop your abilities to effectively use your peripheral vision. The sooner you see an attack or a foreshadowing movement, the faster your reaction. This drill also helps you become aware of how relaxed you are.

When working this drill, keep in mind the principle of economy of movement. A straight line is the shortest distance and therefore the fastest approach. Do not reach out to the side to intercept it. Wait until you must strike straight out in front of you.

Enter the Dragon

This fun and effective training game resembles the sparring between Bruce Lee and Bob Wall in the movie *Enter the Dragon*. Stand facing your partner, off to one side. The outside of the right foot of both you and your partner should be touching each other. Raise your right hands, place them together with the backs of the hands touching. The object of the game is to hit your partner in no more than two movements.

For example, you could grab his right arm with your right hand and strike his ribs with your left hand. If he blocks your left hand, the game ends. To use your right hand to attempt another strike would consist of a third movement. Do not use any pads. Strike lightly, especially when going for the head. The feet cannot move. This game teaches you how to move very quickly, how to relax, and how not to telegraph. You learn to read your opponent's movements through the sense of touch. After a while, close your eyes. You should be able to strike your opponent and block his attacks with almost the same rate of success. It's a lot of fun blocking your opponent's attacks with your eyes closed.

Night Vision & Sound Drill

This exercise is a bit more unusual, however, it is an effective means of developing your reactions to sound and using your night vision. With a super ball, go to a grass field with a training partner, or if alone, find some grass next to an uneven wall. The wall must have a surface that causes a ball tossed at it to go off in any direction. Get into a fighting stance or a wrestler's stance. Throw the ball at the wall or have your partner toss the ball at the ground in front of you. In either case, it should be dark enough so that you cannot see the ball until it is within three or four feet of you. Your first awareness of it is the sound it makes as it bounces off the grass somewhere in front of you. You should be able to barely see it. Catch it with a quick grab. If the sound of the ball is five or six feet out and to the side, dive for it. As your body approaches it, spot it, catch it and complete your roll. This drill helps develop sound awareness skills, quick reflexes, rolls and falls, and it clearly demonstrates how depth perception is lost in low light conditions.

Speed Catch Drill

A training drill similar to the one above requires a partner. Stand facing a wall with your hands under your shoulders and your elbows in. Stand three feet away if your hand/eye coordination and speed are already well developed. Stand five or six feet away otherwise. Your partner tosses tennis or super balls over your shoulder. Your objective is to strike out and catch the ball with one quick movement as it bounces off the wall toward you. Your partner should toss the balls at different heights and angles, requiring both hands to strike out in several directions. Your partner can even toss them from around your sides so that you have to kick the ball. As you become skilled at this level, either have the balls thrown faster or move closer to the wall. Both accomplish the same thing. You will have less time to determine the ball's direction and speed before striking.

Partial Rep Shadow Boxing

Shadow boxing can be used to directly increase the speed of your movements. If you throw a jab/cross combination, it would take, for example, 10 fractions of a second. If you now throw the combination using only 1/2 to 2/3 of your reach, the combination would take only 5 or 6 fractions of a second. You can incorporate kicking with this type of training as well. Of course, when sparring, use proper technique and execute the combination fully, delivering as much force to your opponent as possible. However, by using a shorter range of movements while shadow boxing, your techniques are MUCH faster. Your neuromuscular system adapts to these quicker movements, making your techniques faster while shadow boxing and sparring as well.

Overspeed Training

There is another type of training that is effective via a similar mechanism to partial rep sparring. It is called overspeed training. The theory of overspeed training relies on the neuromuscular system adapting to a speed that the body cannot produce on its own. A common example frequently employed by track coaches involves runners sprinting down a slight down grade. You can overspeed train your punches using bungee cords. Secure two cords to a wall. Each hand should then grab the loose end of one of the cords. Step back stretching the cord. Get into your fighting stance. You should be facing the wall and the cords should be exerting a slight pull on your hands. Throw your straight punches. Throw one and two punch combinations. This training does not work well with curving techniques. The pull from the cord should be slight. It should not be difficult to maintain your balance and not so strong that you might involuntarily hyperextend your elbow.

Kicking Speed & Precision Drills

Partial Range Kicks

You can increase your kicking speed by using the partial range drill. It works best if you kick a hanging piece of paper, a belt, or best of all, a bush with many leaves. That way you do not have to wait for the belt to return to its place if you kick it. Stand facing a bush, right leg in the air. Execute a front snap kick at a leaf. Try to come as close to the leaf as possible without touching it. Kick at the leaf four or five times. The speed of your kick is the primary goal. This drill also helps fine tune your precision. Similar to partial rep shadow boxing, do not completely re-chamber your kick. That would slow you down. This training works well for front snap kicks and roundhouse kicks. Mix the two kicks up. Throw a front snap kick, then snap out a roundhouse kick, followed by a roundhouse kick a few inches higher, then finish with two front snap kicks. The kicks should not be any higher than thigh level. Otherwise, they are too slow and you lose the adaptation stimulus for speed enhancement of the neuromuscular system. This training is also an excellent drill to increase your ability to relax the antagonist muscles.

This training is very effective in pointing out any problems with your balance. The dynamic movements amplify any imperfections in your balance and this dramatically slows down your movements. It's not be possible to attain several kicks per second if you are struggling to maintain your balance because your struggling generates muscular contractions. Observe how you cannot fully and completely relax the antagonist muscles whenever you must compensate for a loss of balance.

Strive for economy of movement. The principles of economy of movement apply to all parts of the body, not just the legs. Wasted upper body movement can slow your kicks and telegraph your intentions. Do not move your arms, shoulders or hips any more than necessary. These drills are similar to plyometric training because of the sudden changes in muscle length and contraction. Therefore, it is important to adhere to the safety standards explained under plyometric training in *Chapter 10* when performing these dynamic kicking drills.

Hanging Paper Drill

Hang a piece of paper from the ceiling with string. Attempt to hit it as fast as you can and as lightly as you can, thereby working on both your speed and precision. Imagine that it is a fly on a wall. Attempt to squash it without hurting your hand or foot on the wall. Every time a side exposes itself to you, snap out a jab, finger jab, back-fist or roundhouse kick.

Bag Work

Working on the heavy bag will not directly increase your speed, however, it can aid you indirectly by teaching you combinations, economy of movement and rhythm. Work on the heavy bag, experimenting with every kind of combination imaginable. Investigate which ones flow from one technique into the next. Many techniques naturally lead into another because the body is already moving in a manner appropriate for the next technique. A perfect example is the jab, cross and rear-leg kick combination. Develop as many of these natural combinations as possible. With the above example, you can throw the three-hit combination almost as fast as you can execute just the kick.

Repetition alone does not program you to automatically respond in a certain manner. The training must concentrate on developing a response to a stimulus.

Chapter 12
SKILLS OF THE EXPERTS

As explained previously, repetition alone does not program you to automatically respond in a certain manner. The training must concentrate on developing a response to a stimulus. It is advisable to develop some conditioned responses to a few situations in sparring and self defense. In doing so, your actions are faster in both situations. It may also help prevent paralysis caused by fear or panic.

Not only does reducing the number of options your brain has to consider increase your speed, but preprogramming your mind to automatically respond to a certain stimulus also makes you faster. For example, program yourself to throw a jab every time your opponent lowers his hand. Or every time he throws a hay maker, step in with a stiff jab. Your jab is a straight technique compared to his curving punch and your jab hand is closer to his head than his hay maker is to yours. Therefore, it will win the race of the punches if you throw it early enough.

Preprogramming works well for going toe-to-toe. Whenever boxers go toe-to-toe, they obviously are close enough to hit and get hit at any moment. Therefore, they take great care in covering up. However, whenever your opponent is punching you, he has created an opening. Train going toe-to-toe with your partners. Move at half speed and half power at first. Experiment with different combinations and look for openings when your opponent is attacking. Do not look at the ground, look at him.

Look for situations that give you an advantage. For example, when he throws a hook, not only is your hand close to his chin for an uppercut, but you can deliver the uppercut without exposing as large a target as he has with his hook. You may be able to score with an uppercut before he goes on the offensive. You can sometimes slip an uppercut through his guard by throwing it without turning the hand. In other words, your palm will remain facing across your body. This makes it easier to slip your glove through a small opening between his gloves.

On the down side, there is the possibility of such programming becoming a detriment when going against a skilled opponent. If he notices your pattern, he could set you up by intentionally lowering his hand, only to take advantage of you by knowing what you are going to do.

Preprogramming Self Defense

Working with a partner, develop your self defense skills addressing numerous scenarios, using various techniques. Start slowly at first until you have chosen what techniques come naturally and smoothly for you. Close your eyes and do not open them until told to do so by your partner. Your partner launches any kind of attack. If he starts with a sucker punch, he should say something as he starts to punch. At that time, open your eyes and respond without thinking. If you do not like the technique you instinctively reacted with, choose another one and do it again. Repeat it until it feels comfortable.

Have you partner continue with random techniques, only to throw a sucker punch again. Hopefully you automatically throw your preferred technique. If not, do it again a few more times using your preferred technique. If your partner grabs your collar or throat, he should do so quickly while simultaneously shouting or saying something to increase your level of confusion and surprise. This prevents you from having time to think of a response.

If he starts with a technique that requires some time to get into, perhaps a nelson or a headlock, try to help him get into position quickly and try not to think of your response. You want to respond instinctively. This way you learn more about how you respond to such situations and more about the types of techniques you instinctively prefer. Make a note of your responses, preferably on paper.

Repeat the drill next week, or in two or three weeks. Before beginning the training, do not practice your defensive drills. Test your current abilities without cheating (without refreshing your memory and reflexes with practice beforehand). Which responses did you use this time against the same attacks? Were they the ones you used last time? If they were and if they are your preferred responses, great, continue programming yourself to respond with those techniques.

If you seem to automatically revert to a previous technique after trying to preprogram yourself for a preferred technique, stick with the instinctive response if it is effective. If for some reason you choose not to go with your subconscious mind's automatic response and decide to reprogram it with your preferred response, know that unless you do this type of training frequently, you may revert to your former technique under stress. Or worse, you may hesitate or freeze as your subconscious mind starts to take over and runs into a road block created by your conscious mind attempting to respond with the reprogrammed response.

This hesitation causes an increase in stress because you are not responding to the problem effectively and decisively. The inability to remember your preferred technique causes a loss of clarity in thought. These factors combine to cause frustration. The result can lead to an increased sense of fear and a significant decrease in your confidence in getting out of a situation. This in turn goes back to the beginning, further affecting your level of stress, the loss of mental clarity and the tendency to hesitate. Also, the technique that your subconscious wanted to use will be delayed, if not blocked entirely. If you condition yourself to respond with the technique preferred by your subconscious, your response will be quick as a cat's, instantaneous and automatic. The technique may not be the BEST response, but it will be more thoroughly ingrained in your neuromuscular system because it is a technique that flows naturally from within yourself.

When under a great deal of stress, you are not physically capable of performing fine motor skills. If your preferred technique involves any fancy moves, twists, or balancing acts, discard it. When the pulse rate reaches 150 beats per minute or higher, you lose your ability to perform such a technique. You then have to switch to another technique. This of course wastes time and slows your response. If you encounter an actual street confrontation, especially if you are surprised by it, your pulse rate could easily climb to 150 beats per minute, or higher, instantly. This depends on the circumstances involved, your confidence level and your mental preparation.

The closer to reality your training comes, the more effective it is. Use your imagination and ingenuity to design realistic training sessions. An example may include training in a hallway or on a cluttered floor. The primary drawback to realistic training is that the risk of injury increases as the realism increases.

Hypotheticals

Two elements that slow reaction time are identification and decision making. How long does it take you to identify the threat and how long does it take you to choose a plan of action? For many situations, these elements can be taken care of in advance through hypothetical situations. Think of what situations you could possibly walk into someday. Imagine you walk into a situation and are completely surprised by what is happening. What would you do? Is that the best response? Can you think of another response?

Change the situation a little. Now what would you do? Perhaps your spouse is with you this time. By running these scenarios through your mind over and over, you can significantly decrease the time it takes to perceive the threat and the time it takes to accurately ascertain what is happening. This also reduces the time it takes you to respond. Better still, the response selected is most likely a better one than had you not run that scenario or a similar one through your mind. Hypothetical training is a training method you can perform at almost any time.

<u>Balance</u>

Having a good sense of balance and maintaining that balance can dramatically improve speed of movement. Not having proper balance when you decide to attack slows down your movements in the following ways:

1) If you become off balance while, or after, launching an attack, it becomes necessary to regain balance before you can withdraw from the attack or continue with your combination. For example, a right cross should be thrown from the body. The rear foot should turn, driving of the ground, followed by a twisting of the hips, torso and shoulders. The arm should extend out straight, elbow down, hand rotating over at the last moment. The head should look down a straight arm, as if looking down the barrel of a rifle.

Body weight should be sinking into the right foot as it is driving off the ground. The hand should be retracted by a reverse twisting of the body, not by pulling the hand back to the chin. Many fighters get carried away and continue with the punch until they are off balance with most, or all, of their weight on their front leg. The punch circles down and across their body in some kind of wild follow through. Not only are they wide open to an attack on their right side, but they are vulnerable to a sharp opponent who recognizes that they are off balance and that they cannot quickly twist their body and snap back into their defensive/offensive position. Recovery time is at least twice as long when balance is sacrificed.

2) Errors in balance increase muscular tension. Below are a few drills that improve balance and demonstrate the relationship between balance and tension.

Lights On, Lights Off

This drill requires the students to assume a fighting position. Turn the lights out. An instructor/training partner moves around the room with a flashlight and turns it on for a fraction of a second. The students should turn toward the light and quickly strike with a designated technique or combination. This drill helps develop explosive techniques from a stationary position.

It is also good training for remaining relaxed. If you start to get jumpy, anticipating the strobe of light, you will be able to feel your tension and how it slows you down. This drill demonstrates how sight can be your primary sense for balance, not the ears. Like another exercise to follow, it demonstrates how minuscule disturbances in your balance cause a tensing of your muscles, thus slowing you down. The room must be totally dark. Your eyes must not be able to see anything. This way their function in the maintenance of balance is negated. As you patiently wait for the strobe of light, you will most likely make small corrections in your balance. Observe what happens when you do this. If the strobe flashes during one of those corrections, are you in your best position to react quickly and powerfully?

Blind Balance

Blindfold yourself. Get into your fighting stance. At the sound of a clap, quickly perform a specific technique that was called out by your training partner. Do it again. Continue this drill for five or ten minutes, changing the technique every time or two. People make most of their adjustments to balance through information they receive through their eyes, not from their ears as you might have been told. Don't believe it? Try standing on one leg. It's easy enough. Now tilt your head a little. Move your head around, disrupting the fluid in your ears. It's still pretty easy, isn't it?

Now close your eyes. Did you start swaying like a tree in the wind? Being blindfolded causes you to make minor errors in your balance. Notice that the minute adjustments in balance cause muscular tension and notice how this slows you down. Even after learning this lesson, you may wish to repeat this drill periodically to improve your ability to maintain balance without the use of your eyes. Close the blinds and turn the lights off. If it's dark enough, you will not need a blindfold.

Speed Kicks

This drill involves multiple kicks. Throw a front snap kick, followed by a low roundhouse kick, followed by a side kick, all with the same leg. Do not extend the kicks fully. The only objective is to kick as fast as you can. Do not return to your fighting stance after each kick and do not re-chamber fully. Execute the kicks as fast as possible. Repeat the series or use a different combination. Each kick should be lightning fast, taking only a fraction of a second. If not, chances are the problem lies in your balance.

To throw a kick as fast as possible, re-chamber quickly, re-kick without touching the ground, re-chamber and do it again at full speed requires great balance. Making minor adjustments to your balance slows the movement of your kicks. Each kick and re-chamber is a dynamic action. It takes maximal muscle firing accompanied by maximal antagonistic muscle relaxation to kick, re-chamber and kick again. Plyometric training should help maximize the muscle firing and the relaxation of the antagonist muscle. However, an increase in your balance during execution increases your speed more than any neuromuscular benefits derived from plyometric training. If your balance is off, there is no way you can fully relax the antagonist muscle. Nor can you fully stimulate the firing of the working muscle. Also, when off balance the inhibitory reflex activates more forcefully because it is attempting to prevent an injury to the muscle that is twitching to maintain balance.

If holding on to a support helps, that is more evidence the problem lies in your balance. Attempt to feel the minor imbalances and the minute tension within your muscles. By learning to recognize this, you can continue making improvements to your balance and speed during all training sessions.

Lastly, set up a speed/force measuring device on your heavy bag. If you don't have one, don't worry about it. You can practice this drill without one. Stand facing the bag, close your eyes and strike it with a right cross when you hear the random beep, or when your partner claps his hands. Do not worry about power, only speed. As you wait for the sound, anticipating it at times, you may inadvertently tense up as you focus on responding as fast as humanly possible the instant you hear the stimulus. Of course this tensing up slows you down, but it also throws you off balance and you will notice how this slows you down even more. When you notice that you are off balance, you will tense up to regain your balance. There is a direct relationship between balance and tenseness. This drill enables you to feel how a loss of balance to just the slightest degree causes you to tense up and how tensing up causes you to lose your balance. Try it!

Timing and Rhythm

Fighters are like dancers. They each have their own style and rhythm. Every fighter naturally develops a rhythm as he learns techniques, combinations, foot patterns, etc., and places the ones he likes in his own personal repertoire. Skilled fighters learn to observe this rhythm, using it to fool their opponent, to conserve energy and to avoid having it used against them. New fighters do not have much rhythm. For this reason, they are dangerous. Many superior fighters have been hit by these greenhorns because they throw punches that are totally unexpected. There is no rhythm to their attacks and they do not flow from one to another. Use this method to your advantage. Break up your rhythm. Not only can you unexpectedly tag your opponent, but you can prevent him from using your rhythm against you.

If your opponent has an established rhythm, he will have a tendency to continue with the same pattern of movement, usually at the same tempo, or speed. This rhythm is programmed into his neuromuscular system. He is 'motor set', or on auto-pilot, to continue the sequence. You can take advantage of this by: 1) predicting where he will be; 2) by hesitating or speeding up your rhythm to interrupt his rhythm and/or surprise him by doing the unexpected; and 3) by timing your slip and counter. It takes him a moment to recover from his own ongoing rhythm, which he must first interrupt, before he can respond to your attack. Hopefully, you have already hit him by that time. (48)

Slipping, Bobbing and Weaving

Effective slipping, bobbing and weaving have numerous advantages. By causing your opponent to repeatedly miss you, he will lose confidence in his abilities and therefore develop an increased respect for your abilities; waste his energy and tire more easily; try harder; and possibly tense up resulting in decreased speed, increased telegraphing and over-commitment. Such effective avoidance skills benefit you by, in addition to the above, boosting your confidence, saving energy, avoiding the adverse effects of moving backward, creating openings by causing him to over commit, maintaining an aggressive demeanor, and most importantly, allowing you to immediately take advantage of the opening created by your opponent's attack. This greatly increases your speed since you do not have to move out of range and then back into range to deliver your attack.

It's safer to slip to the opponent's outside position, distancing yourself from a punch by his other hand. This outside position also limits your attacks as well. If you slip to the inside, don't stay there long. You are too close to avoid his strikes unless your skills are significantly superior to his. Hit and move out or move to the outside position.

There are many ways to work on slipping, bobbing and weaving. Shadow boxing, focus mitts and sparring all work well. When sparring, have your training partner throw ninety percent of the attacks. Just concentrate on avoidance.

The following are some drills for training bobbing, weaving and slipping:

Padded Shinai Drill

An excellent training drill that works wonders in the skill development arena involves a padded shinai (flexible bamboo training sword). Pad the last twelve inches of a shinai. Glue two 2 by 4's together so that you have a two-foot long 4 by 4. You need two of them. The apparatus will be more stable if you affix each end to a one-foot 2 by 4, making the shape of an "I". For protection, wear a cup, mouthpiece and perhaps headgear. Step onto the boards and get into your fighting stance. The boards should be arranged so that your foot position is natural for you.

Your partner will attempt to hit you and knock you off the beams with the shinai. Most shots should be jabs to the head since the exercise focuses on bobbing, slipping and weaving. The shinai holder can use jabs to the head & body, swings to the head and shoulders and sweeps to the front foot. Sweeps to the body are not allowed because there is no possible way to avoid them. Do not block the attacks, avoid them. Bob, slip and weave! The only block permitted is the stop block. Don't hit it very hard. Just tap it as you slip the jab. Otherwise, you end up pushing the shinai to the side and it slows down the jabs from your training partner. That's cheating.

The jabs should come at about two or three per second. Avoid the jabs to the body by using a glancing block while turning the body. The sweeps to the foot ensure that you maintain good balance as you are forced to pick it up to avoid being swept. Use your legs to lower yourself to avoid the swings to your head and shoulder. Attempt to keep your head as close to the shinai as possible when bobbing and slipping. Your training partner should mostly jab at your head, providing you with plenty of practice. As you improve, the strikes should come very quickly and relentlessly.

During the padded shinai drill, keep the hands up and avoid the shinai by bobbing, weaving and bending the knees, not by blocking or bending forward.

Shadow Boxing

Shadow boxing is a very effective training method. It helps develop fluidity, smoothness, combinations, and all around good habits, including guard, proper technique, evasive maneuvers and continual movement. In addition, it helps you develop a thorough understanding of all the above elements even if you do not have a sparring partner every day. Fifteen to twenty minutes of shadow boxing in place of sparring can work wonders. As previously stated, by familiarizing your mind and body with your fighting techniques, they will come naturally when sparring or fighting. Many of the above listed benefits increase your fighting speed.

Chapter 13
TACTICS

Tactics is defined as the art or science of directing forces in battle; the science of disposition and maneuver; and the methods or procedures to gain advantage. This section includes some tactics not previously discussed. This chapter is not all inclusive. The more variety you incorporate in your sparring, the more thoroughly you will understand tactics and strategy.

Strategy differs from tactics in that tactics are used to win a battle and strategy is used to win a war. A coach uses tactics to prepare his athlete to fight a specific boxer. The coach uses strategy to develop his athlete's over all skills and style.

Precede Your Attacks with Punches

Punch as you initiate an attack to conceal the nature of your true attack. For example, if you are planning to kick your opponent, by throwing some punches at the same time he will not be thinking about your kick. He will be focusing on your punches so he will be unprepared for a kick. Besides increasing the effectiveness of your attack, this also increases your level of safety. If your opponent happens to attack simultaneously, or attempts to counter your attack, hopefully he will walk into one of your punches.

If the gap is wide and you are attempting to close it with one long lunge, you will have the tendency to thrust your arms out when you lunge. This tendency is automatic because thrusting your arms out when you lunge aids the biomechanics of the lunge. Disciplined training can break most fighters of this habit, however, punching when you lunge provides the advantages stated above while also delivering the biomechanical advantage realized from the thrusting of the arms.

Anticipating Your Opponent's Moves

Anticipating your opponent's moves increases your speed and effectiveness substantially. If you know what your opponent is going to do, you know where he will be open, from what angle the opening will be created and to a degree, how long the opening will last. You can then plan how best to take advantage of this opening.

In addition to using methods of perception to anticipate his moves, you can encourage specific attacks by leaving an opening in your defenses. By adding feints to this strategy, you can draw his attack out. Now, you not only know to where, and most likely, with what he is going to attack, but you also know when. It is always preferable to feint him into attacking, than it is to wait for him to decide when to attack. The more control you have over the situation, the greater the edge you have.

Fakes

There are many types of fakes. For instance, you can feign an injury, as if you stepped on something that hurt, you can pretend that the referee or someone else said something, you can fake high and go low, fake hands and attack with the feet, or you can pretend to develop a pattern. This pattern can include slow movements to fool your opponent about your speed. It may also include repetitive attacks, footwork or hesitation. Any action you can think of that fools your opponent in any manner is a form of a fake. They all increase your speed by changing his mindset and/or increasing his perception time.

One Style of Fake: Leave an Intentional Opening

Example: Sticking your elbow out to expose your ribs.

Benefit: If you know when and where your opponent is going to attack and you have already planned your counter, his attack will seem very slow. Your counter will be very fast because the analysis and decision stages were already completed.

Common Methods of Feinting

- Half way extended hand attacks.
- Snapping the head forward.
- Stomping of the front foot.
- Partial step forward, or to the side.
- Snap torso forward.
- Snapping twist of hips and or shoulders.
- Bend forward knee.
- A quick shout combined with any of the above.

An effective combination is to feint, shout and then strike. The amount of time between the feint, the shout and the strike is minimal. The strike should begin approximately one half second after the feint began.

Any combination of the above.

Work on Your Defense!

If your defensive skills are good, then your opponent has to work harder, probably a lot harder, to strike a blow. This increased effort on his part slows him down. It should also provide you with more time to perceive his attack. His increased effort and frustration cause him to tense up, providing you with more clues to pick up on. Like everything else, minor decreases in his confidence and minor increases in your confidence affect the speed of both of you. Each of these points helps in a small way, but taken together, the result is substantial.

Try to immediately follow each of your defensive techniques with an offensive one. You may initiate a counter using a technique that flows from your current body positioning. In doing so, your movements will be smoother and faster. However, your opponent may know what technique to expect because he can see, and/or feel, your body position. Since your opponent may be expecting the technique that flows naturally from your current position, your chances of catching him off guard should increase if you throw a technique that feels unnatural. The technique may be a little slower, however, its unexpectedness can overcome this downfall and become what appears to be a fast counter. This strategy of doing the unexpected can be employed in many situations. You can create situations or patterns that facilitate your opponent's expectation of a certain technique or behavior. Use your imagination. For example, begin the round retreating from your opponent's attacks. Then after you have established a pattern, the next time he attacks, stand your ground and counter.

Aggression is an effective tactic. The charger, or offensive strategist, has many advantages. He can move forward faster than you can move backward. He can develop far more speed and power than you can while you are moving backward. He has the action/reaction principle in his favor. He appears aggressive and confident to himself, you and the judges (if in competition). If you're not naturally an aggressive fighter, experiment with it. You may like the results.

Fight a Boxer

Oppose the tactics of your opponent. Fight your fight, not his. Make him fight in a manner that he is not accustomed to, or at least not comfortable with. If he prefers to fight by countering, then make him attack. If he prefers to attack, continually driving his opponents back, then you should be more aggressive. Make him defend your continual attacks. The saying, "box a fighter, fight a boxer" has much wisdom behind it. Strive to learn what your opponent likes and don't allow it. Take it away from him. If he regularly attacks by hitting his opponents on the hands, then continually move your hands. Take that sensation of touch away from him. This simple change may be very disconcerting to him. (48)

Vary Your Techniques

Do not get stuck on one particular fighting strategy. Everyone has their own favorite techniques, but if you become locked into one particular fighting style, or series of techniques, it can easily become a disadvantage for you. If your favorite technique fails, or your opponent has a good counter, then you may be left at a loss for how to continue your attack and beat your opponent.

One way to prevent this is to vary your sparring partners, forcing you to deal with different techniques, styles and body sizes. Your adaptability increases, enhancing your ability and confidence, and reducing your stress. Your speed improves as a result. By using numerous techniques, combinations and fighting styles, you make it harder for your opponent to learn, and therefore predict, your style. You also develop the ability to alter your style to one that frustrates your opponent.

Reach

When your opponent has a reach advantage, he has an advantage in speed. He may be able to hit you without having to lunge forward, whereas, unless you slip and counter, you always have to lunge on your attacks. As you know, a punch is faster than a lunge and punch. And a lunge gives your opponent more visual stimulus to perceive when your attack begins.

An effective method of taking this advantage away from him is to increase the distance even farther. This has two ramifications. First, a tall opponent is not used to fighting from this exaggerated distance. He will foreshadow his techniques in his attempt to compensate for the increased distance, providing you with more reaction time. He also may tend to overextend himself in his attempt to hit you. This overextending slows his combinations and his recovery. The second ramification is that the first attack in your combination will not come close to hitting him. There is no need to feint. The first strike essentially is your feint but do not treat it as a feint. Keep it as an actual strike. This way, he will be sure to respond to it. All you have to do is continue with your combination, taking advantage of the openings created when your opponent reacts to your first strike.

Using this tactic, your first strike has become your feint and your opponent's first strike has become an error because his distance is off. Not only will you see it coming a mile away, but his technique will have run its course too soon. You simply have to react after his strike. Now he has closed the gap and missed his strike and you are in a prefect position to deliver a counter.

A way to change this tactic a little to prevent your tall opponent from catching on too quickly is to lunge when your opponent lunges. Not only will he be surprised by your aggressive move, but his distance and timing will be off. All of a sudden you're too close to hit and he does not have sufficient time to complete the strike. Your timing and distance will be right on. This technique can be very demoralizing to your opponent. Your decisive, aggressive move against a taller opponent looks very impressive as well.

Follow Up

Follow up quickly on your opponent's loss of poise. Your follow up should be aggressive, designed to prevent your opponent from recovering. Make this the number one goal of some of your sparring sessions. This focused training decreases your hesitation, increases your effectiveness and speed, and makes it more difficult for your opponent to successfully analyze his mistake that provided you the advantage. In this way, you'll be able to use the same tactic against him more often. (56)

Chapter 14
STRATEGY

Attack whenever you perceive an advantage, for example, when your opponent is flat-footed, unbalanced, in the middle of a step or does not seem prepared.

Attack when your opponent is preparing to attack. At that moment he won't be psychologically (and possibly not physically) prepared to defend himself. For example, when he is thinking about a combination of moves he plans to execute, or when he sees an opening that you have intentionally left for him, he is not prepared to counter your attack because he is not in a countering, or even in a perceptive, mindset. Thus, you have a higher probability of success. This strategy will frustrate him to no end.

If you attack him whenever he is preparing to attack, it will demoralize him and lower his confidence. This slows him down even more because of his non-focused mental state. He can't be frustrated and in the zone at the same time. His lack of confidence in his ability and technique will cause him to hesitate, thus further slowing him down. All the above cause anxiety, resulting in tension and mental delays as he first must set aside any stress before he can process the stimulus of an incoming attack.

Attack when he changes his stance. If your opponent has raised a foot off the floor while moving or changing his stance, he cannot make any alterations to his direction of movement until the foot re-contacts the floor again. This gives you the edge. Attack when your opponent lifts his front foot and begins to move forward. You can initiate this scenario by advancing and then retreating. He should follow. When he picks that foot up and steps forward, attack him or sweep his forward leg.

Time your opponent whenever he is advancing. In other words, attack when your opponent is moving toward you. This makes you appear faster because you don't have to move forward as much. It also significantly increases the power of your technique. Similar to attacking when your opponent is preparing to attack, this strategy builds your effectiveness and confidence, and demoralizes your opponent, weakening his confidence.

When your opponent tries to get out of the way, you have already won for two reasons. First, because you are moving forward and he is moving backward, you are faster, more powerful, better balanced and in a better position to follow up with combinations. Also, if he is on the defensive, your opponent most likely lacks the confidence and determination to overcome your attack and feels that he must avoid it altogether.

Another excellent time to attack is just after your opponent launches his attack. Yes, he has the action/reaction principle on his side, but through your excellent perception, you knew he was about to attack. Because of your practice in this area, you knew when and how he was going to attack. When he moves forward in his attack, blitz him. Attack straight forward as aggressively and explosively as possible. Move like a freight train. Very frequently, this completely overwhelms his attack and reveals his lack of confidence and conviction in his attacks. His attempt at defense is futile because he is not in a mental or physical position to defend. It's also too late for him to defend. This significantly boosts your confidence and kills his. Watch your speed increase and his decrease before your eyes. To everyone present, you appear lightning fast and effective. Besides all of these benefits, it's a lot of fun.

Just as emotions and feelings are contagious, the fighting attitudes and perceptions of your opponent can be influenced. This applies to most fighters, but works especially well against new sparring partners. When sparring against a new opponent, start with relatively slow movements. This has two effects. First, it creates a false sense of security. Second, the tempo may be contagious, causing him to fall into a less than 98% level of attentiveness and commitment. This can set him up for a rude awakening when you change the tempo with a fast strike to the face.

This ploy also works for distance. Besides the tricks to fool your opponent into thinking that you are farther away than you really are, throwing short punches and kicks can have the same effect. Not extending your shoulder or hip on punches and kicks shortens your attacks. He may begin to think that he is safe from that distance. When the opportunity presents itself, hit him with a combination or hit him once and back up. That way he probably won't be able to figure out his error.

The following increase your opponent's reaction time:

· Attack immediately after he completes a technique, while he is executing an attack, or while he is stepping.
· Attack when the number of stimuli that he perceives is increased, including visual, auditory and tactile stimuli.
· Attack when he is inhaling.
· Attack when your opponent is distracted by a feint, a shout, a spectator, coach, etc.
· Attack after you connect well with a hard blow. He may be dazed, his confidence may be shaken and he may fear additional pain.

Fighting Distance

Distance is extremely important. Immediate recognition of distance variations, and skill in controlling distance, are two factors that increase your speed and effectiveness tremendously. Many people have a hard time judging distance. Experiments have shown that women have a harder time with spatial relationships than do men. It has not been determined if this difference is due to gender or social factors. The author does not know of any studies specifically targeted at differences in judging distance among groups of men and women, but based on studies concerning geometry, hand-eye coordination, and the author's experience in developing fighters' abilities to judge distance, this is a learned skill. Training increases your ability in this area.

The best method for developing this skill involves placing the student in sparring sessions where the distance varies from one partner to the next and from one weapon to the next. Train with people of varying builds. Fight a range of opponents from tall, slender boxers to short, stocky kickers. The more variation the better. To further enhance the training, add weapons. Knives, staffs, swords and padded sticks of 15 inches, 22, 26 and 30 inches all work great. Eventually, you will be able to know 'exactly' where you and your opponent are while fighting.

When you have reached this level and your opponent has not, you can hit your opponent almost at will, frustrating him as you appear to remain just outside his range. Once you have mastered distance control, you will encounter this situation fairly frequently because many people are not skilled in the judgment of distance. They either get too close or allow you to get too close, resulting in your quick, successful attack. They cannot understand how you are hitting them. They will conclude that your speed is incredible. Others skilled in distance judgment will recognize your opponent's mistake. When watching others spar, practice your distance judgment, observing who has the advantage, how, and why.

There are numerous ways to work with distance skills, including two practical strategies:

1. Stay at the very end range of your opponent's distance. Don't get too close or the action/reaction principle will work too much against you. Remain just at the very edge. Use your avoidance skills, bobbing and weaving, etc., to avoid his attacks. He will step in closer to hit you. In his attempt to successfully hit you, he will make errors in distance. When he starts to move in, tag him.

2. Stay far away. So far away that he has to over-exaggerate his movements to close the gap. Not only do you have plenty of time to perceive his attack, but his over-exaggerated attack requires more commitment. This makes it hard for him to stop or change his actions once they have begun. Blitzing, or simply countering his over-committed attack is easy.

Focus on your Opponent's Concentration

For most people, concentration is cyclic. Learn to perceive when your opponent's concentration lags, then strike. This may occur just after an attack by either you or your opponent, after a minor distraction, as your opponent anticipates the end of the round, or for any number of other reasons. By being aware of this and looking for it in your opponent, you are less likely to fall victim to it.

Attack Against His Inertia

This strategy was previously touched upon at the beginning this chapter. Attack when your opponent is moving, such as stepping forward, attacking or moving to the side. This gives you the advantage because he can not adequately respond. He is committed until he finishes the movement. When there is a wide gap he must make a preparatory move, a gap closing move. Attack as he makes his move to close the gap. Create this wide gap by stepping back. When he steps forward to close the gap, launch an aggressive, backward driving attack. He cannot stop moving forward and start moving back until his forward foot reaches the ground and starts pushing back.

Other ways to lure your opponent in include leaving an opening, looking tired or unfocused, off balance or intimidated. Then, not only will you know when he is going to attack, but you also know how he is going to attack. Your timed counter is planned, set and waiting to strike.

Power Hitting

You do not need power to be a powerful hitter. It certainly helps, but a small person can deliver a devastating punch or kick without relying on power. The trick is timing, combined with a little technique. Use your confidence to stand your ground and your speed of perception, decision making and movement to deliver your attack when your opponent is moving toward you. Put his weight behind your punch. Without getting too technical, you are adding his weight to your body weight and his speed of movement to your speed of movement. That all adds up to one powerful strike. How does this relate to speed? Through timing your opponent, you increase your speed by adding the speed of your opponent to the speed of your attack.

Timing takes a lot of skill in perception. You must be able to perceive the attack, analyze your opponent's movement and the opening, and initiate an appropriate attack of your own. Straight line attacks are best because you want to add the movement of your opponent to your technique. A circular attack undermines that goal.

Timing takes a lot of confidence. You must have full confidence in your ability to stand your ground and counter with a strike that will land. Timing also takes a lot of experience. Spend hours in the ring until you develop the skill of timing. Don't worry about getting hit. A hit taken that teaches you something pays off later, perhaps in a tournament or a street fight, by allowing you to slip an attack or beat your opponent with a quick straight punch. Your confidence is augmented by developing this attitude because, not only are you developing the skills necessary to perceive the attack, slip the attack, and counter the attack, but you learn not to fear being hit. Fear becomes unjustified when the fear of getting hit hinders your performance more than the actual hit would. Having full confidence in your abilities and lacking any unjustified fear of getting hit goes a long way in making you a power hitter.

Hand Positioning

Boxing Stance vs. Karate Stance

Should the hands be placed, chambered, at the hips as in the classical karate position, or up near the shoulders as in boxing. Sorry to tell you this my karate friends, but boxing is by far the better way to go, especially where speed is concerned. Punches are much faster from the boxer's position simply because they are much closer to the target. Less distance equates to faster delivery time. It also provides less time for the opponent to perceive the attack and less time to react to it.

The trajectory of a jab or a cross from a boxer's stance is much harder to perceive than from a karate stance. The left jab starts at or near eye level. It goes out straight, horizontally, and contacts at or near eye level. A karate punch starts at or near the hip and rises toward its target. Think of it from this perspective. Which is harder to see, an arrow coming straight at your eyes or an arrow traveling across your field of view? Obviously, the arrow heading straight for you. Because of this principle, it is much harder to perceive the initial movement of the straight arrow, or the jab. The result is somewhat of a stealth technique, at least when compared to the alternative.

The classic punch may be powerful, however, besides all the above, it exposes more of the body. By using the boxer's stance, keeping the elbows in to protect the sides, hands up and chin down, the head and torso are much less exposed than compared to the classic stance. This position of superior protection results in less defensive movement. This alone increases your speed for numerous reasons. Some of them include:

1) Your opponent has to work harder to successfully attack you.

2) This increases your confidence, decreases his and provides you with more reaction time and better stimulus with which to perceive his attack

3) Since your body positioning may do the blocking for you, it may not be necessary to move your hands to block, thus they remain close and ready to instantly counterattack.

4) Because of your protected position, instead of having to move back, you are in a better position to stand your ground and counter. Not having to move back and then re-close the gap increases your speed by 400 or 500 percent.

Hand Positioning/Body Mechanics

It's a rule that the closer you keep your limbs to your body, the more strength you have. As with everything in life, there are limits to this rule. Having your hands and arms too close to your body will not allow you to exert maximum force in either pushing or pulling. However, referring to the rule, most of your strength is lost when the arms are far away from the torso. For example, if someone grabs your wrist, you have more control over the movement of your hand if your hand is near your torso instead of being stretched out, away from you.

Here's an exercise to illustrate the biomechanics involved. Place your palms together and extend your arms out in front of you. Now push your hands together forcefully. Relax. Now, keeping the palms together, bring your hands in toward your chest. Try pushing your palms together again.

The pressure generated with the hands close to your body will be substantially greater. Think about the bench press or the leg extension. The point when you are the strongest is at mid-range, just a few inches out from the body. For the same reasons, muscle contraction is fastest when the muscle is neither excessively stretched nor shortened. (38) Therefore, do not fully chamber punches or kicks.

For fighting purposes, if your hands are too close to your body, they have to travel too far to the target. Your attack is slower because of the increased distance traveled. Your opponent has more time to perceive the attack and to respond.

Having the hands too far out has several problems as well. Your hands and arms are vulnerable to your opponent. Your torso is unnecessarily exposed and your punches lack power. Yes, the shorter distance to travel increases your speed, but you need some distance to build up sufficient momentum. The opponent may use the extended hand against you by hitting your fist out of the way, hitting it as a distraction, or pulling you off balance. Some people argue that you should keep both hands in front of your cheeks for better protection. That's a valid point, however, doing so slows you down for reasons stated above. The optimum positioning for your arms, both offensively and defensively, is the boxer's position. The right hand is back on the cheek and the left hand is approximately 10 inches out from your face.

Foot Placement

Kicks are faster from a boxer's stance because the feet are closer together and because you are much more mobile than in a classical karate stance. It is true that kicks from a cat stance are fast, but this stance is not very mobile, nor effective for quick lunges, quick retreats or maintaining your ground against a fighter. From a boxer's stance, small steps are easily performed and recommended. Small steps are best for continual movement, balance maintenance, and combinations. It should go without saying that the knees should always be in a slightly bent position, ready to spring into action.

Which Side to Train On?

If you are right handed, your right hand and leg will be faster because those limbs are more coordinated and often stronger. The myelination is thicker on the dominant side. Therefore, if you are interested in a quick response scenario to a self defense situation, place your right side forward. If you are a boxer, kickboxer or wrestler, you most likely fight with your strong side back.

There are two valid arguments whether you should train on both sides or only one. Both corners agree that you should be able to throw any technique from either stance because of the dynamic nature of fighting. In an actual fight, especially against multiple attackers, you will find yourself, at least momentarily, moving through both stances. Here's where some experts differ. One side argues that you should train 50% from a right stance and 50% from a left stance. This ensures that your techniques are near equal on both sides. This increases your confidence in competing with your strong side forward.

The other side feels that, because of the myelination principle, you will increase your speed, fluidity and coordination most if you train on one side. By sparring with your strong side back, the techniques that you use most often increase in speed more than if you switched back and forth. These movements become more coordinated because of the additional time spent training on this side. Therefore, these techniques will be faster. On the other hand, your confidence and performance suffer when forced to switch to the weaker side.

Note: If you are right handed, most likely you prefer to jump off your left leg. This often develops the left leg into the stronger leg. The right leg usually remains the more coordinated. This difference has implications regarding which kicks are faster and which are stronger. These implications are explained under *Using Your Dominant Leg* in *Chapter 17*.

Even though the force of impact increases as the object's speed increases, this relationship is not necessarily the same when it comes to fighting. Generally, as you increase the speed of a technique, the power of that technique decreases.

Chapter 15
TRICKS OF THE TRADE

1. There is a relationship between speed and power. Even though the force of impact increases as the object's speed increases, this relationship is not necessarily the same when it comes to fighting. Generally, as you continue to increase the speed of your technique, the power of that technique decreases. This is because, to increase the speed of a punch or kick, you put less of your body mass behind the technique. By decreasing the amount of mass behind the technique, you can generate more speed because you can move a limb much faster than you can move your entire body. The reduced mass impacting on the target results in loss of force.

2. Any wasted time, or movement, results in a loss of speed.

3. Keep your hands, and preferably your feet, mobile. You can initiate a punch or a kick faster from a hand or foot that is already moving than you can from a hand or foot that is stationary. Continually move your hands and upper body. Even if your hands happen to be circling back when you start to punch, it is generally faster to make a change in direction than it is to start movement from non-movement. The exception to this rule would be if your hand is moving straight back and you punch straight out in the opposite direction.

4. For speed of movement, any series of punches, kicks and jabs should be like one movement. Your techniques need to flow together for maximum speed. Use your hand techniques to get yourself in position to throw a kick. For example, first throw a jab, follow it with a cross that brings your shoulder forward and pivots your hips. This positions you to throw a kick, such as a roundhouse or side kick.

Give It 98% Effort

Give your technique a 98% effort. Why not 100%? Because people tend to tense up when giving a technique their all, or 100%. You will need to practice this for it to become automatic. Start at a full 100% and then back off just a little. Strive for a fast, fluid motion. Don't have in your mind the commands, "faster, faster, faster." That builds tension. This slightly less than 100% effort will be faster because your muscles will be looser, more relaxed. Your techniques will be smoother.

Clothing

You know from earlier in the book that tight clothing adds friction and resistance to your movement. For top speed, clothing should be loose and light. Sweat increases the weight of the clothing and friction.

A sweaty and sticky gi can be a pain in the neck. Not only do the pant legs stick to your thighs, slowing down your kicks, but many people have a habit of pulling them up when they are about to kick to reduce friction. This slows them down by telegraphing that they are about to kick, by tying up the hand so they cannot punch while kicking or just before kicking, and it creates an opening for the opponent. Two tricks help prevent these problems. The first is to wear thin and very loose pants. The second is to wear thin nylon running tights under your gi. The nylon should go down to the lower thigh. This allows the gi to slide over your legs even when it is wet and sticky.

Clothing can also be used to hide your movements and muscle contractions. The samurai wore the hakama. The hakama is kind of a cross between a skirt and a pair of baggy pants. It provided easy leg movement and it concealed the leg and foot movements from the opponent. Champion kick boxer Dennis Alexio was sanctioned during a bout because he wore a

Hawaiian grass skirt. The skirt hid his thighs and made it harder for his opponent to perceive the initial leg movement of an attack.

Traction

Many people spar with socks on. The advantage to this is that it reduces friction, decreasing the chance of your knees locking up while your upper body continues to turn, potentially tearing a ligament. However, if you lose traction, you will be slower. If you wear sparring shoes, lace them up tightly. You don't want any extra room in the shoe. The shoe should be part of your foot. Regardless of what you have on your feet and where you spar, search for something on the floor or ground that gives you traction. If sparring on irregular or uneven surfaces, such as a garage with pieces of carpet layered over it, look for areas of raised surface.

If sparring on grass or some other outside area, look and/or feel for anything that might provide better traction for your rear foot, such as a rock. These areas provide a good foothold, much as the sprinter's block does. Use whatever you find to your advantage to launch your offensive and defensive techniques while attempting to maneuver your opponent to a disadvantaged location. A disadvantageous position would include having him face uphill, face the sun or lights, stand in front of obstacles, or on a slippery surface, and even face the tournament judge so that the judge can not see whether his techniques land.

First Moves

Which should you move first when attempting to strike quickly with a hand technique, the hand or the foot? It depends on the distance and the technique. For most techniques, if you are close enough to the target without having to step forward, then the fastest method to hit the target is to strike without stepping forward.

There are a few exceptions to this rule. Some techniques are sped up by snapping the upper body forward or by twisting the shoulders as you strike. This snapping of the torso forward and twisting of the shoulders can provide a few extra inches of reach. The sliding back-fist is an odd ball punch that does not follow any rule. The speed of the back-fist is increased by sliding your feet together and rising up on the balls of your feet as you strike.

If the target is far enough away to require a small step to be taken, two or three inches, the fastest method is to move the hand first, then explode forward a fraction of a second after beginning your hand technique. It will appear that the hand and foot begin to move simultaneously.

If the distance to the target is significant, it is necessary to begin stepping first. Otherwise, the strike will have completed its course before reaching the target. Combinations and evasive maneuvers of the upper body while bridging the gap increase the probability of hitting your opponent, while decreasing the chances of being countered.

Techniques & Tactics to Increase Speed

When a body is involved in a circular motion, the diameter of the body affects the speed of movement. For example, spin around on the ball of one foot. Attempt to spin about three revolutions. While spinning, hold your arms out to your sides horizontally. Now do it again, only, after you have gone about 1/2 to 3/4 of the way around, quickly pull your arms into your chest. The speed in which you turn will increase dramatically.

You can use this same law of physics on some of your techniques. The most appropriate technique is the ridge-hand. When you throw your ridge-hand out, just as it nears your opponent's head, snap it back in, bending the elbow, twisting the hand and forearm down as it makes contact. This snapping back dramatically increases the speed of the ridge-hand. Twisting the hand and forearm (in a counterclockwise motion if using the right arm) facilitates the shortening of the arc and increases the speed of the technique. The twisting of the hand and forearm also generates more power upon impact. This additional power is generated in the same manner as the power generated by the twisting of a straight punch as it makes contact.

Which is faster, a jab that whips out as the opponent steps in, or one that the whole body is behind lunging toward the opponent? Which has more power? The technique involving the entire body has more power, which should not be a surprise. But it is also faster, at least in one sense. When performed correctly, the pushing off the toes, driving through the knees and straightening out the hips, all add to the speed of the previous motion. In other words, the speed created from the drive off the toes is added to the speed generated by the quadriceps, and so on through the body. This continues through the shoulder. From here, the punch and the lunging punch consist of the same movements. Both culminate with the hand snapping over the wrist.

From a technical aspect, the lunging punch produces the faster strike because you have the speed of the punch and the speed of the lunge. The combination of this additional speed and having more weight behind it enhances the power. From a different aspect however, the technique is slower. Since the technique begins with a push off the ground and works its way upward, it can be detected much earlier. This may provide the opponent time to react, effectively making the strike slow. If you initiate the lunge at the same time you strike, you minimize your opponent's ability to perceive the attack and take action to some degree. Of course, for every gain there is a loss and doing that decreases the maximum possible speed of the punch. Since you initiated the punch at the same time you initiated the lunge, you can not add the speed of each successive body part because you have lost the coiling effect. Much of this action is now occurring simultaneously. Therefore, this method of simultaneous lunge and punch is slightly slower, as far as the speed of movement goes, when compared to the technique that begins with a lunge and rolls up the body.

The simultaneous lunge-punch technique may be slower than the lunge-punch technique that rolls up the body, but as stated above, it is harder for your opponent to perceive. Since the punch starts when the lunge starts, it reaches the target earlier. Yet, it is not traveling as fast as the rolling technique.

The slowest moving jab, or back-fist, is the one that does not incorporate body movement. It comes out from the shoulder only. This method is the hardest for your opponent to perceive. There is no body movement for him to observe, only the hand moving straight at him. Remember the zero perception angle? Since the moving hand is the only thing he can perceive, his perception time will be quite a bit longer because of the reduced amount of visual stimulus and the zero perception angle.

If speed is your goal and power is not an important factor, then don't wait for your body to get behind your punches. Do not wait for your foot to hit the ground, or to approach the ground before striking your target. You can move your hand much faster than you can move your body weight by stepping. Execute the technique as the foot lifts off the ground and by the time it approaches the ground, you should be completing your next strike. Strikes of this type are only applicable for tournaments, light contact sparring, or soft tissue targets, such as the throat, eyes and groin.

Keeping the above in mind, why do many experts say that the hand should move first? Bruce Lee, fencing experts and swordsman Miyamoto Musashi have all stated that the hand should move first. As far as fencing and sword fighting go, it is important to move the hand, and therefore the sword, before lunging forward. Since the stakes are grave if an error is made, it would be foolish to step forward without first taking a measure to prevent your opponent from wounding you. The first movement is directed, not at your opponent, but at his sword. Deflecting or faking for his sword can usually be accomplished without lunging or by taking only a small step. Once the gap has been made safe to enter, then the lunge and strike occur. Therefore, for survival reasons, the hand moves first when sword fighting.

As far as punching goes, it depends on the circumstances. For instance, if the distance to your opponent is such that an average size lunge is required to reach him, it would not be beneficial to start your strike by moving the hand first. If you did, the strike would have completed its path before the movement of your lunge carried you close enough to hit him.

When throwing an arced strike, such as a back-fist, ridge-hand, spinning crescent kick or roundhouse kick, the momentum starts at one end of the body and moves along it like a wave toward the point of impact. The same mechanics are involved when throwing a ball. All the accumulated speed is present at the elbow when the forearm snaps over it. When the wrist and fingers come into play, even more speed has been generated. To take advantage of these mechanics, it is important to involve each segment of the movement as late as possible. If one segment is started too early, the previous segment will not be able to reach its peak speed. The resulting summation of speed of the two segments will then be diminished.

You can also increase the speed by fully stretching the part of the body that is about to snap forward. Referring to the baseball example, before the elbow is snapped forward, the chest and front deltoid muscles of the pitcher should be stretched back and out. This provides for maximum range of movement for acceleration and it incorporates the intrafusal fibers (stretch receptors). Before snapping out the elbow in a back-fist, the shoulder should be pulled in, across and in front of the chest. This stretches the upper back and the rear deltoid muscles. These are muscles involved in the pulling of the elbow outward. This increases the top speed of the back-fist. Again, by allowing each segment of the body to complete its movement, and by providing a full range of movement and stretch to increase speed further, the actual execution time of the technique will be slower. The hand moves faster, but the time from start to finish is longer.

The final segment of the technique, such as the wrist snap in the back-fist, should be postponed until the instant before contact. The final phase of the technique should be the fastest. Visualize maintaining the acceleration as long as there is contact with the target. This is what instructors mean when they say to punch through your opponent. It is not simply allowing your momentum to carry your punch after contact has been made. Continue driving, accelerating through the opponent. However, only allow your technique and inertia to continue carrying you into and beyond your opponent if this follow through will not interfere with the speed of the next movement. (48)

Here's an example of the above when performing a spinning crescent kick. The kicking leg should be dragging slightly behind the spin of the body. As you are completing your spin around toward your opponent, the position of this leg, which has not caught up with the body, should be causing a stretching feeling in the outside buttock, thigh and lower back muscles. By doing so, you are in the proper mechanical position to develop the maximum possible speed. Incorporate this stretch with the above principle of initiating each segment at the last possible moment, along with coordination, fluidity of movement, and control over the antagonist muscles, to create perfection in motion.

The following is a list of common telegraphing mistakes:

- Looking/glancing at where you are about to strike.
- Dropping your hand prior to punching.
- Chambering your hand before punching.
- Raising your shoulders prior to attacking.
- Leaning forward before lunging.
- Turning your feet and or hips prior to a spinning kick.
- Making facial expressions prior to attacking.
- Tensing up before attacking.
- Pulling up your pants prior to kicking.
- Attacking in stages instead of creating an instantaneous explosion of movement.
- Shifting your feet and or weight prior to kicking or lunging.
- Making minor movements, especially with the hands, before attacking.

Many of the above mistakes, but especially the last two, can be masked by continual movement of the hands, head, torso and feet.

*To develop a fast jab and back-fist, imagine a fly
on the wall. Not only is the fly incredibly fast,
but if you hit the wall too hard, you will injure
your hand. Try to smack the fly as quickly as
possible, remembering that power is your enemy.*

Chapter 16
FASTEST HAND TECHNIQUES

This chapter is a comparison of the speed values of various techniques and why one style can be superior to another in terms of execution time. As a rule, hand techniques are faster than foot techniques. This is primarily due to two reasons:

1) The arms are much lighter than the legs.
2) You are standing on your legs, so before you can kick, you must first take your weight off one foot, transfer your weight to the other foot and then kick with your free leg. Besides being slower, maintaining your balance and landing a successful kick is trickier. And of course, leg techniques require a greater expenditure of energy.

Finger Jab

As far as hand techniques go, the finger jab/flick is the fastest for several reasons. First, comparatively speaking, it requires very little power. Furthermore, it is a relatively safe technique because there is virtually no commitment to it. The faster the technique, the less power generated, therefore, more precision is required because you must make contact with a more vulnerable area. The most obvious target of the finger jab would be the eyes.

Another reason the finger jab is faster than a punch is because the hand remains open. You do not have to exert any energy clenching your fist as you do with a punch. This allows you and your arm to remain more relaxed, resulting in a quicker attack. You may also have less psychological tension with this technique because it requires less commitment. Some fighters do not hold back as much under these circumstances.

There is an increase in the length of your weapon with the finger jab as opposed to the punch. This means you will not have to move your body forward as much to close the gap between yourself and your opponent. Since striking out with the hand is significantly faster than closing the distance, the less you have to move the body forward, the faster the technique. The finger jab provides approximately four additional inches. If you incorporate the shoulders and a twisting of the body, you can continue to increase the reach of this technique. To illustrate, when performing a finger jab with the right hand, turn to the left, pointing your right hip toward your opponent, and extend your right shoulder. This adds roughly an additional five inches. That means this style of finger jab would have about nine inches over the traditional or standard jab, cross or middle punch.

Another reason this technique is faster is its zero perception angle. The hand moves out straight toward the eyes, not arcing or in a line across the path of the eyes. Remember the example of watching an arrow shot directly at your eyes versus watching one moving across your field of vision.

Disadvantages:

Difficulty in hitting a small, mobile target.

Cross

When throwing a right cross, pull your left arm & fist back to your body. Bringing your left arm back while extending your right helps rotate your hips, increasing your power. Timing is crucial. The technique starts with a drive off the ball of the rear foot, continues through the legs, hips, torso, shoulder and finishes with the rotation of the arm. The arm goes out straight. The arm also comes back straight. When retracting a cross, reverse the body mechanics that extended the punch. Don't simply pull the arm back. Use the reverse snapping of the body to snap the hand back into place. The result is a faster withdrawal.

Advantages:

Performed properly, the cross is a fast and powerful punch. Also, it is harder to perceive something, in this case a hand and arm, coming directly toward you, as opposed to a technique coming from the side, such as a hook. This is especially true when aimed directly at the eyes. This increases your opponent's perception/reaction time, which adds to your speed in the sense that you have additional time to complete the maneuver before he realizes it's coming.

Back-Fist

Relaxing with this technique is very important. Many people try too hard with the back-fist. When attempting to develop a fast jab and back-fist, imagine a fly on the wall. Not only is the fly incredibly fast, but if you hit the wall too hard, you will injure your hand. Try to smack the fly as quickly as possible, remembering that power is your enemy.

When withdrawing the back-fist, use the same method as for other techniques. Snap it back by moving the body. Not only does this help to quickly retract the fist, but it increases the effectiveness of the technique. To reverse the wrist snap as it makes contact, the wrist must be kept loose. If it is tensed up, the snap will be greatly diminished, both forward and backward. Therefore, the reverse snap ensures that the wrist is held loosely. This, in turn, increases the speed of the forward snap, resulting in an overall increase in the speed of the fist as it contacts the target. This also increases power.

Referring to the subsection on physics regarding snapping techniques, the shorter the time the hand is in contact with the target, the better. The opponent must absorb the power in less time resulting in a more effective technique.

Performance Tip

When throwing a back-fist, keep the wrist loose, allowing the hand to whip forward and then back upon impact. This increases the snapping effect and the speed of the technique by allowing for a maximum level of relaxation in the arm and by increasing the whipping action of the hands.

Jab & Step

It is a good habit to extend your jab before your front foot hits the ground. Not only is it crucial to get the jab out and back quickly when there is an opening, but, you also want your weight behind the jab. If your foot hits the ground first, or at the same time, some of your weight that could be behind the jab is now going into the ground.

If the jab is a feint, then it does not matter when the forward foot hits the ground, except that the jab is much faster than the foot and you do not want to slow it down by timing it with the foot. Many people time their punches with their steps. Don't get into this habit. Few things will slow you down more than this. You can throw several punches in the time it takes to step. Some people have a tendency to fall into this rhythm. Not only does this make them slow, but also vulnerable to sweeps.

When your opponent jabs at your face, as soon as he starts to retract it, follow it back into his face. Imagine there is a string attached to both gloves. When he starts to pull his jab back, launch your jab, staying as close to his hand as possible, one to two inches away at the most. Your hand should follow the same path as his. This hides your jab in the shadow of his jab. When his jab gets back, your jab comes crashing through, too late for him to react. This simple strategy makes your jab seem incredibly quick.

Performance Tip

Twist the jab as you throw it. The left hand should rotate in a clockwise manner in the same way that a middle punch does. This last minute twist increases the speed and power of the punch.

Sliding Back-Fist

To increase your speed, abruptly move/snap your feet closer together as you punch. Rise up on your toes and slide each foot together, meeting directly under your body. The rear foot moves forward, the front foot moves back. You will end up on the balls of your feet. As unusual as it may sound, this increases your speed and reach.

Advantages:

Increases your speed and reach, therefore, the chances of striking your opponent have increased.

Disadvantages:

High center of gravity. Not well balanced. This technique requires a relatively high level of commitment.

This illustration depicts the final position of execution for the sliding back-fist. Both feet slide together and up onto the balls of the feet.

The Blinding Jab

This technique works best on southpaws, although it is also effective with right-handed fighters. Throw your jab at his eyes. If you hit him, great, if not, it's still effective because it blocks his vision. Either way, leave your hand in front of his eyes for a fraction of a second to blind him.

At the same time as you launch your jab, step forward and a little to the left. This will not raise his suspicions because people frequently step with their jab. As your glove is blinding him, and at the same time you are stepping, bend your legs and get low, preparing to hook him in the floating rib. As you are getting into the final position, bring your jab down and hook him. This should all be one movement. When done properly, your movement is obscured by your jab and you are able to successfully hook him. If the hook is successful, he will most likely drop his hands to protect his ribs. This gives you an opportunity to throw a second hook to his exposed head.

Double Jab/Kick

Doubling up on your jab can increase your speed in two ways. First, the second jab does not re-chamber completely. It only travels back part way, just enough to have sufficient space to generate adequate power. The shorter distance results in a faster delivery time. Second, it can frequently catch your opponent off guard. Perhaps the first jab caused him to blink, or better yet, hit him in the eyes, disrupting his vision. Possibly, your opponent thought that the attack was over, or that you were going to follow up with another technique. The result is a jab that appears to come out of nowhere, so quickly that there is no time to react.

Doubling up on your kick has the same effect for the same reasons. If the kick is not toward the eyes, obviously you do not generate the same blinding effect. However, you could use hand movements to distract your opponent just as you are finishing the first kick. This can have the same effect, causing the second kick to be perceived only after it's too late.

Opposing Forces Punch

This technique increases the actual speed of your punch. To illustrate how it works, snap your fingers. Create that loud popping sound as your middle finger slams into the base of your thumb. Now try to create the same sound without first bracing your middle finger against the tip of your thumb. Attempt to slam your finger into the hand without using the thumb as a releasing mechanism. You can't do it can you? You can't produce nearly the same volume of sound because you can't develop the same speed that's produced when you snap your finger. The reason your finger moves so much faster when you snap it is because you have already begun contracting the muscles involved in its movement. When you don't snap it, the finger's movement is initiated by starting to contract the muscles. When you snap the finger, the muscles have already begun to contract. They are not starting out from ground zero. In fact, they are starting at nearly their maximal firing rate. The finger is attempting to contract as fast and as powerfully as it can. Only, its movement is blocked by the thumb. Allow the finger to slip over the thumb and the "horse" comes out of the blocks at or near it's maximum speed. There is no time wasted for acceleration. When you don't snap the finger over the thumb, the finger never has the opportunity to even approach the same speed achieved through the snapping method. This principle can be applied with punches.

Take the back-fist as an example. The back-fist will shoot out substantially faster if you use the principle of opposing forces. Instead of simply executing the punch, hook the thumb of the hand about to punch with the index finger of the other hand. Forcefully contract the muscles of the punching hand. Don't contract all the muscles, only the ones involved in executing the punch. The hand should be exerting a lot of force on the index finger in its attempt to break free and fly forward. Now release the hook of the index finger and allow the fist to fire forward. This technique dramatically increases the speed of the punch during the extension phase, however, it does not increase the speed of the return. Experiment with different methods of executing this technique with different punches.

Performance Tip: Punches

If you can maneuver yourself or your opponent into a position where you can hit him without having to lunge forward, your speed will increase dramatically. Or at least, your opponent will think so.

Another method of being able to hit your opponent without having to lunge forward is to turn your hips and bend your knees. This technique is only practical for one-shot scenarios, such as tournament fighting or for some street applications. Take, for example, the scenario that someone grabs you by the throat with one or two hands. It does not matter if his arms are longer than yours. If they are, you cannot strike or gouge him without changing the situation. If you attempt to punch him in the throat, you will be unable to reach. To reach him, turn ninety degrees to your left, bending the knees. Your right knee ends up facing to the left. Your right hip and shoulder end up pointing toward your opponent. Your right punch has gained several inches in distance. By turning your body this way, you have increased your reach and power significantly. You have also increased your speed because you hit him without having to move your body forward.

Performance Tip: Straight Punches

Straight punches are the fastest because they travel the least distance to their target. The shortest distance between two points is a straight line. Therefore, keep all your straight techniques straight, both on the delivery and the return. Any variance to this slows down the technique. Most people have a tendency to circle their techniques, on the way out, on the way back, or both. The two most common examples of this involve the jab and the cross. Most people begin the jab with good form, shooting it out straight, turning the hand over as it nears the opponent. However, at that point, it tends to go downhill. The jab then takes a dive downward, making a semicircle back to the on-guard position. A good fighter knows that his straight jab can beat your circular jab and will effectively counter your primary offensive and defensive technique.

Performance Tip: Crosses

The cross is even more commonly flawed. Frequently, the elbow is lifted up and out to the side. This not only reduces power, but it telegraphs your attack. Keep the elbow down. After the cross is extended, it should appear that you are looking down the barrel of a rifle with your chin down, arm and body lined up. Most fighters however, do not stop and retract here. They continue the cross in an inwardly curving and downward arcing direction. This robs the technique of speed and power. This also exposes you to a counterattack for a substantial amount of time. Shoot the cross out straight and then snap the body back. The cross should come back straight. You want to use the principle of a straight line being the shortest distance in both your attack and recovery.

Performance Tip: Hooks

The most common error with hooks causes them to be extremely slow. Many people drop their arm and pull it way back before launching. It begins to resemble your basic hay-maker. The dropping and pulling back telegraph your intentions a mile away. Your grandmother could slip that one. The hook doesn't need any chambering at all. Simply lower the hand from eye level and whip the body. This action flows smoothly from a slip. The bending and slight twisting away of the upper body hides the lowering of the hand and provides a natural chambering.

As the body turns, starting at the ball of the front foot, moving through the waist and continuing with the upper torso, the shoulder lags behind. The shoulder must remain loose to execute the hook this way. As the upper torso continues turning away from the hooking shoulder and toward the target, it reaches a point when the shoulder must begin turning because it is at the end of its range of flexibility. As the arm begins to be pulled around, start driving the arm with your chest and shoulder muscles. This delayed whipping of the arm across the body combined with the normal muscle mechanics results in a fast and powerful hook.

Performance Tip: Withdrawal of Punches

Many people get lazy and allow for extra time during the withdrawal of a kick or punch. Don't let yourself become one of them! Not only are you more vulnerable to being countered because of your slow withdraw, but this slows down your next movement as well. You should work at top speed, the 98% level as discussed in *Chapter 14*, during every aspect of your attack. If you retract your kick at full speed, not only are you able to continue with your combination faster, but you are in an accelerated mental state, ensuring that your next attack is at full speed.

Stop Block

A stop block is a parry of a jab. The rear hand moves out across the face and taps the incoming jab just before it would land. Do not reach out for it. Parry it at the last second. If you reach out for it, your opponent will observe this fault and next time, he will throw a feint jab and hook your head as you reach out for the jab. When you stop block correctly, it frequently causes the withdrawal of your opponent's jab to move in an arc. As you know from above, your straight jab can beat his arcing jab. Just after you stop block, shoot out your jab and beat him back.

Sticks & Other Weapons: Increasing the Speed

One method of increasing the speed of a stick this is to hit the stick with another stick. This technique is most easily performed if you hit the stick downward then allow the stick to circle around and up into your opponent. This technique is designed to add the speed obtained from hitting your striking stick to the speed of your normal swing. To clarify, if you wish to strike with your right stick, initiate movement of the right stick by hitting it with the left stick. To maximize the speed gained, hit the right stick near the tip. This technique increases the speed at which the stick moves, however, it involves a circling first. Therefore, the actual time from initiation to reaching the target is increased because of the distance traveled.

It is possible to take advantage of this principle without the circling of the stick. This method is more difficult, but since the distance traveled is less, the technique is faster. To illustrate the basic idea, hold the right stick up in front of your face. Snap it out into your target. Now, initiate the snap action by striking the stick with the left stick.

You can also apply these tactics when sparring with just one stick. Hit the stick with your left hand to speed its movement. For example, if you are going to circle the stick down and back up into your target, begin the circle by hitting the stick downward with the left hand. If the stick is across your body and you are about to swing it to the right into your target, begin the swing to the right by hitting it with the left hand.

Another tactic to increase the speed of the stick involves a form of bouncing. For illustration purposes, snap the stick at a wall, attempting to come within one inch of the wall without touching it. Do this as fast as you can. Now do it again, hitting the wall. You are able to complete your technique, the strike and retraction, much faster bouncing off the wall. Next, with the right hand, swing the stick as if making a strike to the left side of your opponent's head. It does not matter if the right palm is facing the ground or facing to the left as the stick nears the target. Before hitting the target, with your left hand, strike your right forearm just below the wrist. This causes the hand and stick to snap over the wrist, greatly increasing your wrist snap, and thus, increasing the speed.

Technically speaking, the above comparison is not accurate. The wall example involves a bounce, whereas the wrist example involves an increase in the whipping action of the wrist. However, both examples illustrate how you can increase speed by incorporating bouncing and whipping actions into your techniques. Think about how you may be able to incorporate these tactics into your sparring using the weapons and techniques you already know.

Remember the technique involved in the opposing forces punch? Remember the example of how snapping the finger increases the speed of movement of the finger? You can use the same technique to increase the speed of your stick. This technique won't work if the stick is held up above your head. You can apply it if you are holding the stick in front of your chest, however. Holding the stick in front of your chest, brace the tip of the right stick against the left stick. Contract the muscles of the right arm in an attempt to strike your target with the right stick. The stick should be flying toward the target except that the left stick is preventing it from doing so. Allow the right stick to slide off the end of the left stick when your want to strike. The speed of the movement is increased because the muscles involved in accelerating the stick have already begun to contract prior to the beginning of the actual strike. If you are sparring with only one stick, you can block the right stick with your left index finger to accomplish the same results. The technique is easier using your finger rather than another stick.

Here's another method of increasing the speed of your strike. The same rules apply to this technique as they do to most others. That is, by gaining one aspect of speed, the speed of execution, you sacrifice the top speed of movement and the power of the technique. As you know, many techniques obtain their top speed by adding the speed generated from one part of the body to the speed generated from the next part of the movement. Recall the example of the baseball pitcher where the speed produced by the arm moving over the fulcrum of the elbow is added to the speed already generated by the movements of the pitcher. The movements of the wrist and fingers snapping forward increase the speed of the throw even more. As explained earlier, the same technique can be employed to deliver a fast, powerful punch or kick.

You can use the same technique when delivering strikes with sticks. This technique will generate fast execution speed, however the speed of movement and the power of the strike may leave something to be desired. From the basic striking position, with the right hand up near the face, position number one in some styles, perform a strike directed down at your opponent's neck. (Note: This technique is much more effective for a left foot forward, right hand back stance with the right hand striking. If the right foot is forward, most of the shortcut gained through this technique is lost.) Notice how your hips and shoulders rotate to the left during the strike. Strike again, only this time, rotate the hips and shoulders to the left prior to starting. The strike will not be very powerful, but you'll be able to snap the stick out at your opponent's wrist more quickly. Rotate your torso and wait for the right time to strike. Or create a striking opportunity. If you employ this technique sparingly, your opponent won't learn to recognize the preset position.

You can also increase the speed of the stick by increasing your skill in snapping the wrist. Practicing the snap increases the myelination, which increases coordination and fluidity.

If your weapon requires the use of both hands, remember to use opposing forces to your advantage. In other words, if wielding a sword or a staff, when you move the weapon in just about any manner other than a thrust, push down with the hand that will end closest to the opponent and pull up with the other hand. If you are right handed, grip the sword with your right hand near the tsuba and your left hand at the end of the handle, near the kashira. When you make a downward slice at your opponent's shoulder, the right hand pushes the sword down and the left hand pulls up on the handle. When stick fighting with only one stick, if you want to increase the speed of the stick for one strike, you can use the same tactic. Grab the very end of the stick with the left hand and apply the opposing forces technique as described above.

Another way you can significantly increase the speed of your sticks, and all weapons for that matter, is to increase your strength. Snapping a stick out and back requires a lot of strength. The heavier the stick is and the faster it moves, the more strength it takes to stop and reverse the action. Recall the discussion about inertia in *Chapter 1*. The moving stick wants to continue moving in the same direction. It takes strength to overcome this inertia. The faster it moves and the heavier it is, the more inertia it has.

By increasing your strength, you are able to stop the stick and change directions more quickly. You are also able to initiate movement faster from a stationary stick. To increase your strength, train with heavy weapons and lift weights. If you train with sticks, spar with PVC pipe, wrapped with insulation foam and then duct tape. To further increase the weight, tape a cut out tennis ball at the end of the stick. This also makes for good negative reinforcement training. The welts you receive on your body continually remind you not to make the same mistake again.

If you train with a staff, try performing your katas with a barbell. Train with this exclusively for one month. Then pick up your wooden staff. You'll be amazed at how fast you can manipulate it. You may want to tape your wrist when training with the barbell, otherwise it could prove to be stressful on the joints. This type of strength training can be devised for any type of weapon.

You can obtain several inches of extra reach
and increase your speed by bending the knee of
your supporting leg.

Chapter 17
FASTEST KICKS

Front Leg Groin Kick

This is one of the fastest kicks because the foot is close to its target. The short distance to the target translates to less perception and reaction time for your opponent and therefore a faster technique. In addition, less power is necessary because you are targeting a vulnerable area.

When kicking your opponent's groin or a higher target, the kick is a two part technique. First raise your knee and then snap out the kick. If you are kicking your opponent's shin and it is within one or two feet of your foot, the kick is faster if you execute it as a one part technique. Start kicking your foot out at the same time that you begin raising your knee. This may take a little practice, but it's definitely faster. For both forms of front kicks, relaxation of the kicking leg is of the utmost importance for the production of speed.

You can obtain several inches of extra reach and increase your speed by bending the knee of your supporting leg. Skeptical? Try this easy experiment. Keeping your supporting leg nearly straight, hold your foot out as if kicking your opponent's knee with a front leg kick. Now bend your knee. Observe how your foot extends a few additional inches. This trick also works for side kicks, however, the gain in reach is not as dramatic.

Slightly leaning your upper body back in the opposite direction of the kick, facilitates the bending of your knee. You can also obtain a few more inches of reach by simultaneously skipping your supporting leg forward. This skip occurs simultaneously with your kicking motion.

Front Leg Knee Kick

This is also one of the fastest kicks because your opponent's front knee is the closest target to your front foot. Any number of kicks can be used to target this vulnerable area. If you can get him to straighten his knee first by leaning back in reaction to a punch to the face, the knee becomes even more vulnerable.

Spinning Crescent Kick

There are two primary tricks to learn and one common fault to avoid to increase the speed of your spinning crescent kick. The mistake almost everyone makes to some degree is telegraphing. Most people warn their opponent of their intentions by preceding the kick with a slight turn of the front foot or hips. You have to avoid this at all cost. The two tricks soon to follow help, but most of the work must come from an effort to avoid telegraphing. You will find it helpful to use this kick as a combination, starting with other punches or kicks that start the body making the appropriate movements.

To increase your speed, first think of lifting and turning with your back knee. The more powerfully you drive the knee up and around, the faster you move. When practicing the technique, feel your knee, nothing else. Don't extend your leg. Let the momentum of your knee turn you too far. Then you'll know you're doing it right. Extend the kicking leg at the last possible moment. The tighter you keep your body, the faster you'll rotate. This goes for your arms as well. Throw a jab prior to starting the kick. Then as you start to turn around, bring that arm in to protect your head. You will also be increasing your speed of rotation.

The other trick for increasing the speed of this kick is to rise up onto the ball of the front foot. Do not keep your body weight on the front foot as you are turning. Your weight should be lifting up, driving your knee up and around. You should feel as if the ball of your front foot is about to lift off the ground. When you feel this, you are executing the kick near top speed. Of course, you lose a little balance and control by using these tricks, but your kick will be much faster.

Lunging Crescent Kick

Assume your fighting stance. For example purposes use a left leg forward stance. Quickly shuffle your feet forward so that your right foot lands a little beyond where your left foot was. It may seem as if both feet leave the ground at the same time, however when done properly the right foot leaves the ground before the left foot does. As a martial artist, you should have this shuffle down smooth, both forward and backward.

Shuffle forward again, only this time, finish with your left knee up near your chest. Do it again and execute a crescent kick that would sweep across your opponent's face from your right to your left. Feel your lower leg snapping out and back down in an arc. Your knee acts as a loose hinge. It should feel as if your leg is whipping out and in, with your knee as the fulcrum point. Remember how it feels when your hand whips over your wrist in a loose back-fist? Try to achieve the same kind of speed by generating whipping action with your lower leg.

This technique can also be used to bring down your opponent's guard. Remember to jab when you start this kick.

Advantages:

This kick is very fast and it covers a lot of ground, making it good for closing the gap. It's also an unusual kick, making it unexpected, and therefore fast.

Disadvantages:

This kick requires that both feet leave the ground at the same time. Because of this and because it is a crescent kick, it's only a tournament technique. Though it's effective and pretty for point fighting, don't try it on the street.

<u>Rising-Heel Groin Kick</u>

Facing forward in your fighting stance, swiftly twist halfway around, shifting all weight to your rear leg. From a left foot forward stance, twist to the right 180 degrees so that your back is now facing your opponent. Quickly lift your left foot up, keeping your left leg fairly straight. This becomes a rising heel strike to your opponent's groin.

This needs to be done as one continuous movement and as quickly as possible. You should practice this technique frequently not only to ensure accuracy and smoothness, but to keep your mental circuitry wired to execute this kick automatically when appropriate.

The technique primarily works as a counter to a kick, when your opponent's groin is vulnerable. It can be used as an attack as well, i.e.: jab to distract and execute the kick. However, because many fighters keep their groin closed off with their forward knee, you will find the kick most effective as a counter.

It is a fast kick because your foot is so close to the target. You should be able to kick him in the groin before he kicks you. Also, your torso bends forward significantly, away from your opponent, moving out of your opponent's range. You have another advantage. You are most likely targeting a more vulnerable area than he is. Not only is this a fast and frustrating technique to your opponent, it is an extremely powerful one.

Disadvantages:

Your back should be exposed to your opponent for only a fraction of a second, otherwise you'll be leaving yourself open to attack.

This is the final position as your heel slams into your opponent's groin. The hamstrings, gluteus and spinal erectors all work throughout the techinque, continually increasing the speed and power.

Accelerated Rising Heel Groin Kick

To increase the speed of the last technique, start with a push upward and backward with front leg while pulling forward with rear leg. Perform the kick as described previously, but push off the ground with your front leg. Continue the kick, snapping your hips around and over. The difference with this version is that along with using a seesaw motion to raise your striking leg, you are always pulling it up with your muscles, continually increasing your speed.

After you have initiated movement by pushing with the front leg and pulling with the rear leg, immediately follow by snapping the hips and body over so that they are facing the ground. Now you can use the hamstring, gluteus and spinal erector muscles to pull the leg up into his groin. The torso continues to drop down, using the seesaw action to increase the speed even more.

To ensure top speed, the snapping of your hips around should be more of a jump than a turn. You have to practice this one a lot (as with any new technique), but it is well worth the effort.

Advantages:

This is a very fast, very powerful kick aimed at a vulnerable target. Not many fighters are aware of this kick and still fewer use it. Not only does it surprise your opponent, but it causes him to significantly reduce the frequency of high kicks. This unplanned change in his fighting style increases his frustration, decreases his confidence, and causes him to hesitate. It's also a relatively safe kick because your torso moves out of range of your opponent, and since it is a counter to your opponent's kick, he is not in any position to counter your kick or to lunge forward.

Side Kicks

The four most common types of side kicks are:

1) The rear leg side kick. From a stance where the left arm and leg are forward, the body turns in a counter clockwise direction as the right leg extends out toward the target. The foot of the left leg turns up to 180 degrees, often ending with the heel pointing toward the target.

2) Spinning side kick.

3) Stepping through side kick. In this technique, the rear right leg steps forward and behind the left leg. The hips turn toward the target and the left leg extends out into the target.

4) Sliding side kick. This kick is similar to the stepping through side kick, except the left leg extends out to the target as the right leg moves forward. Both feet push off the ground simultaneously. The right foot lands about where the left foot was, with the heel pointing toward the target. The instant movement begins, the left leg shoots up for the kick.

These side kicks all include closing the gap. If an opponent lunges at you, close enough to side kick him without having to move forward, then the fastest type of side kick would be to simply thrust out your front leg into his on rushing body.

By far the slowest and the most powerful is the spinning side kick. The second slowest is the stepping through side kick. When the gap is small between you and your opponent, there is no difference in speed between the rear leg side kick and the sliding side kick. For purposes of this section, a small gap is defined as one where the target is close enough to reach with the rear leg side kick without having to move forward at all, other than the rotating of the left foot on the ground.

As the gap increases, the sliding side kick is faster than the rear leg side kick. In addition to arriving at the target sooner, you have much more reach with this kick. If the opponent moves back, you may not be able to reach him with the rear leg side kick, but with the sliding side kick you still may be able to kick him because of the extra reach of this kick.

The least powerful is the sliding side kick. The stepping through side kick and the rear leg side kick are more powerful than the sliding side kick for two reasons. When using the sliding side kick at close range, there is not sufficient distance to develop enough forward momentum of your body to create power. Since both feet are airborne simultaneously, you can't drive off your legs into your target. All power must come from the jump and the thrust of the leg.

With the other side kicks, you can continue driving off the ground as you kick your target. With a farther distance, for example, seven feet, the sliding side kick is faster and more powerful than the stepping through side kick. The rear leg side kick and the spinning side kick can't reach the target from long distances. At close ranges, the order from most powerful to least powerful is as follows: spinning side kick, stepping through side kick, rear leg side kick and the sliding side kick.

Performance Tip: Side Kick

The counterpart to the finger jab is the side kick, at least as far as reach goes. It is not the fastest. A front kick is faster. However, if the distance is relatively short, it would be faster to throw a side kick than to step and deliver a front kick. As always, use your hands to distract your opponent. An instant before you start to deliver a side kick to his knee, throw a jab and follow with a cross as your body starts to turn. The three-part combination flows very smoothly, each technique making the next one easier.

Use the same combination while adding another technique. The combination goes as follows: left jab, right cross with a simultaneous right leg sweep, immediately followed by a right leg side kick. The jab and cross combination sets up the body mechanics for the sweep, just as they do for the side kick. They also distract the opponent, allowing you to sweep his leg out from under him. At this point, circle your right leg around and deliver a side kick. The side kick is effective if the sweep drops your opponent, if he picks his leg up and you miss, if he blocks it, or if he places his weight on it and your sweep bounces off. Regardless, the side kick flows perfectly from the sweep and he won't be expecting it or prepared for it. This is a very effective four part combination.

Back Kicks & Side Kicks: A Tip to Increase Speed

Execution:

Include an act of deception.

Examples:

Pretend to hear something, or someone, and act as if you are turning in the direction of the 'noise', when in reality you are beginning to turn to execute a back or side kick.

-or-

'Preface' your technique by turning as if you are going to walk or run away.

Advantages:

This can undermine any foreshadowing of your technique and increase your opponent's perception time.

Disadvantages:

This is generally not practical for sparring. However, you may find it a useful trick in street fighting. But don't let your guard down. He may think that you are turning to run and use it as an opportunity to attack.

Side/Back Kick Hybrid

The following technique will not increase your speed, however, it will give you one or two more inches of reach and quite a bit more power. As your side kick is nearing the end of its extension and your target, roll your hips over so that your rear end is now facing upward and not to the side. The heel of your supporting foot is forced to turn more to accomplish this. The completed kick resembles a back kick.

Like most techniques, increasing the power usually increases your commitment and decreases the speed. This technique is no different. By increasing your commitment, the speed is decreased, at least as far as the recovery is concerned. The advantages include slightly more reach, therefore more penetration, and more power because there is additional hip torque. In addition, there is more power because the muscles involved with this kick, the hamstrings, glutei and spinal erectors are all stronger than the muscles along the outside of the leg and waist. True, these muscles are not the driving force, however, they play a part in the delivery and transfer of the force. This kick is also more powerful if the heel is used to deliver the kick versus the side or bottom of the foot as with the normal side kick. The heel has a greater tendency to contact the target using this technique than it does with the standard side kick.

Spinning Side Kicks vs. Spinning Back Kicks

Spinning Side Kick

Advantages:

Turning 3/4 of the way around, you are able to focus both eyes on your opponent, giving you better depth perception and greater clarity, which translates into better accuracy.

Disadvantages:

First, it is slower than a back kick since you have to turn farther around. Second, you are more likely to telegraph your move to your opponent because most people shift, reposition their feet and/or pivot their hips just before they execute this technique (because they have so far to turn). Third, a side kick is less powerful than a back kick. The major muscles used are the tensor fasciae latae (runs alongside outer thigh), the gluteus medius and gluteus minimus, quadriceps and the external obliques. Since this is not a common movement for one's thigh, the body has not dedicated many strong muscles for this purpose. Compare the size and strength of those muscles with the ones used in the execution of a back kick. They are the gluteus maximus, hamstrings, quadriceps and spinal erectors. Lastly, the point of contact is often the side of your foot, as opposed to your heel with the back kick. The greater surface area means that the force is dispersed over a larger area, resulting in less damage to your opponent. In addition, the side of your foot is mostly soft tissue, which also translates into a softer impact due to less energy transfer.

Spinning Back Kick

Initially facing your opponent, turn 1/2 way around (so that your back is facing your opponent) and lift your kicking leg up and back toward your opponent. (Kind of like a donkey kick.)

Advantages:

First, it's a faster technique than a spinning side kick because you do not have to turn around as far. Second, you are less likely to tip off your opponent by repositioning your body prior to executing it; and if you do have this habit, it's easier to break. Because the kick is faster and because there is less telegraphing with this technique, speed is also increased in the sense that you have cut down on the perception time of your opponent. Third, much more powerful muscles are used which means there will be more power to your technique. The major muscles used are the hamstrings, the gluteus maximus, the quadriceps to a degree and the muscles of the lower back, such as the erector spinae. Finally, the point of contact is the heel of your foot. The smaller surface area concentrates the force generated, and the heel bone also increases the force of impact by permitting more energy transfer, resulting in an overall greater impact.

Disadvantages:

You can only focus one eye on your opponent, so your accuracy may suffer.

Front Kick & Roundhouse Kick

You can increase the power of these kicks without decreasing the speed if your hands and arms are initially extended as opposed to holding them close to your body. As you kick, draw your hands into your body as you extend your kick. For the front kick, the hands are drawn in as the body tilts backward in a seesaw manner. The act of drawing the hands in increases the effectiveness of the seesaw action, thus increasing the power of the kick. For the roundhouse, the arms are drawn into the body in the opposite direction that the kick is traveling.

To provide cover and distraction, don't just extend your hands. Throw a few punches, then draw them back as you are performing your kick.

When performing a rear leg roundhouse kick, (left leg back), your leg moves in a circular direction to the right while the arms are pulled in a circular direction to the left. This action increases the ability of the muscles powering the kick to stabilize, thus increasing their ability to deliver force. This stabilization, caused by better balance, is due to the effect of the arms pulling in the opposite direction. The result of this is a minimizing effect on the net angular momentum. (23)

Advantages:

When kicking, maintain cover. Drawing in your arms helps ensure this.

Front Thrust Kick

You can move faster going forward than your opponent can going backward. Moving forward helps add power to your techniques. When your opponent is moving backward, it is very difficult for him to deliver a powerful strike. It is therefore advantageous to get your opponent moving backward. If he is hard to get to move backward, either because he stands his ground and fights or he side-steps well, a front thrust kick usually does the job. A good front thrust kick makes it hard to stand your ground and it is fast enough to prevent most people from side-stepping it. This kick works better at moving an opponent back than a right cross does because the upper body is much more mobile than the lower body. Many fighters can slip a cross without much trouble. Of course, you want to throw a jab/cross combination simultaneously with the kick.

There are many methods of executing a rear leg front thrust kick. Remember, as a rule, the faster the technique, the less power it has. The most powerful rear leg front thrust kick initially includes a lean forward with the torso. As the rear leg drives up and thrusts out, snap the arms and torso back so that your shoulders end up behind your hips. This movement causes the force generated from the seesaw action to be combined with the drive off the legs.

Using Your Dominant Leg

If you attempt to dunk a basketball, which leg do you take off from? If you are right handed, you most likely jump off the left leg. Odds are again that this leg is your stronger leg. If that is true, then the following rules should also hold true. When in the usual left leg forward stance:

1) Your front leg snap kicks are stronger. They probably won't be faster than your right leg front snap kicks because the right leg is more coordinated.

2) Your left leg front thrust kicks are weaker because your weaker leg is the one driving off the ground.

3) Your retreats are faster because the stronger leg is available to drive you backward.

4) Your lunge forward is slower because the weaker leg is responsible for the lunge.

This last point is the most important one concerning speed. Your attacks are slower than they could and should be. If maximum speed is needed for one technique or one combination, put your strong side forward. For most people this is the right hand and foot. This places the strongest leg in a position to power the lunge and/or the front leg thrust kicks. It also places the strongest and most coordinated hand and arm in the closest position to deliver the hand attacks. If you are involved in sustained sparring and want to incorporate the power techniques involving the rear limbs, spar with the dominate, usually the right, side back. In order not to let the speed of your forward lunge suffer, you need to increase the strength of your right leg, from the calf to the gluteus muscles.

High Kicks vs. Low Kicks

High kicks are slower. There's no getting around it. They take longer to execute for the following reasons:

1) The target is farther away. More distance to travel equates to more time.

2) Flexibility plays a role. Even if you are flexible, there is still resistance that your muscles must overcome. This includes the general viscosity of the muscle and the specific viscosity at the time, i.e., how warmed up are you. Also, recall the previous discussion of the stretch reflex in *Chapter 2*. It takes work to stretch the rubber band. All this results in a slower contraction.

3) Gravity. Your muscles must overcome the force of gravity. Therefore, of the strength supplied by the muscular contraction, less is available for speed production. This slows you down and decreases your power. In addition, you are more vulnerable when kicking high, and, as Christensen says in his book, *Speed Training*, (11) why pass up all those lower targets on the way to a higher, smaller and more mobile one?

Chapter 18
FAST ON YOUR FEET

The stance that provides a balance between the elements of power and solidarity and those of speed and mobility requires that your feet be under your body, approximately shoulder width apart. As a rule, the wider your feet, the more stable your stance and the more power behind your techniques. The narrower your stance, the more mobile you are and the faster your techniques are.

Some techniques are more forceful if initiated with the feet close together because the longer step now possible allows gravity to help generate inertia. For the proper stance, both knees are bent and the center of gravity is a little forward. The heel of the rear foot is raised and the foot is pointed forward, toward, or almost toward, the opponent. The front foot points in a little. Most or all of the weight of the front foot is on the ball of the foot. Depending on your style, the front heel can either be raised or touching the ground. If you don't have to worry about kicks to your front knee, keep the heel touching the ground. This slight contact aids in balance and decreases muscular tension.

Boxer's/Sprinter's Stance

Positioning:

- · Position your feet and legs as you would if about to sprint forward.

- · Place your left (or right) foot forward, in front of you, with the knee bent.

- · Place your rear foot behind you, knee bent, with the ball of your foot on the ground and your heel raised.

- · Weight distributed 50/50 on each foot.

- · Both feet and knees are facing forward, toward your opponent.

- · Your torso is slightly hunched over, leaning forward. This forward leaning stance makes you better able to absorb an attack and makes your forward lunge faster. The lean is very slight. You must be perfectly balanced. You don't want to be perfectly upright and definitely not leaning back.

- · Your shoulders should be rotated to the side a little. Only square your shoulders when going toe to toe with your opponent. This allows you to incorporate hooks, uppercuts, knees and elbows, with both sides. You don't have to square off for headbutts, but they will be more powerful if you do.

Advantages:

Increased speed and mobility. When you attack you are basically sprinting or lunging toward your opponent, so you want to have your entire body already positioned to execute this one step sprint or lunge. This is an ideal position to either lunge forward or backward. Initially faster, this standard type of lunge is better when your opponent is relatively close to you. It can also be used for long distances because it is effective for maintaining balance. To maintain balance, mobility and to avoid overcommitting, it is best to make two or more short steps rather than one long, deep lunge.

Tips (Do's & Don'ts):

Practice this stance until it becomes second nature to you. Once it has, you'll see how beneficial it is to your entire fighting style. Learn to move in this stance in all directions, incorporating your defensive and offensive maneuvers while moving.

Some Muay Thai kick boxing schools teach fighters to stay up on the balls of both feet. This position provides additional protection from leg kicks to the front knee. It adversely affects balance, however. If balance is a concern, keep the heel of your front foot on the ground to aid in balance while keeping most of the weight of the forward foot distributed to the ball of that foot. This adds a factor of safety to the front knee and maintains your balance.

Disadvantages:

The standard lunge from this stance is not as fast for longer distances. It is slower after the first ten inches or so.

Long Distance Lunge

From the same stance as in the standard lunge, initiate the lunge with a pulling action of the front foot. It's kind of like a skip. This technique is faster than the standard lunge when covering long distances for two reasons:

1) It uses the muscles of both legs to propel the body forward, rather than simply pushing off the rear leg in a standard lunge.
2) Because of the active role the front leg plays, the body never becomes overextended, therefore, negating the need to make two or more smaller lunges. This technique takes a lot of practice to develop a smooth lunge that you feel comfortable with. The rear foot leaves the ground first, but the front foot starts pulling before the rear foot starts pushing. That is crucial. The order of movement in its execution is as follows:

   1. Front foot pulls against the ground, as if pulling the body forward.
   2. Rear foot pushes, driving forward as in any lunge.
   3. Rear foot lifts off the ground.
   4. Front foot, still on the ground, changes from a pull to a push as the body moves over, and then forward of, the front foot.
   5. Front foot lifts off the ground.
   6. Rear foot contacts the ground.
   7. Front foot contacts the ground.

Advantages:

This is a faster lunge for longer distances. It can be very helpful when there is a wide gap, i.e.: when sparring someone very tall who has a longer reach than you, or when sparring with sticks or other types of weapons.

Disadvantages:

There are three primary disadvantages to this technique.

1. Because the first 12 inches of movement in this technique are slower than the first 12 inches of movement in the standard lunge, for short distances the standard style lunge is faster. (Note: the 12 inch mark is an approximation, it differs for everyone.)

2. Because this lunge is so much more complicated, it is harder to avoid telegraphing your initial movements. The movements must be explosive and coordinated smoothly or the lunge will be telegraphed.

3. Since both feet are off the ground at one point, you are more committed to the attack. You obviously cannot make any alterations to your forward movement while both feet are airborne.

Tips (Do's & Don'ts):

This is a unique and difficult long distance lunge. It was discovered while searching for optimal techniques for speed and power. You need to practice it frequently to develop coordination, but once you do, you will have added a valuable new technique to your repertoire.

Tips For All Lunges

Keep your body level. Any unnecessary change in height while executing a lunge wastes energy and slows you down. If you need to lower your center of gravity upon impact, that's OK. Raising your body means that instead of moving forward, some of your effort is wasted on overcoming gravity. Also, those

This illustration is a freeze frame of the technique at its midpoint. The martial artist started by pulling his left leg and pushing with his right leg. At this point, the right leg begins to pull, contracting the hamstrings and the left leg begins to push forward. The left leg is about to leave the floor as the right leg re-contacts the floor.

that raise up when they lunge frequently do it at the beginning, telegraphing their intentions.

Opposing Forces Lunge

This technique can be used for the standard boxer's lunge described previously. The trick is to drive off the rear leg without lunging, yet. You prevent any forward motion by pushing back with the forward leg. Then when you decide to lunge, all you have to do is to relax the forward leg. The muscles in the rear leg are already contracting. This makes for a faster contraction of the rear leg muscles. In theory, it should therefore translate to a faster lunge. This does not hold true for everyone. It depends on how quickly you can relax the quadriceps, the muscles of the front leg opposing the contracting muscles of the rear leg.

Disadvantages:

Since your opponent is able to see your quadriceps flexing if you are wearing shorts, you can't decide to do this only occasionally. Otherwise you will be telegraphing. Performing this technique frequently consumes a significant amount of energy.

Plyometric Lunge

Recall from *Chapter 2* that concentric contractions are more powerful when preceded by fast and deep eccentric contractions. In other words, they are more powerful when preceded by a plyometric movement. You can use this fact to increase the speed of your lunge.

Initiate your lunge with a quick bending of the legs. Dip down and then spring back, lunging at your opponent. Think of it like a broad jump. Before you attempt to jump as high or as far as you can, you first bend the legs. It's not the extra distance your legs have to contract that helps you. Even if you were to start at this position with the deeper bend, you wouldn't jump as high as you would if you started with the plyometric movement. The benefit also does not come from the inertia generated because you are moving in the wrong direction. The benefit comes from the physiology of plyometric movements discussed earlier in this book. Therefore, a faster method of performing the standard lunge is to initiate it with a plyometric movement.

Disadvantages:

The disadvantage to this technique is that the overall time of the plyometric lunge is slower that the standard lunge. The lunge is faster as far as the speed of movement goes, but the opponent has more time to perceive the attack. The dipping of the legs is also a form of foreshadowing, alerting the opponent that you are beginning to attack. You can overcome this disadvantage by faking the lunge or through constant movement. The constant movement helps hide the dipping of the legs and the fakes prevent the opponent from accurately associating the dips with the lunge.

Weight Distribution when Lunging

This section is a theoretical discussion about how body weight should be distributed to lunge forward at maximal speed. Tactics and mobility are not factors of consideration in this discussion. To increase the speed of your lunge, place more than 50% of your weight on your front foot and position your hips forward of your rear foot. The primary reason you need a good deal of your body weight on your rear foot is to provide friction. The less friction your rear foot has with the surface of the ground, the more weight you must place on that foot to keep it from sliding backwards when you push off it. You will also notice that as you move your hips over your rear foot, more weight is placed on that foot.

You want to have your hip forward of your rear foot because that is the direction you wish to move, forward, not up. If your hips are over your rear leg when the rear leg starts extending, the hips will be driven up. The farther forward the hips are, the more efficient your technique is because less energy is used to drive the hips up, resulting in a larger portion of the energy being used to drive the hips forward. Think of a sprinter in a sprinter's block. The reason he gets down so low is to position his hips forward, and not over, his driving legs. It's also important for the sprinter to begin his run in this leaning position. Many sprinters waste energy by standing up to quickly. This slows them down.

You do not want to have more weight than necessary on your rear foot because you have to move all of that weight forward at the very start of the lunge. For example, if 98% of your weight is on your rear foot, your rear foot has to push all 98% of that weight forward from the very beginning of the movement. If 40% of your weight is on your rear foot, assuming that you perform the lunge properly, your rear foot only has to push 40% of your body weight for the initial part of the lunge. This smaller amount of work translates to a faster muscular contraction. Also, when you are standing, you are fighting gravity. The more weight on your rear foot, the more work that leg is doing to fight gravity. Therefore, when you go to drive forward, less of the total power available in that leg is available to drive forward, because a larger portion of it is being used to fight gravity.

Performing the lunge properly means lifting the front foot off the ground, pushing up with the front foot as little as possible. If you drive up off the front foot, the hips are moved up and backward. This not only wastes energy, but it slows down the drive of the rear foot because the hips are now moving back, into the rear foot. The rear foot catches up to the remaining 60% of the body weight sooner, thereby slowing down the speed of its contraction because the amount of work it must perform is increased, and because the hips are moving in the wrong direction. You want to pick the front foot off the ground just enough to move it forward, or to allow the momentum of the body weight that is being driven forward, to push the front foot forward for you.

What is happening is that the hips and therefore the forward mass of the body, is falling forward. This is good. It's moving you forward. The amount of your fall is insignificant. The initial speed of a falling object is quite slow and you are only falling for a fraction of a second. At the same time, your rear leg is driving you forward. After 2-5 inches, the rear leg catches up with the fall. The speed of the forward fall is added to the speed of the driving of the body. The combined speed of the two parts means that you reach the place where the front foot contacts the ground quicker. The actual amount that you fell is indiscernible.

One of the disadvantages of this method of lunging is the short distance of the lunge. By not driving the hips up, the front foot must contact the ground closer than it would if you were to drive the hips up with a push off the front leg.

To position the hips farther forward of the rear foot, you can move the rear foot back or the front foot forward. This aids the drive forward, but the distance of the lunge is reduced by the same amount that you separated your feet. Other disadvantages to this wider stance are the decreased mobility if your opponent was to attack you and the foreshadowing it may provide to your opponent if he sees you separate your feet farther. How weight distribution and hip placement affects lunging is a difficult concept to grasp cognitively. However, if you stand up and experiment with the different positions and weight distributions discussed, you will quickly observe how the position of the hips influences the direction of the drive of the rear foot. Also notice how weight distribution affects the position of the hips and how the push up with the front foot affects the movement of the hips.

Again, this is a theoretical model. It may never be practical for you. However, if you are in a situation where you only need to lunge forward a few inches to deliver a hand strike and you have excellent traction for the rear foot, (perhaps a curb to push against), your forward lunge will be faster if you place the majority of your weight on your front foot and you refrain from pushing up any more than you have too with the front leg.

Side Stepping

The fastest method of side stepping is to take a small step with the right leg if moving to the right. If moving to the left, take a small step with the left foot while driving off the right leg explosively. Just as you begin to move, bend the upper torso to the left. This bend is not a forward bend. Imagine that a punch is coming at your head. Bend the torso to the side, allowing the punch to fly past your head. This bend increases the speed of your avoidance maneuver.

Sweeps

Sweeps can be devastatingly effective and demoralizing to an opponent not accustomed to them. When an opponent is not familiar with defending against sweeps or when he develops a pattern with his foot movements, sweep him and follow up. Of course, sweeping your opponent does not increase your speed, but if you can demoralize him, robbing him of his confidence slows him down.

The best time to sweep is when your opponent is stepping forward, when he is just about to transfer his weight onto his front foot. A sweep at that time often sends him to the floor. Look for a pattern in his steps. If there is one, time him and drop him. If he does not fall, for whatever reason, perhaps you were late and he had too much weight on his foot, the sweep often causes him to lose his balance. Immediately follow up. Take advantage of his vulnerability. Don't sweep without planning to follow up.

If you do not see a pattern in his foot movements, create one. Cause him to step in, chasing you. You could throw a jab and front kick combination and then step back. When he steps forward, sweep him. Again, always conceal your intentions with movement. While stepping forward to sweep, throw a jab and cross combination. He will focus on your attack and not take action against your sweep.

If you are fighting a southpaw or if he switches to this stance, you can effectively sweep him with your front leg. Wait until he steps forward, throw a jab and sweep the leg. Remember to follow up. You can also wait until he steps forward with his jab. Slip, or parry his jab, and sweep. When both of you are in a right hand back stance, you can also sweep with your front leg to the inside of his front leg, however, this technique is usually forbidden in schools and tournaments because of the increased risks to the knee.

Beginning fighters often commit themselves when kicking. In other words, they cannot retract the kicking leg because their weight is moving forward. They have to finish the kick with a step forward. The best way to correct this bad habit is to sweep them when they are dropping all their committed weight onto their front foot, just after they finish kicking.

Another sweep technique is to wait until your opponent is flatfooted. When he appears flatfooted or sluggish, sweep and follow up with a same-leg side kick. If both fighters are in a right hand back stance, with the left leg forward, move to sweep his left leg with your right leg while concealing your intentions with a jab and cross. Notice how these techniques flow together. Sweep the leg. If his weight is on it and it only knocks him off balance a little, that's okay, you can then drive your right leg into him with a side kick. After the sweep, the leg makes a small circle and delivers the kick. If he picked his foot up to avoid the sweep, now he is much less mobile, so make the small circle and deliver the side kick. This sweep also works as a very effective fake, leading into the side kick. The combination is jab, cross, fake sweep, side kick. Remember, start the sweep just after you start the jab.

Chapter 19
SUMMARY

Becoming an incredibly fast fighter is within the realm of possibility for everyone. Even those of you who believe that it's not in the cards you were genetically dealt, as this book has illustrated, the deck can be stacked. You can make significant improvements in every aspect of fighting speed, including increasing the velocity of your muscular contractions. If you train diligently in each of the areas of speed covered in this book, the resulting increase in your overall speed will be incredible. It just takes work.

In a study of motor expertise, Doctor Abernethy determined that "the amount of effortful practice is the single most important determinant of the acquisition of expertise." (1) To any martial arts instructor, and to the students as well, it's obvious which students really want to improve. It later comes as no surprise to everyone when those students are the ones to improve. Therefore, if you want to become a fast fighter, practice. Use the information in this book to make your training more effective and efficient, and practice. Most people only train when they are in some kind of formal setting, such as class. The vast majority do not practice what they were taught during the time between classes. If you practice just ten minutes every day, you will improve much more quickly than those who don't practice between classes.

Physical training is fun. It has immediate gratification and we live in a world where a pleasing physical appearance and good health are rewarded. Don't neglect the mental aspects of training however. Mental training is an integral element to your speed training. Just as with physical training, ten minutes each day of mental training will work wonders compared to a session with your instructor every now and then. This doesn't mean practice only ten minutes a day. It means that if you are going to make the excuse that you do not have enough time for a full practice each day, train for ten minutes on those days. Short practices done on a consistent basis can be very effective. You will find mental training especially effective when you come to a plateau and the gains from the physical training seem to slow significantly or stop altogether. During those times the mental training can be effective in breaking through the barrier and preparing you for another period of improvement.

As far as physical training goes, refer to *Chapters 2, 4* and *10*. Just kidding. To increase the speed of your lunges and side stepping, use heavy resistance training on your legs. The king of leg exercises is the squat. If you have a healthy back and knees, do squats regularly and follow a heavy weight, low rep routine. On a safety note, keep this in mind. Squats and skiing enable orthopedic surgeons to buy fancy cars. Maintain strict form with squats. Train your calves hard also. Remember to add plyometrics. They make your training program more effective. To increase the speed of your kicks, develop a flexibility routine based on the guidelines set forth in *Chapter 9*. Also include resistance training and half rep kicks which emphasize speed of movement and balance. The resistance training should involve explosive movements using approximately 33% of your one rep max.

To increase the speed of your hands, your training regimen should include half rep, speed shadow boxing, and explosive resistance training. As with the kicks, the explosive resistance training should involve explosive movements using about 33% of your one rep max. Remember, regardless of the weight used, on every repetition, on every set, for every muscle, the effort should be at 100%. The motor-neurons should be firing at your maximal rate. Always! If you are going to be wielding weapons, the stronger your upper body and arms, the faster you can manipulate the weapon. Therefore, like training your legs for lunges, include some heavy resistance training that allows you to perform no more than six to eight repetitions per set.

The best way to improve your speed skills in perception, analysis and decision making, in deceiving your opponent, and in defense, is through sparring. The more hours you spend sparring, the better and faster you will become. It's as simple as that. For those of you who do not like sparring, keep at it. You will learn to like it, especially if you like contact and/or competitive sports. It will most likely become a form of addiction, bringing you up when you are feeling down. Vary the types of sparring as much as possible. Fight different people, under different rules, with different weapons.

This way you develop a more thorough understanding of distance, perception, deceptive maneuvers, etc.

As a final note on training commitment, always strive to win, or to be the best you can possibly be. It makes the intensity and sacrifice of training easier to bear. Don't settle for, "I'd like to place in the top three," or "I hope I do well." That is a form of negative or defeatist thinking. It can hamper your progress. If it is within the realm of possibility, plan on winning.

Only settle for a lesser achievement if it helps you more thoroughly believe in your goals and mental imagery. The goals must be realistic. If you set unrealistically high expectations, or schedule an insufficient amount of time to achieve the goals, you will probably be disappointed with your performance and with yourself. This is one more reason to have detailed goals and to know where you stand in relation to your goals. It makes setting realistic, yet substantive, goals all the easier. You can, and should, be constantly reaching for ever higher accomplishments. But no one becomes an expert overnight. Set each new goal in a time frame that you truly believe you can achieve. And think positive. Don't let little set backs get you down. Whenever the course becomes frustrating, remember these wise words:

"The control of our being is not unlike the combination of a safe. One turn of the knob rarely unlocks the safe; each advance and retreat is a step toward one's final achievement." Author unknown.

GLOSSARY

Adrenaline: A hormone released to create an immediate, highly aroused state. Adrenaline overrides neurological safety mechanisms, permitting the individual to obtain a voluntary level of strength closer to his absolute strength level. Adrenaline also acts as a pain suppressor, sensory enhancer and a vascular manipulator.

Aerobic: For exercise purposes, it describes the production of energy through the use of oxygen.

Anaerobic: For exercise purposes, it describes the production of energy without the use of oxygen.

Antagonist muscle: A muscle that counteracts the action of another muscle.

ATP (adenosine triphosphate): A chemical compound that is the basis of energy production within the body.

Autonomic nervous system: The part of the nervous system that carries out automatic functions. The sympathetic and parasympathetic nervous systems are branches of the autonomic nervous system.

Basal metabolic rate: The metabolic rate measured during basal conditions: 12 hours after eating, after a restful sleep, no physical activity preceding test, in a comfortable temperature and lacking emotional excitement.

Bulboreticular: A fibrous tissue found in different areas of the body.

Capillaries: The network of microscopic blood vessels that carries blood to the cells of body tissue.

Cognitive: A conscious knowing, perception or awareness.

Collagen: A fibrous insoluble protein found in connective tissue, including muscle, skin, bone, ligaments and cartilage.

Concentric contraction: A shortening of the muscle fibers while the muscle is performing work. There is a corresponding change in the joint angle.

Dendrite: A branched portion of a neuron that conducts impulses to cell bodies and forms connections with other neurons.

Denervation: A loss of nerve supply to a muscle.

Dynamic: In the physical training world, dynamic refers to something that happens quickly. With stretching, it refers to a motion similar to a swinging of the limb. In strength training, it can reference plyometrics, or lifting weights that constitute about 33% of your one rep max, lifting them explosively during every rep.

Eccentric contraction: A lengthening, or stretching, of the muscle fibers while the muscle is performing work. There is a corresponding change in the joint angle.

Electroencephalogram: A device for measuring electrical activity of the brain.

Endocrine system: A system of glands responsible for the regulation of hormones, including adrenaline and endorphins.

Enzymes: Complex proteins capable of producing chemical changes in other substances without being changed themselves. They are capable of accelerating the speed of chemical reactions.

Hypertrophy: Increase in the size of the muscle.

Isometric contraction: There is no lengthening or shortening of the muscle fibers while the muscle is performing work. There is a no corresponding change in the joint angle.

Mitochondria: A slender structure found within cells responsible for energy production. They are also involved in protein synthesis and fat metabolism.

Motor neuron: A neuron that carries impulses initiating muscle contraction.

Motor unit: A single motor neuron and the muscle fibers its branches innervate.

Muscle elasticity: The ability of a muscle to stretch, store and release energy as the result of imposed tension.

****

Muscles

Each muscle is made up of FIBERS. Each fiber is made up of MYOFIBRILS. Myofibrils are further broken down into SARCOMERS. A bundle of sarcomeres laid end to end form one myofibril. Each sarcomere is made up of overlapping thick FILAMENTS consisting of MYOSIN and thin filaments consisting of ACTIN.

Actin: A protein present in muscle fibrils, comprising approximately 35% of total muscle protein.

Cross-bridge: Thick and thin elements of a muscle intermixing in the myofibrils.

Myosin: A protein present in muscle fibrils, comprising about 65% of total muscle protein.

Type I: Skeletal muscle fibers characterized as being slow to contract and slow to fatigue.

Type II: Skeletal muscle fibers characterized as being fast to contract and fast to fatigue.

****

Myelin: A fat like substance forming a sheath around the axons of nerves.

Myelination: The process of acquiring a myelin sheath.

Negatives: Exercises performed eccentrically.

Neuromuscular: Comprising both nerves and muscles.

P-NR-A-NR-D-NR-A: Perception>neurological relay>analysis> neurological relay>decision> neurological relay>action.

Parasympathetic nervous system: Responsible for normal functions necessary for life, including breathing, heart rate and digestion.

Parry: A defensive motion that moves an attacker's strike out of line and away from the original target.

Positron Emission Transaxial Tomagraphy (PET): A machine that utilizes radio labeled substances to measure different bodily functions in specific areas of the body.

Physiology: The science of the functions of the living organism and its components and the chemical and physical processes involved.

Plyometrics: A sudden overloading of the muscle while the muscle is being stretched. It is an eccentric movement, followed immediately by a concentric contraction, performed explosively.

Reinnervation: A return of nerve supply to a muscle.

Resistance training: Generally referred to as weight training, although other exercises such as push-ups and pull-ups are resistance exercises as well. Push-ups and pull-ups use body weight and gravity to provide the resistance.

Riposte: An attack immediately following a parry.

Satellite cells: Cells believed to play a role in the repair of damaged tissue.

Sympathetic nervous system: Responsible for emergency system responses, including but not limited to: the release of adrenaline and endorphins; increased sensory perception; constriction of capillaries at the skin, the extremities and the digestive system; increased blood flow to the major muscle groups.

VO2 Max: The maximal amount of oxygen your body can metabolize during exercise.

REFERENCES

1) Abernethy, Bruce. Training the Visual-Perceptual Skills of Athletes. Insights from the Study of Motor Expertise. Amer. Jrnl. Sports Med. 24/6: S89-S92, 1996.

2) Anderson, John E. If You Really Want to Succeed. At the Center of Sports Psychology, Colorado. By Reader's Digest, 5/1996.

3) Atha, J. Strengthening Muscle. Exerc. Sport Sci. Rev. 9:1-74, 1981.

4) Barnhart, Robert K. American Heritage Dictionary of Science. Boston: Houghton Mifflin, 1986.

5) Brooks, Susan V., and John A. Faulkner. Skeletal Muscle Weakness in Old Age: Underlying Mechanisms. Medicine and Science in Sports and Exercise. 26/4: 432-440, 1994.

6) Burke, Darren G.; Pelham, Thomas W., and Laurence E. Holt. The Influence of Varied Resistance and Speed of Concentric Antagonistic Contractions on Subsequent Concentric Agonistic Efforts. Jrnl. of Strength and Conditioning Research. V/13, #3, 193-197, 8/1999.

7) Cahill, Bernard R.; Misner James E., and Richard A. Boileau. Current Concepts. The Clinical Importance of the Anaerobic Energy System and Its Assessment in Human Performance. Amer. Jrnl. Sports Med. 25/6: 863-872, 12/1997.

8) Caiozzo, Vincent J., and Fadia Haddad. Thyroid Hormone: Modulation of Muscle Structure, Function, and Adaptive Responses to Mechanical Loading. Exercise and Sport Sciences Reviews, American College of Sports Medicine Series. 24: 321-361, 1996.

9) Carson, James A. The Regulation of Gene Expression in Hypertrophying Skeletal Muscle. Exercise and Sport Sciences Reviews, 25: 301-320, 1997.

10) Cartee, Gregory D. Aging Skeletal Muscle: Response to Exercise. Exercise and Sport Sciences Reviews, American College of Sports Medicine Series. 22: 91-120, 1994.

11) Christensen, Loren. Speed Training. How to Develop your Maximum Speed for Martial Arts. Boulder, Colorado: Paladin Press, 1996.

12) David, F. A. Taber's Cyclopedic Medical Dictionary. Philadelphia: F. A. Davis Company, 1985.

13) Delecluse, Christophe; Van Coppenolle, Herman; Willems, Eustache; Van Leemputte, Mark; Diels, Rudi, and Marina Goris. Influence of High-resistance and

High-velocity Training on Sprint Performance. Medicine and Science in Sports and Exercise. 27/8: 1203-1209, 1995.

14) Dengle, D.R.; George, T.W.; Bainbridge, C.; Fleck, S.J.; Van Handel, P.J., and J.T. Kearney. Training Responses InNational Team Boxers. Med. Sci. Sports Exerc. 19:277. 1987.

15) Derse, Ed. Explosive Power. Plyometrics for Bodybuilders, Martial Artists & other Athletes. Los Angeles: Health For Life, 1993.

16) Devor, Steven T, and Timothy P. White. Myosin Heavy Chain Phenotype in Regenerating Skeletal Muscle is Affected by Thyroid Hormone. Medicine and Science in Sports and Exercise. 27/5: 674-681, 1995.

17) Duchateau, Jacques. Bed Rest Induces Neural & Contractile Adaptations in Triceps Surae. Medicine and Science in Sports and Exercise. 27/12: 1581-1590, 1995.

18) Duchateau, Jacques, and Karl Hainaut. Isometric or dynamic training: differential effects on mechanical properties of a human muscle. The American Physiological Society. 296-301, 1984.

19) Ebben, William P., and Phillip B. Watts. A Review of Combined Weight Training and Plyometric Training Modes: Complex Training. Jrnl. of Strength and Conditioning Research. V/20, #5, 18-27, 10/1998.

20) Ekblom, Bjorn. Effects of Creatine Supplementation on Performance. Amer. Jrnl. Sports Med. 24/6: S38-39, 1996.

21) Essig, David A. Contractile Activity-Induced Mitochondrial Biogenesis in Skeletal Muscle. Exercise and Sport Sciences Reviews, American College of Sports Medicine Series. 24: 289-320, 1996.

22) Evans, William, by Bonnie Liebman. Exercise. Use It or Lose It!/ Delaying the Aging Process. Washington DC: Center for Science in the Public Interest. 22/10: 1-7, 12/1995.

23) Feld, Michael S.; McNair Ronald E., and Stephen R. Wilk. The Physics of Karate. Scientific American. 240: 150-158, 1979.

24) Fitts, Robert H., and Jeffrey J. Widrick. Muscle Mechanics: Adaptations with Exercise-Training. Exercise and Sport Sciences Reviews, American College of Sports Medicine Series. 24: 427-474, 1996.

25) Fleck, Steven J. Antioxidants and Athletic Performance. Lincoln, NE: National Strength & Conditioning Association, 1994.

26) Fleck, Steven J., and William J. Kraemer. Resistance Training: Physiological Responses and Adaptations. The Physician and Sportsmedicine. 16/3-6: March-June, 1988.   [4 of 4 parts.].

27) Fry, Andrew C.; Kraemer, William J.; Van Borselen, Fenke; Lynch, James M.; Marsit, Joseph L.; Roy, E. Pierre; Triplett, N. Travis, and Howard G. Knuttgen.

Performance Decrements with High Intensity Resistance Exercise Overtraining. Medicine and Science in Sports and Exercise. 26/9: 1165-1173, 1994.

28) Gaesser, Glenn A., and David C. Poole. The Slow Component of Oxygen Uptake kinetics in Humans. Exercise and Sport Sciences Reviews, American College of Sports Medicine Series. 24: 35-70, 1996.

29) Garfield, Charles, and Hal Z. Bennett. Peak Performance. Mental Training Techniques of the World's Greatest Athletes. Los Angeles: J. P. Tarcher, 1984.

30) Girouard, Cindy K., and Ben F. Hurley. Does Strength Training inhibit gains in Range of Motion from Flexibility Training in Older adults? Medicine and Science in Sports and Exercise. 27/10: 1444-1449, 1995.

31) Gould, Daniel, and Eileen Udry. Psychological Skills for Enhancing Performance: Arousal Regulation Strategies. Medicine and Science in Sports and Exercise. 26/4: 478-486, 1994.

32) Hackfort, Dieter. The Display of Emotions in Elite Athletes. Amer. Jrnl. Sports Med. 24/6: S80-S84, 1996.

33) Haff, Gregory G.; Stone, Michael H.; Warren, Robert K.; Johnson, Robert L.; Nieman, David C.; Williams, Franklin Jr., and K. Brett Kirksey. The Effect of Carbohydrate Supplementation on Multiple Sessions and Bouts of Resistance Exercise. Jrnl. of Strength and Conditioning Research. V/13, #2, 111-117, 5/1999.

34) Hakkinen, K.; Komi, P. V., and M. Alen. Effect of Explosive Type Strength Training on Isometric Force and Relaxation time, electromyographic and muscle fiber characteristics of leg extensor muscles. Acta Physiol. Scand. 125:587-600, 1985.

35) Han, Myung Woo. Psychological Profiles of Korean Elite Judoists. Amer. Jrnl. Sports Med. 24/6: S67-S71, 1996.

36) Health For Life. Secrets of Advanced Bodybuilders. Los Angeles, 1995.

37) Heck, Robert W.; McKeever, Kenneth H.; Alway, Stephen E.; Auge, Wayne K.; Whitehead, Robert; Bertone, Alicia L, and John A. Lombardo. Resistance Training-induced Increases in Muscle Mass and Performance in Ponies. Medicine and Science in Sports and Exercise. 28/7: 877-883, 1996.

38) Herzog, Walter. Muscle Function in Movement and Sports. Amer. Jrnl. Sports Med. 24/6: S14-S19, 1996.

39) Hickson, Robert C.; Hidaka, Karen, and Carl Foster. Skeletal Muscle Fiber Type, Resistance Training, and Strength-related Performance. Medicine and Science in Sports and Exercise. 26/5: 593-598, 1994.

40) Ji, Li Li. Exercise, Oxidative Stress, and Antioxidants. Amer. Jrnl. Sports Med. 24/6: S20-S27, 1996.

41) Jones, Ken; Hunter, Gary; Fleisig, Glenn; Escamilla, Raphael, and Lawrence Lemak. The Effects of Compensatory Acceleration on Upper-Body Strength and

Power in Collegiate Football Players. Jrnl. of Strength and Conditioning Research. V/13, #2, 94-105, 5/1999.

42) Kiester, Edwin, and Sally V. Kiester. Discover Your Achievement Zone. Reader's Digest. 8/1995.

43) Kirkendall, Donald T., and William E. Garrett, Jr. The Effects of Aging and Training on Skeletal Muscle. Amer. Jrnl. Sports Med. 26/4: 598-602, 1998.

44) Kraemer, William J.; Fleck, Steven J., and William J. Evans. Strength and Power Training: Physiological Mechanisms of Adaptation. Exercise and Sport Sciences Reviews, American College of Sports Medicine Series. 24: 363-398, 1996.

45) Kraus, William E.; Torgan, Carol E., and Taylor, Doris A. Skeletal Muscle Adaptation to Chronic Low-Frequency Motor Nerve Stimulation. Exercise and Sport Sciences Reviews, American College of Sports Medicine Series. 22: 313-360, 1994.

46) Kurz, Thomas. Stretching Scientifically. A guide to Flexibility Training. Cypress, CA.: Stadion Publication Company, 1990.

47) La Tourrette, John. Speed Fighting. Medford, OR.: American Sports Training Institute, 1992.

48) Lee, Bruce. Tao of Jeet Kune Do. Burbank, CA.: Ohara Publications, 1975.

49) Leggett, Scott H. and Michael L. Pollock. Effect of Training on the Relationship between Maximal and Submaximal Strength. Medicine and Science in Sports and Exercise. 25/1: 132-138, 1993.

50) Marsit, Jospeh L.; Conley, Michael S.; Stone, Michael H.; Fleck, Steven J.; Kearney Jay T.; Schirmer, Ginger P.; Keith, Robert L.; Kraemer, William J., and Robert L. Johnson. Effects of Ascorbic Acid on Serum Cortisol and the Testosterone: Cortisol Ratio in Junior Elite Weightlifters. Jrnl. of Strength and Conditioning Research. V/12, #3, 179-184, 8/1998

51) Martin, Wade H. III. Effects of Acute and Chronic Exercise on Fat Metabolism. Amer. Jrnl. Sports Med. 26/7: 203-231, 1996.

52) Mayhew, Thomas P.; Rothstein, Hules M.; Finucane, Sheryl D., and Robert L. Lamb. Muscular Adaptation to Concentric and Eccentric Exercise at Equal Power Levels. Medicine and Science in Sports and Exercise. 27/6: 868-878, 1995.

53) MAYO Clinic Health Letter. V15, #12: 12/1997.

54) Morris, Thomas V. True Success: A New Philosophy of Excellence. New York: Putnam Publishing Group, 1994.

55) Morrissey, Matthew C.; Harman, Everett A.; Frykman Peter N., and Han Ki Hoon. Early Phase Differential Effects of Slow and Fast Barbell Squat Training. Amer. Jrnl. Sports Med. 26/2: 221-230, 3/1998.

56) Musashi, Miyamoto. The Book of Five Rings. Translated by Thomas Cleary. Boston, MA.: Shambhala Publications, 1994.

57) Nissen, S. et al., Effect of Leucine Metabolite Beta-hydroxy Beta-methylbutyrate on Muscle Metabolism During Resistance-Exercise Training. Jrnl. Appl. Physiol. 81/5: 2095-2104, 1996. Also found in Amer. Medical News, V39/N31: 40-42, August 19, 1996.

58) Nissan, S.; Panton,L.; Fuller, J.C Jr.; Rice, D., and R. Sharp. Effect of feeding HMB on body composition and strength of women. Jrnl. Appl. Physiol. 1997.

59) Parsons, Steel V. Nightfire Training, Are We Doing It Right? Police Marksman, 12-14, 7/1993.

60) Parulski, George. A Path to Oriental Wisdom. Burbank, CA.: Ohara Publications, 1976.

61) Pendergast, David R; Horvath, Peter J.; Leddy, John J., and Jaya T. Venkatraman. The Role of Dietary Fat on Performance, Metabolism, and Health. Amer. Jrnl. Sports Med. 24/6: S53-S58, 1996.

62) Phillips, Bill. Sports Supplement Review. Golden, Colorado: Mile High Publishing, 1997.

63) Reynolds, Bill, and Negrita Jayde. Sliced. Chicago, IL.: Contemporary Books, 1991.

64) Richardson, Drew; Taylor Shreeves, Julie; Van Roekel, Gary, and Al Hornsby. The Encyclopedia of Recreational Diving. Santa Ana, CA.: PADI, 1996.

65) Robinson, Jerry, and Frank Carrino. MAX O2. The Complete Guide to Synergistic Aerobic Training. Los Angeles: Health For Life, 1993.

66) Rogers, Marc A., and William J. Evans. Changes in Skeletal Muscle with Aging: Effects of Exercise Training. Exercise and Sport Sciences Reviews, American College of Sports Medicine Series. 21: 65-102, 1993.

67) Schmidtbleicher, D. and M. Buehrle. Neuronal Adaptations and Increase of Cross-sectional area studying different Strength Training Methods. Biomechanics X-B, Vol. 6-B, 615-620. 1987.

68) Shepard, R. J. Aerobic versus Anaerobic training for Success in various Athletic Events. Canadian Jrnl. of Applied Sport Sciences. 3: 9-15, 1978.

69) Siddle, Bruce K. Sharpening the Warrior's Edge. The Psychology & Science of Training. Millstadt, IL.: PPCT Research Publications, 1995.

70) Simonsen, Erik B.; Magnusson, Peter; Larsson, Benny, and Paul Dyhre-Poulsen. A New Concept For Isokinetic Hamstring: Quadriceps Muscle Strength Ratio. Amer. Jrnl. Sports Med. 26/2: 231-237, 3/1998.

71) Starkey, David B.; Pollock, Michael L.; Ishida, Yoshi; Welsh, Michael A.; Brechue, William F.; Graves, James E., and Mathew S. Feigenbaum. Effect of Resistance Training Volume on Strength and Muscle Thickness. Medicine and Science in Sports and Exercise. 28/10: 1311-1320, 1996.

72) Tan, Benedict. Manipulating Resistance Training Program Variables to Optimize Maximum Strength in Men: A Review. Jrnl. of Strength and Conditioning Research. V/13, #3, 289-304, 8/1999.

73) Wallace, M. Brian, and Sean Flanagan. Boxing: Resistance Training Considerations for Modifying Injury Risk. Jrnl. of Strength and Conditioning Research. V/21, #3, 31-39, 6/1999.

74) Wilson, Greg J.; Newton Robert U.; Murphy Aron J., and Brendan J. Humphries. The Optimal Training Load for the Development of Dynamic Athletic Performance. Medicine and Science in Sports and Exercise. 25/11: 1279-1286, 1993.

75) Yarasheski, Kevin E. Growth Hormone Effects on Metabolism, Body Composition, Muscle Mass, and Strength. Exercise and Sport Sciences Reviews, American College of Sports Medicine Series. 22: 285-312, 1994.

76) Young, Warren B.; Jenner, Andrew, and Kerrin Griffiths. Acute Enhancement of Power Performance from Heavy Load Squats. Jrnl. of Strength and Conditioning Research. V/12, #2, 82-84, 5/1998.

Index

About the Author

Author Ted Weimann is a Special Agent for the Immigration and Naturalization Service. In addition to being a certified black belt and instructor, he holds instructor certification in defensive tactics, baton, chemical weapons and use of force/confrontational simulations. He has taught these specialized subjects to officers of the Immigration and Naturalization Service, the Federal Law Enforcement Training Center and the Oregon Police Academy.